A Beginner's Guide to Trading - Stock and Forex Technical Analysis

Andy Hai Dinh

Published by Andy Hai Dinh, 2025.

A BEGINNER'S GUIDE TO TRADING - STOCK AND FOREX TECHNICAL ANALYSIS

First edition. February 6, 2025.

ISBN: 979-8227515308

Written by Andy Hai Dinh.

Also by Andy Hai Dinh

ACRYLIC AND DIPPING POWDER - Product Knowledge and Applications
The Nail technician's Career Guide
A Beginner's Guide to Trading - Stock and Forex Technical Analysis
WIN MORE, TRADE BETTER - A Practical Guide to Trading and Investing

Watch for more at https://pensight.com/x/lona.

Table of Contents

To my beloved children, Audrey An and Neal Phong,

May you always have the courage to chase your dreams, the wisdom to navigate life's challenges, and the curiosity to keep learning.

This book is a testament to the power of knowledge and perseverance, and I hope it inspires you to approach every opportunity with confidence and an open mind.

With all my love,

Andy Hai Dinh

INTRODUCTION:

This book aims to help you master the fundamentals of technical analysis in trading. You will learn to read price action, identify market trends, and spot high-probability trading opportunities. This book is a manual equipping you with essential skills to analyze charts and make informed trading decisions. Upon the completion of the book, you should be influent in chart reading, pattern recognition, and stock market analysis.

What will you learn from studying this book:

- Candlestick Analysis: Interpret various candlestick patterns and their implications for market movements.

- Market Conditions: Identify bullish, bearish, ranging, and choppy market conditions to adapt your trading strategy.

- Support and Resistance: Recognize key price levels that act as barriers to price movement, including angular support and resistance.

SECTION 1: TRADING FUNDAMENTALS

This section provides a comprehensive introduction to the world of trading, designed for beginners who want to build a solid foundation in financial markets. Through interactive lessons and practical examples, you will learn the essentials of trading, from understanding market dynamics to developing a personal trading strategy. The section emphasizes the importance of risk management, accountability, and continuous learning in achieving long-term trading success.

Received skills:

RISK MANAGEMENT

FINANCIAL PLANNING

STRATEGIC DECISION-MAKING

What will you learn from this section:

- Trading basics: Understand what trading really is, beyond the common misconceptions, and learn how to analyze market trends and patterns.

- Financial expectations: Gain realistic insights into the potential returns and risks associated with trading and learn how to set achievable financial goals.

- Accountability systems: Learn how to develop and maintain an accountability system that will help you stay disciplined and continuously improve your trading performance.

Chapter 1: Introduction to Trading

Lesson 1: Section Overview

Trading isn't just about buying low and selling high. It's about understanding market patterns, managing risk, and making informed decisions. Don't worry if this sounds complicated - we'll break it down step by step. By the end of this section, you'll have the tools to navigate the financial markets with confidence.

Trading is actually about analysis, strategy, and discipline. While quick thinking helps, success comes from careful planning and informed decision-making.

Let's test your instincts:

Look at this chart. It shows the price of a stock over the past month. There's a sharp spike at the end. What do you think this means? What would you do if you saw this chart?

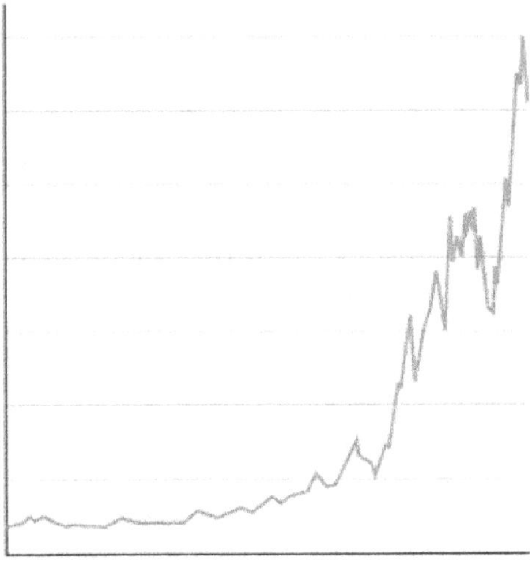

Answer: The best choice is to wait and gather more information. A sudden spike could mean many things - good news, market manipulation, or a temporary trend. In this course, you'll learn to analyze these situations and make informed decisions.

Throughout this section, we'll cover everything from basic market concepts to advanced trading strategies. You'll learn how to read charts, understand market trends, and develop your own trading plan. But most importantly, you'll gain the confidence to make your own decisions in the market.

While trading can be profitable, it's not a quick path to riches. Success comes from education, practice, and disciplined decision-making over time.

Remember, trading is not a get-rich-quick scheme. It requires patience, discipline, and continuous learning. But if you're willing to put in the effort, the potential rewards can be life-changing. Are you ready to take the first step on your trading journey?

Your trading toolkit:

Throughout this book, you'll build your own trading toolkit. This includes technical analysis skills, fundamental analysis techniques, and a solid understanding of market psychology.

A combination of all these skills is indeed the most important for successful trading. Technical analysis helps you read charts, fundamental analysis helps you understand the bigger picture, and market psychology helps you navigate the emotional aspects of trading. Together, they form a powerful toolkit for any trader.

In our upcoming lessons, we'll dive deeper into the basics of trading, explore different financial instruments, and learn how to analyze market trends. We'll also discuss the importance of risk management and developing a trading mindset.

Lesson 2: What Is Trading?

Your first trading mission!

Imagine you've decided to start trading and have chosen a popular stock to buy. You see that the price of TechCo stock has increased by 5% over the past two days. This has caught your attention.

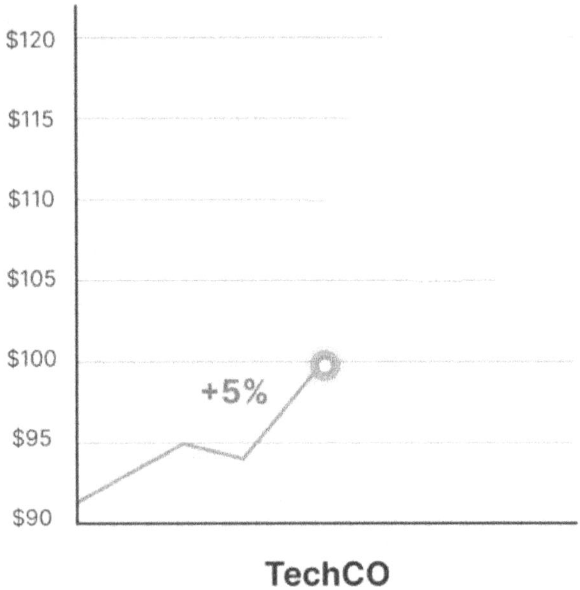

Now, you're faced with a decision: should you enter the market now? Before we decide, let's think about why the stock price might be rising. What factors could influence its movement?

There could be several reasons for the price increase. Maybe TechCo announced a new product or their quarterly earnings were better than expected. The entire tech sector may be performing well, or there's a general market uptrend.

What's your move?

You now have two options: buy the stock and hope for further growth, or wait to see how the price will move further. What do you think is the best thing to do now?

Answer: Waiting and gathering more information is often the wisest choice. Before buying, we should understand why the stock is rising and whether the trend is likely to continue. This involves analyzing company news, financial reports, and overall market conditions.

Let's continue our scenario. After your analysis, you decide to buy TechCo stock at $100 per share. Two days later, the price has risen to $110. Now you have a new decision to make: sell the stock and take a $10 profit per share, or hold on for potentially higher gains.

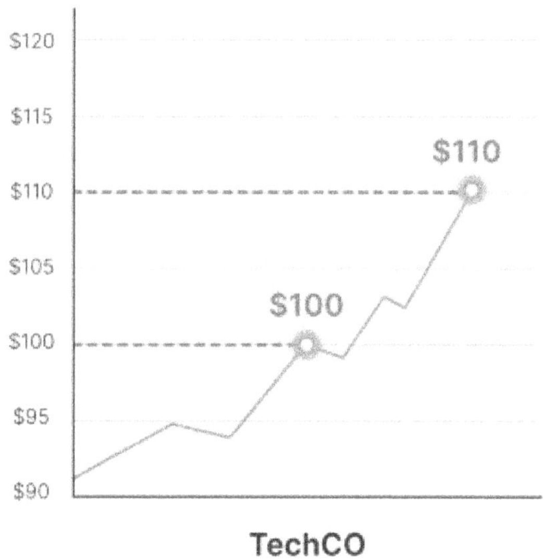

Time to decide:

You're facing a classic trading dilemma: take profits now or hold for more. There's no universally right answer - it depends on your strategy and risk tolerance. What would you do in this situation?

Answer: While there isn't exactly a wrong choice here since each strategy has its merits, aligning your decision with your personal investment goals and risk tolerance is crucial. Whether you decide to hold, sell, or even buy more, the key is that your decision aligns with your financial goals and risk profile. Each option has potential benefits, and what matters most is how it fits into your overall investment strategy.

Now, let's fast forward three days. Suddenly, negative news about TechCo causes the stock price to drop to $95. You're now facing a loss. This is where risk management comes into play.

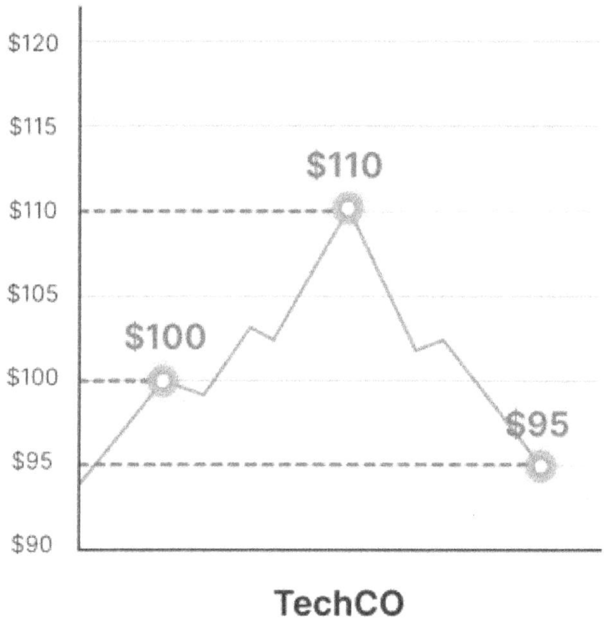

One tool traders use to manage risk is a stop-loss order. This automatically sells your shares if the price falls below a certain level, limiting your potential losses.

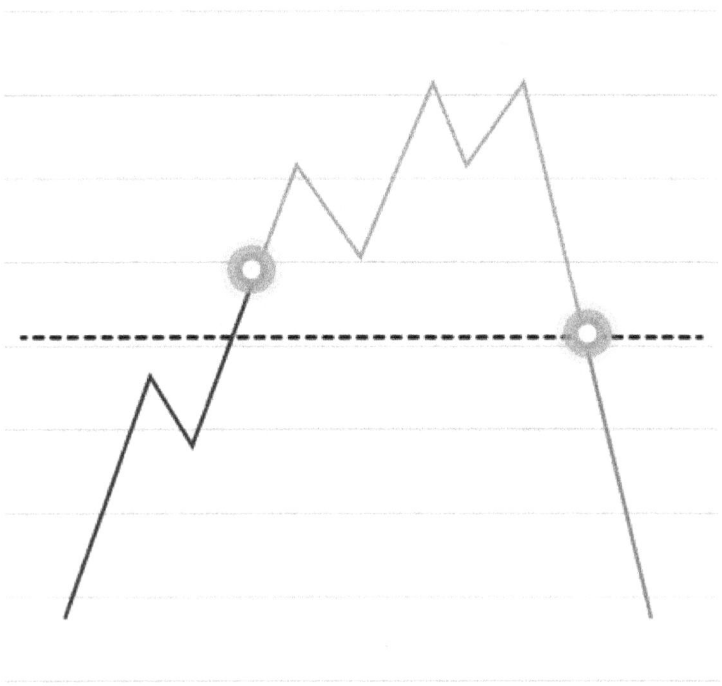

Managing risk:

Reflecting on this scenario, do you think you should have set a stop-loss order? How would you act now, seeing the price drop?

Answer: Setting a stop-loss order is often a wise choice. It helps you manage risk by limiting potential losses. For example, you might set it at $90, giving the stock some room to fluctuate while protecting you from severe losses. Remember, preserving your capital is crucial in trading.

Now that we've walked through this scenario, let's reflect. How would you answer the question: what is trading?

Trading is about making decisions based on market data. It involves constant work with risks and an attempt to maximize profits while minimizing losses. It's not just about buying low and selling high - it's about strategy, analysis, and risk management.

You've learned that trading requires evaluating the market, using tools like stop-losses, and not relying solely on luck. In the following lessons, we'll look at how professional traders manage their trades and make decisions.

Don't worry if it feels complicated now. We'll take it step by step, building your ability to make informed decisions. Remember, trading is a skill that grows with knowledge and hands-on experience.

Chapter 2: Time and Money

Lesson 1: Time Investment in Trading

Many people think trading is a quick way to make money. The reality? It takes time to learn, practice, and become proficient. Let's break down what this means for you as a beginner trader.

On average, it takes between 6 to 12 months to learn the basics of trading. But becoming consistently profitable? That usually takes 12 to 18 months of dedicated effort. Don't let this discourage you - remember, you're learning a valuable skill!

But how much time should you dedicate daily? A good rule of thumb is at least one hour per day on average. This could mean 3 hours on Sunday and an hour each on Tuesday and Thursday. Consistency is key!

Allocating 1 hour every evening after work and 3 hours on Saturday or Sunday is a good balance. It allows for consistent daily engagement with the markets and provides a longer session on the weekend for deeper analysis and learning. Remember, consistency is more important than the total number of hours.

Now, let's look at different trading styles and their time commitments:

1. Day Trading: Requires several hours during market hours daily.

2. Swing Trading: 1-2 hours daily, often outside market hours.

3. Position Trading: A few hours per week for research and adjustments.

Let's say you've decided to try swing trading. You've identified a potential trade in TechCo stock. The current price is $50, and you believe it will rise to $55 over the next week based on upcoming earnings.

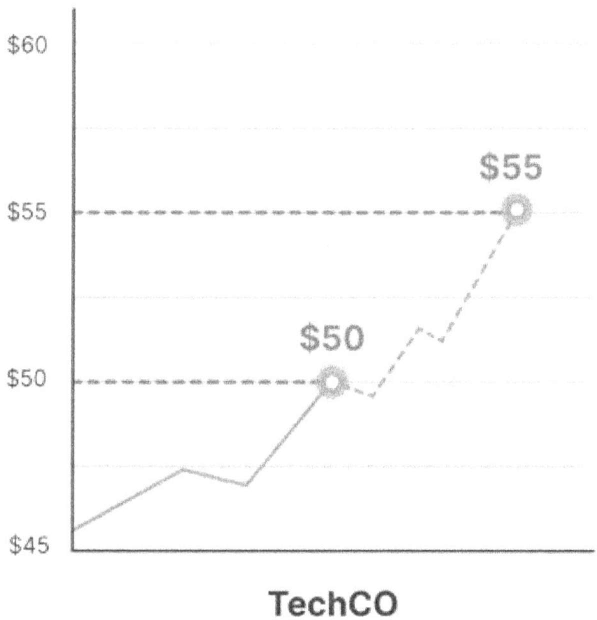

Time management scenario:

You've set an alert for when TechCo reaches $52. The alert goes off during your workday. You have a 15-minute break. What do you do?

Answer: Quickly checking the news, setting a limit order, and returning to work is a balanced approach. It allows you to act on the opportunity without disrupting your work. Remember, part of successful trading is integrating it into your life sustainably.

As you progress, you'll find that experience makes you more efficient. Tasks that initially took hours might eventually take minutes. But this efficiency comes with time and practice.

One way to maximize your learning time is to create a trading journal. Spend 15 minutes at the end of each trading session recording your trades, thoughts, and lessons learned. This reflection is crucial for improvement.

Trading journal example:

Let's practice journaling. You made a trade today: Bought TechCo at $50, and sold at $52. It took 2 days. This is how you would record it for future learning: "Bought TechCo $50 on 12/28/2024, sold $52 on 12/30/2024. Profit $2/share. Reason: Positive earnings report. Lesson: News can drive short-term price movements."

The detailed entry including the buy and sell prices, the reason for the trade, and the lesson learned is most useful. This type of journaling helps you identify patterns in your trading and learn from each experience.

Remember, the time you invest in trading is an investment in yourself. It's not just about the immediate profits, but about developing a skill that can serve you for years.

We've covered the typical timeline for learning to trade, daily time commitments, and the importance of consistent practice and journaling. In our next lesson, we'll dive into financial expectations and realities in trading. See you then!

Lesson 2: Financial Expectations and Realities

"How much money do I need to start trading?"

The answer isn't one-size-fits-all, but let's break it down with some realistic figures.

Imagine your goal is to generate an extra $500 per month from trading. Sounds great, right? But here's where reality kicks in: you'll need more than $500 in your account to consistently generate that income.

To generate $500 monthly, you might need:

- $25,000 at 2% monthly return.

- $12,500 at 4% monthly return.

- $8,333 at 6% monthly return.

Remember, these returns aren't guaranteed. They're examples to illustrate the relationship between account size and potential returns.

While having more capital can provide more opportunities, you don't need millions to start. Many successful traders begin with modest accounts and grow them over time through consistent, disciplined trading.

Let's practice with percentages:

You have a $10,000 trading account. You're aiming for a 2% monthly return. How much would you expect to make in a month?

Answer: The correct answer is $200. To calculate this, we take 2% of $10,000, which is 0.02 * $10,000 = $200. This illustrates why a larger account balance can generate more income, even with modest percentage returns.

Now, let's talk about risk. A common rule in trading is to risk no more than 1% of your account on any single trade. This helps protect your capital from significant losses.

Let's say you have a $10,000 account. Following the 1% rule, you wouldn't risk more than $100 on a single trade. This might seem small, but it's a crucial part of long-term success in trading.

Risk management scenario:

You're considering a trade on TechCo stock. Your account is $10,000. The stock is at $50, and you'll sell if it drops to $48. How many shares can you buy while risking only 1% of your account?

Answer: The correct answer is 50 shares. It's tempting to buy more shares, thinking it will lead to bigger profits. However, this often leads to taking on too much risk. Here's the math: You can risk $100 (1% of $10,000). Each share risks $2 (the difference between $50 and your stop loss at $48). So, $100 / $2 = 50 shares. This way, if the trade goes against you, you'll only lose 1% of your account.

Now, let's address a crucial point: the reality of returns. While you might hear stories of traders doubling their money in a month, this is extremely rare and often involves taking on enormous risks.

Realistically, many professional traders aim for returns of 10-30% per year. This might seem low compared to the get-rich-quick stories, but it's sustainable and can lead to significant wealth over time.

Compound interest magic:

Let's see how a 20% annual return can grow your account over time. You start with $10,000. Try to guess how much your investment might grow after 5 years without calculating exactly. Just a rough estimate!

Answer: If you guessed around $25,000, you're pretty close! The exact amount would be about $24,883, calculated by compounding the growth annually. This demonstrates how powerful compound interest can be for growing your investments.

Remember, these examples assume consistent returns, which aren't guaranteed in real trading. There will be ups and downs. The key is to focus on long-term performance rather than short-term fluctuations.

It's also important to consider the costs of trading. These can include commissions, spreads, and potentially subscriptions to trading tools or data feeds. These costs can eat into your profits if you're not careful.

For a beginner trader, aiming for 15-25% annual returns, with some winning and losing months, is a realistic expectation. This allows for the natural ups and downs of trading while still providing solid long-term growth potential. Remember, consistency and risk management are key to long-term success in trading.

Great job on completing this lesson! Let's recap what we've learned about financial expectations and realities in trading:

1. Starting capital varies, but you don't need millions to begin.
2. Realistic returns are often in the 10-30% annual range for professionals.
3. Risk management is crucial - the 1% rule helps protect your capital.
4. Compound interest can significantly grow your account over time.
5. Consistency and a long-term perspective are key to success.

In our next lesson, we'll explore the importance of accountability in your trading journey.

See you there!

Chapter 3: Accountability in Trading

Lesson 1: Importance of Accountability

Accountability: Your secret weapon in trading

We're exploring a crucial aspect of successful trading: accountability. Ready to level up?

Accountability in trading means taking responsibility for your decisions and actions. It's about being honest with yourself about your performance, both good and bad. Let's see why this is so important.

Imagine you're tracking your trades in a journal. You notice that every time you deviate from your trading plan, you lose money. Without accountability, you might ignore this pattern. With accountability, you'd recognize it and make changes.

Accountability is crucial in both winning and losing situations. It helps you understand what leads to success and what causes failures, allowing you to replicate good practices and avoid mistakes.

Journal Insights:

You've been keeping a detailed trading journal. Over the last month, you've made a total of 20 trades. Your journal shows that 15 of these trades followed your established trading plan, and 12 of those 15 were profitable. However, the 5 trades where you deviated from your plan resulted in losses. What pattern can be observed from your journal entries?

Answer: The pattern observed is that deviating from the trading plan tends to result in losses, highlighting the importance of sticking to a proven strategy.

One key aspect of accountability is tracking your trades. This means recording not just your entries and exits, but also your reasons for making each trade and your emotional state at the time.

Let's say you made a trade based on a "hot tip" from a friend, even though it didn't fit your usual criteria. The trade was profitable.

Without accountability, you might think this was a good decision. With accountability, you'd recognize that it was a risky deviation from your strategy.

Emotional accountability:

You're feeling frustrated after a losing trade and considering making a larger trade to "make back" your losses. What's the most accountable action?

Answer: Stepping away from trading for the day and reviewing your plan is the most accountable action. It acknowledges your emotional state and prevents impulsive decisions. Reviewing your plan helps reinforce your strategy and can calm your emotions.

Another important aspect of accountability is seeking feedback. This could be from a mentor, a trading group, or even by reviewing your own performance regularly. External perspectives can help you see blind spots in your trading.

For example, you might think you're great at picking entry points, but a review of your trades shows you often enter too early. Without accountability to others or yourself, you might never notice this pattern.

Accountability partners:

You're considering finding an accountability partner for your trading. What would be the most valuable quality in this partner?

Answer: Honesty, even when giving difficult feedback, is the most valuable quality in an accountability partner.

This ensures you get truthful insights about your trading, helping you identify both strengths and areas for improvement. Remember, constructive criticism is a powerful tool for growth.

Accountability also extends to your overall trading goals. If you set a goal to learn a new trading strategy this month, being accountable means following through on that commitment, even when it's challenging.

Timing Analysis:

After reviewing your trading journal with a mentor, you realize that most of your losing trades share a common trait: you entered the trades too early, before confirming trend stability. What should be your next step to improve your entry timing based on this observation?

Answer: Waiting for additional confirmation signals before entering future trades is a wise approach to enhance the accuracy of your entries and likely improve your success rate.

Remember, accountability in trading isn't about being perfect. It's about being honest with yourself, learning from both successes and failures and consistently working to improve your trading performance.

Great job completing this lesson! Let's recap why accountability is crucial in trading:

1. It helps you stick to your trading plan and strategy.

1. It encourages honest self-assessment of your performance.

2. It aids in managing emotions and preventing impulsive decisions.
3. It promotes continuous learning and improvement.
4. It helps you stay committed to your long-term trading goals.

In our next lesson, we'll explore practical ways to develop an accountability system for your trading. Get ready to put these concepts into action! See you there!

Lesson 2: Developing An Accountability System

Your trading took an unexpected turn:

You've just closed five trades. Three were winners, two were losers. But something doesn't feel right. Let's investigate.

As you review your trades, you realize you deviated from your trading plan on the two losing trades. You followed your emotions instead of your strategy. This moment of realization is the perfect time to start building your accountability system.

An accountability system in trading is like a personal coach that keeps you on track. It helps you stay disciplined, learn from your experiences, and continuously improve. Let's explore how to build one that works for you.

Journaling your trade details:

After completing several trades today, including a notable one with XYZ stock, it's time to update your trading journal. The depth of your entries can significantly impact your growth and accountability as a trader. What entry format provides the most comprehensive

accountability for your trade with XYZ?

Answer: "XYZ trade: Bought at $50, sold at $55, profit $500. Plan followed? Yes. Emotion? Calm" provides a clear, accountable record. It details not just the financial outcome but also reflects on strategy adherence and emotional control, key for reviewing trading performance and strategy improvement.

Now that you have a solid journaling system, it's time to implement regular performance reviews. Think of yourself as both the trader and the trading manager. Every week, put on your manager hat and analyze your performance objectively.

During these reviews, look for patterns. Are there particular market conditions where you perform better? Are there emotional states that lead to poor decisions? Use these insights to refine your strategy and improve your self-awareness.

Spotting patterns in trade performance:

After reviewing your trading journal for the past six months, you've documented that your most significant losses occur during high-volatility market openings. You also note that your successful trades typically happen during midday market stabilizations. Based on your journal findings, what trading adjustment might improve your performance?

Answer: Limit trading during market openings and increase focus during midday sessions.

External accountability can significantly boost your trading discipline. Imagine joining a small group of committed traders who meet weekly to discuss their performance, challenges, and lessons learned. This external perspective can provide new insights and motivation.

In these meetings, you might share your trading journal entries, discuss your performance reviews, and get feedback on your goals. The key is to be open to constructive criticism and willing to learn from others' experiences.

Handling a losing streak:

You've had five losing trades in a row, despite following your plan. Your accountability group meets tomorrow. How do you approach this situation? What's the most accountable way to handle this losing streak?

Answer: Analyzing each trade, preparing a summary of lessons learned, and presenting it to the group for feedback is the most accountable approach. This demonstrates a commitment to learning from both successes and failures, and leverages the group's expertise to gain new insights. Remember, even losing trades can be valuable if you learn from them.

The final piece of your accountability system is a commitment to continuous learning. Set aside time each week to study market conditions, learn new strategies, or refine your existing approach. This might involve reading trading books, taking online courses, or analyzing historical market data. Remember, a trader's journey is one of constant education; this book's guidance is just one part of a vast universe of knowledge you will explore.

Lesson 3: Section 1 Review

We started by exploring what trading really is. Remember, trading isn't just about buying low and selling high. It's about analyzing markets, managing risks, and making informed decisions based on data and strategy.

What is trading?

Let's test your understanding of the fundamental concept we started with. Think back to our discussions about what trading really means. How to best describes trading?

Answer: Trading is a disciplined approach to analyzing markets and making informed financial decisions. It involves studying market trends, managing risks, and executing a well-thought-out strategy. Success in trading comes from consistent application of knowledge and skills, not from luck or hasty decisions.

Next, we delved into time investment in trading. Remember, becoming a proficient trader doesn't happen overnight. It typically takes 6-12 months to learn the basics and 12-18 months to become consistently profitable.

Dedicating at least one hour on average daily is a realistic and effective approach for beginners. This allows for consistent learning and practice without overwhelming your schedule. Remember, consistency is key in developing trading skills and knowledge.

We also explored financial expectations and realities.

Remember, while trading can be profitable, it's not a get-rich-quick scheme. Successful traders often aim for returns of 10-30% per year, focusing on consistent growth rather than explosive gains.

Risk management in trading:

Risk management is crucial for long-term success in trading. Let's revisit one of the key principles we discussed about managing risk per trade. What's the recommended maximum risk per trade?

Answer: Risking no more than 1% of your trading account per trade is a widely recommended practice. This approach helps preserve your capital, allowing you to withstand a series of losses without significantly impacting your overall account balance. It's a crucial aspect of sustainable trading.

A crucial part of our learning was understanding the importance of accountability in trading. We learned that being accountable means taking responsibility for your decisions, learning from both successes and failures, and consistently working to improve.

A comprehensive trading journal entry should include trade details, your reasoning behind the trade, your emotional state during the trade, and lessons learned. This thorough approach allows you to review not just what happened, but why it happened and how you can improve. It helps you identify patterns in your trading behavior and decision-making process over time.

Throughout the book, we emphasized the importance of continuous learning and adaptation. The markets are always changing, and successful traders commit to ongoing education and refinement of their strategies.

Congratulations on completing this section! You've learned the fundamentals of trading, explored time management and financial expectations, and now built your own accountability system. But remember, this is just the beginning of your trading journey. And when you're ready to dive deeper, join us for our next section of this book on advanced trading strategies. Your journey to becoming a disciplined, accountable trader is well underway. Keep learning, stay accountable, and happy trading!

SECTION 2: TECHNICAL ANALYSIS BASICS

Master the fundamentals of technical analysis in trading. Learn to read price action, identify market trends, and spot high-probability trading opportunities. This section equips you with essential skills to analyze charts and make informed trading decisions.

Received skills:

CHART READING

PATTERN RECOGNITION

MARKET ANALYSIS

What will you learn from this section:

- Candlestick Analysis: Interpret various candlestick patterns and their implications for market movements.

- Market Conditions: Identify bullish, bearish, ranging, and choppy market conditions to adapt your trading strategy.

- Support and Resistance: Recognize key price levels that act as barriers to price movement, including angular support and resistance.

Chapter 1: Basics of Price Reading

Lesson 1: Introduction to Technical Analysis

You might be wondering, "Why should I care about technical analysis?" Well, let me put it this way. Have you ever looked at a price chart and felt like you were staring at a foreign language? That's totally normal. But imagine if you could actually read those charts, if you could spot patterns and trends that most people miss. That's what technical analysis is all about, and it's a game-changer.

In this section, we're gonna cover four big topics.

First up is reading price. This is the foundation of everything we do in technical analysis.

Then we'll talk about something called opportunity confluence. Sounds fancy, right? But it's actually pretty simple.

It's about finding those sweet spots where multiple factors line up to give you a high-probability trade. It's like catching the perfect wave.

After that, we'll get into angular trend lines. Now, I know "angular" might sound a bit math-y, but trust me, this stuff is really powerful. It's all about understanding the psychology of the market.

And finally, we'll wrap up with indicators. These are like the high-tech gadgets of the trading world. They can give you extra info to confirm what you're seeing in the price action.

Now, I'm not gonna lie to you - this book isn't about a magic formula for predicting the future. If anyone tells you they can do that, they're probably trying to sell you snake oil. What we're doing here is learning to read the market, to understand what's happening right now, and to make smart decisions based on probabilities.

After completing this section on technical analysis basics, you will gain the ability to interpret any market chart and understand the underlying market dynamics.

By the time we're done, you'll have a solid set of tools to tackle any market. You'll be able to look at a chart and actually understand what's going on. And let me tell you, that feeling is pretty awesome.

So, are you ready to level up your trading game? Let's jump in and start cracking the code of technical analysis together!

Lesson 2: Understanding Price Action

Reading price:

Alright, let's get started with the fundamentals. Before we can identify trading opportunities or place trades, we need to understand what we're looking at. It's important that we learn to read the markets and interpret charts effectively.

At its core, understanding markets begins with interpreting price movement. The candlesticks you see on charts represent price movement within specific time periods. Each one tells a story about market activity.

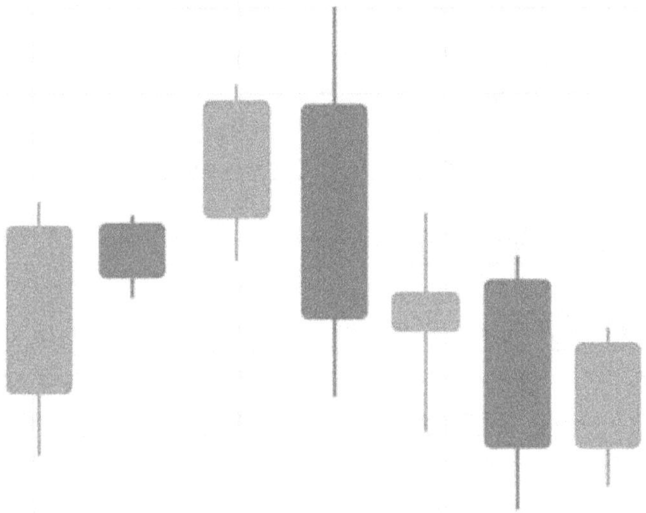

What I want to do now is break down the structure of these candlesticks for you. We'll look at what each element means and how to interpret them in the context of price relative to time.

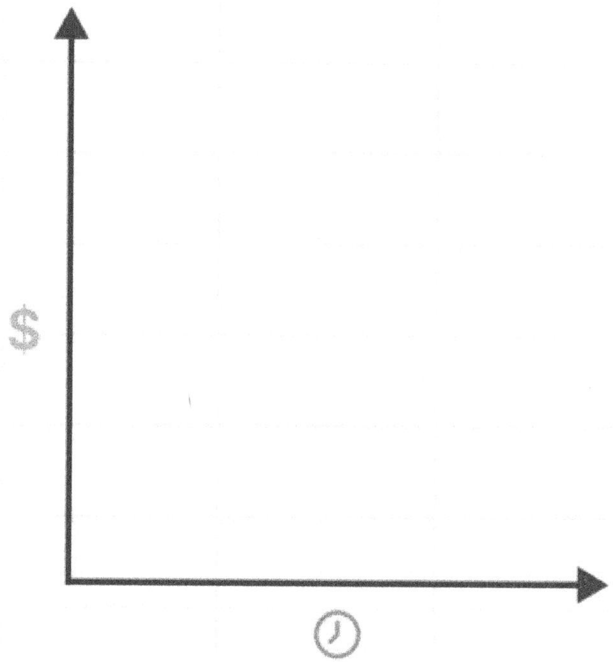

Each candlestick consists of four main components: the open price, the close price, the high of the session, and the low of the session.

Remember, a candlestick could represent any time frame - be it an hour, a day, a month, or even 15 minutes - but it will always include these four elements.

Let's just say that these

candlesticks here in front of you are the hourly candles, which means, on the hour, we're going to have the opening of a new candle and the close of the previous candle.

Now, you're probably looking at these candlesticks and thinking, "Wait a sec, why are some green and some red?" Well, there's actually a good reason for that. The colors aren't just for show - they tell us something important about the opening and closing prices.

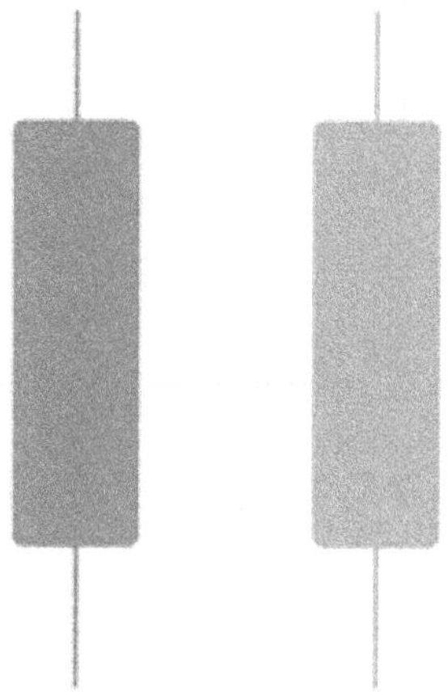

A green candle means that we closed (1) at the end of the hour higher than we opened (2).

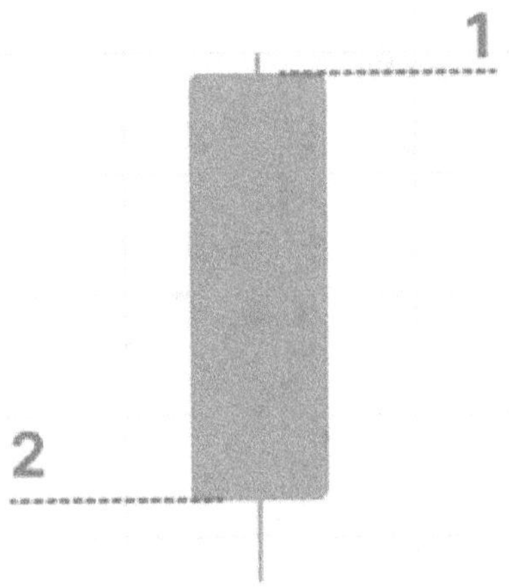

A red candle is simply the opposite of a green one. It means the closing price (1) is lower than the opening price (2), indicating that the price decreased during that time period.

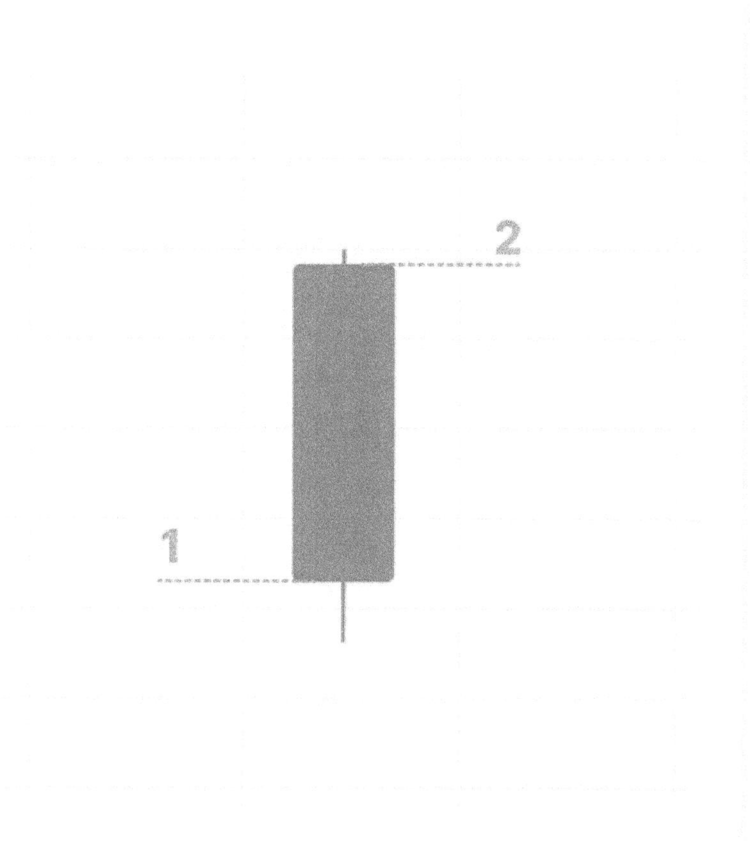

For example, from the candle below, you can see that the shares were traded at $10 at the beginning of the hour and at $20 by the end of the hour.

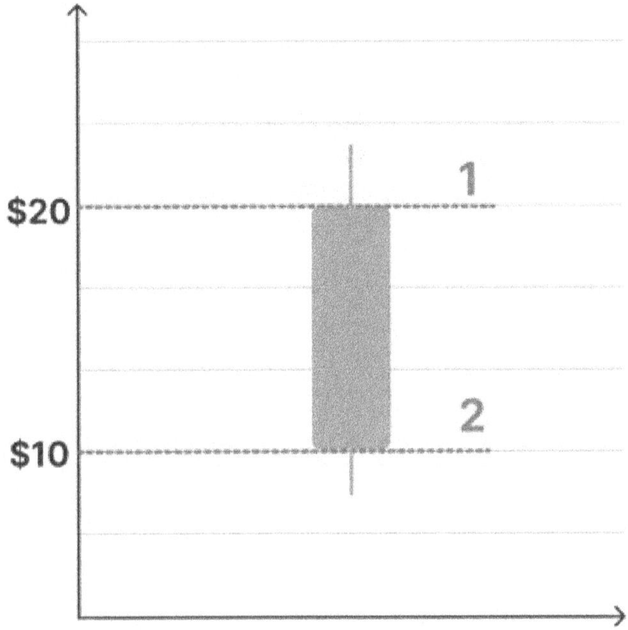

Then obviously, in between that, this would be the high (3) of the session, meaning the highest price that the market pushed up to during that hour, and there would be the lowest (4).

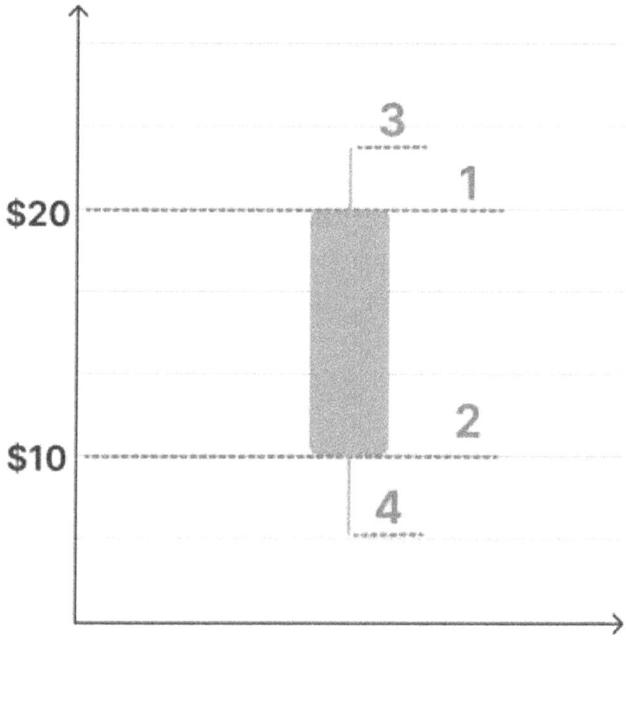

Guess the color:

Let's put that knowledge to the test. Take a look at this candlestick. Based on the relationship between the opening price (2) and the closing price (1), what color should the candlestick be?

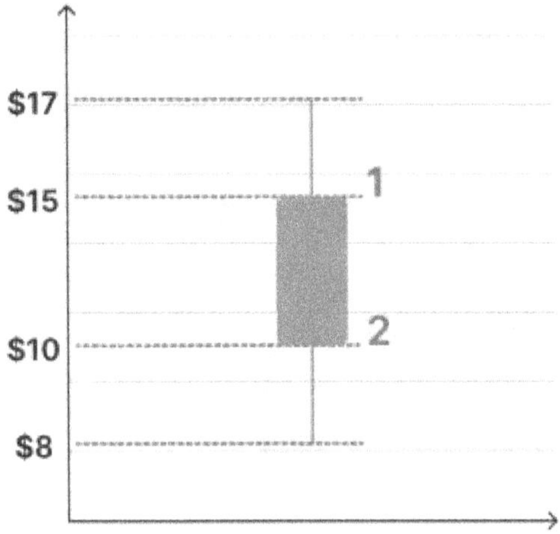

Answer: This candle should be green. The closing price ($15) is higher than the opening price ($10), which indicates an upward price movement during this period. Green candles always show a closing price higher than the opening price.

Essentially, each candle represents the story of that hour. We can see the highest price it reached (3), the lowest price it dipped to (4), where the candle opened (2), and where it closed (1) for the hour.

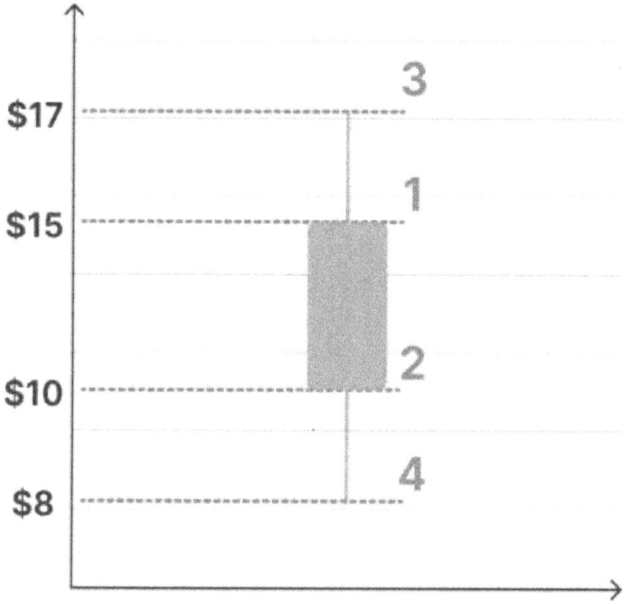

Now, on the red candle, we've got exactly the same points, except, the price closes (1) lower than it opens (2).

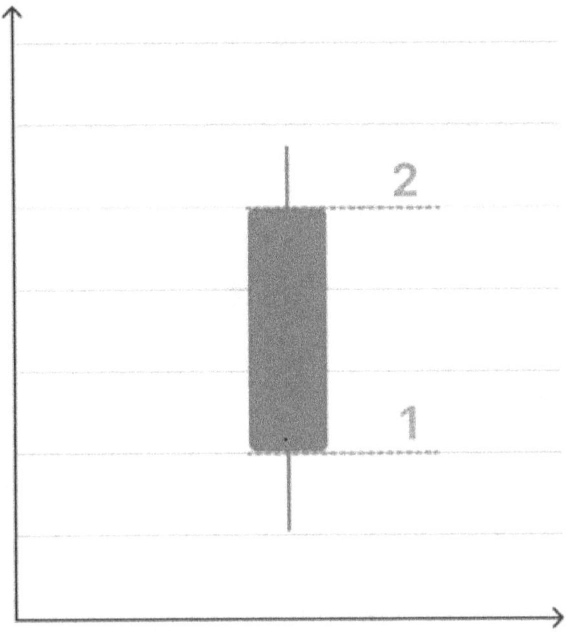

Similarly, this candle can show when it pushes up to the high (3), or it pushes down to the low (4), and then it closes lower than it opens, so this is the close of the candle.

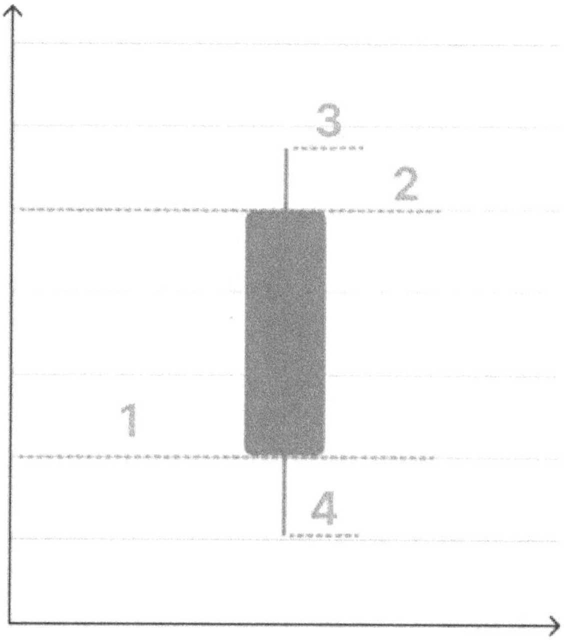

Let's consider the candle below, you can see that the shares were traded at $20 at the beginning of the hour and at $10 by the end of the hour.

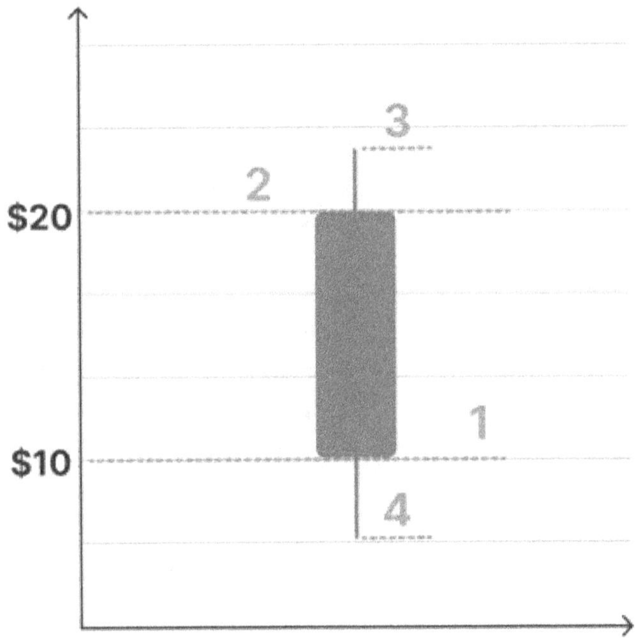

Interpreting the candle's story:

Let's practice interpreting what a candlestick tells us about market

activity. Illustration: A green candlestick with labeled components: Open at $50, Close at $60, High at $65, Low at $48. Based on this candlestick, which statement best describes what happened in the market during this period?

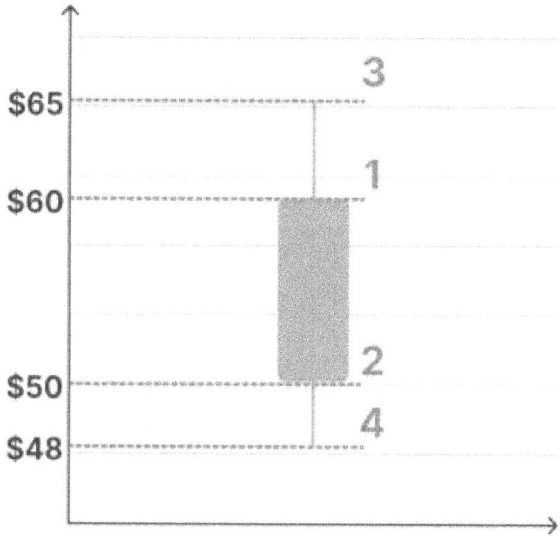

Answer: This green candlestick indicates strong buying pressure with some volatility. It shows: 1) Upward movement (opened $50, closed $60); 2) Bullish momentum (high $65); 3) Some volatility (low $48); 4) Buyers prevailed (closed $10 higher).

One last important thing to understand is how candlesticks connect to each other. Take a look at how each bar's opening price matches the closing price of the bar before it. They line up like links in a chain.

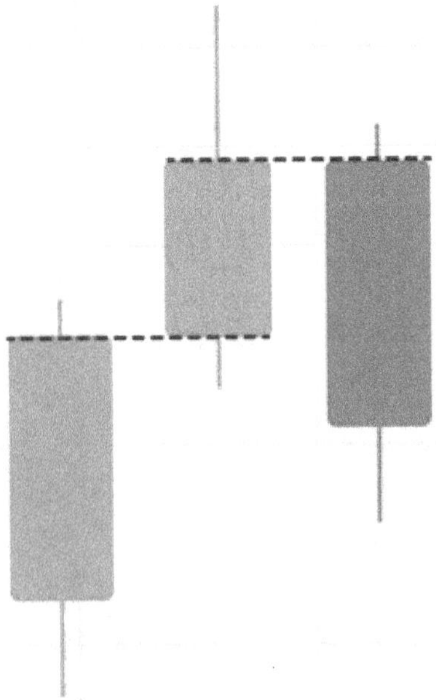

Connecting the candles:

Now, let's look at how candlesticks connect to tell a broader story of price movement. Based on the relationship between the opening price (2) and the closing price (1) in the first candle, what is the correct sequence of colors for all four candlesticks, from left to right?

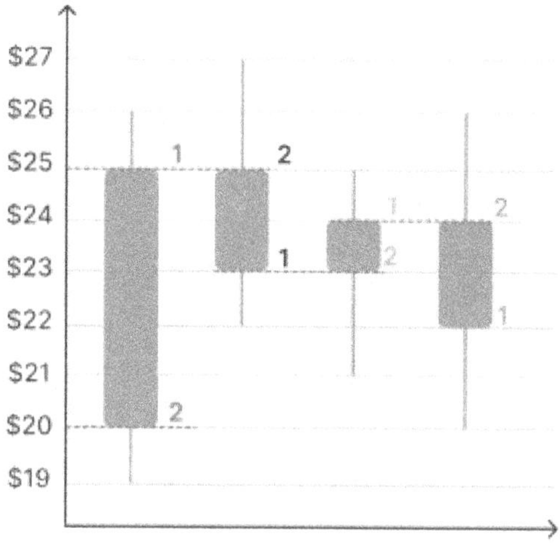

Answer: The answer is "Green, Red, Green, Red". Remember, green means the closing price was higher than the opening price, while red means it was lower.

Great job! You've cracked the code of candlesticks. Each one tells a story of price movement - opens, closes, highs, and lows. Green means up, red means down. This is your first step in reading the market's language. Keep practicing, and you'll be trading with confidence in no time

Lesson 3: Candlestick Anatomy

What more can candlesticks reveal? We've learned that a single candlestick reveals a lot about a specific time period, showing us the opening and closing prices, as well as the highest and lowest points. Yet, there's more it can tell!

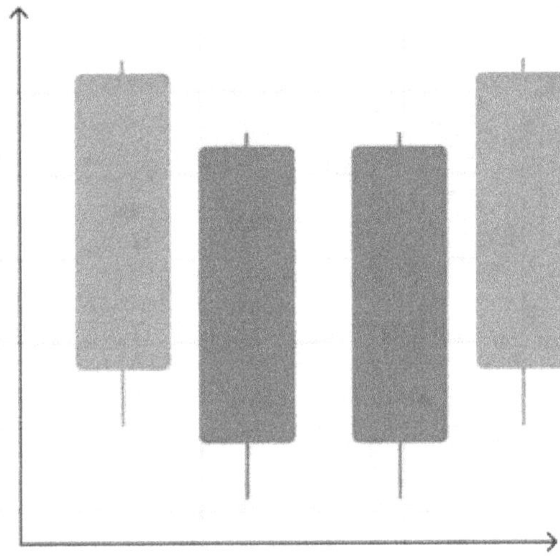

There are two important parts of a candlestick that help us understand market trends. The first is the closing (1) position, which tells us where the candlestick ends. This is key to knowing the final value.

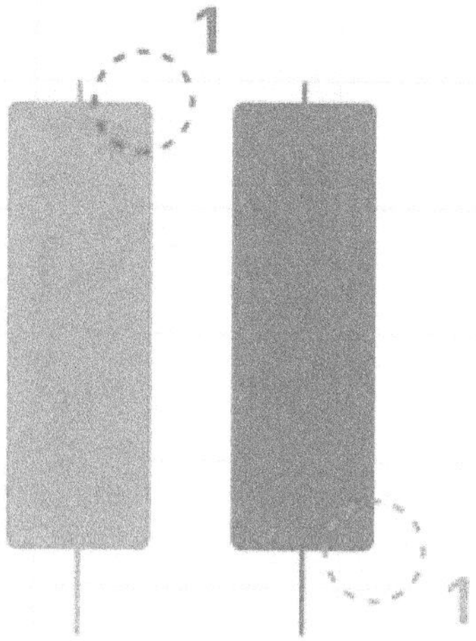

The second part is the candle wick (2), which can stretch up or down. Both these features are super important because they give us clues about how people feel about the market and what might happen to prices.

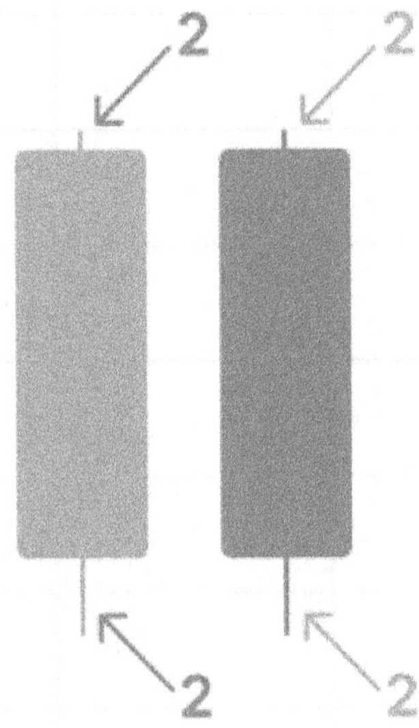

What do they show us? The green candle shows that the price ended up much higher than where it started. The bigger the gap between the starting and ending price, the more people were buying.

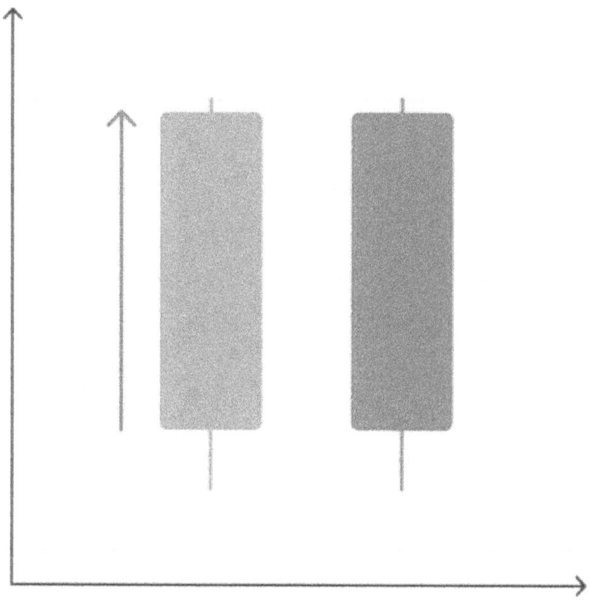

The second red candle tells us that the price ended up a lot lower than it started. The bigger the gap between the start and end price on the red candle, the more people were selling.

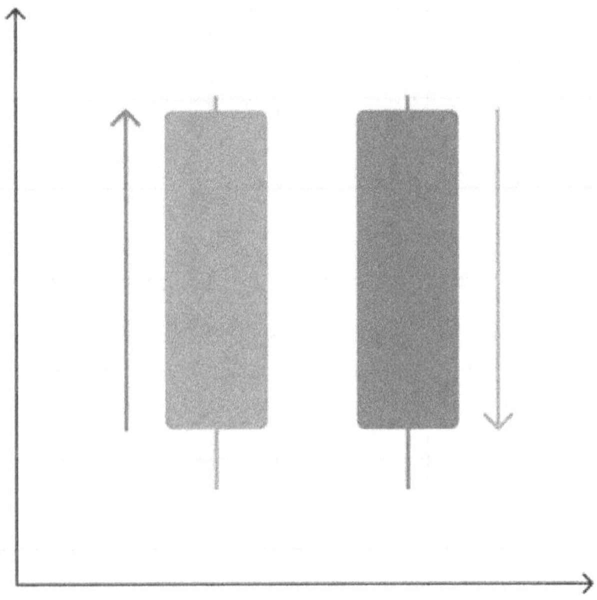

However, you won't always see those kinds of candlesticks. Instead, you might see something like the candle shown below. What happens if the candlestick looks like that?

When we start to look at these candles, we can start to form stories about what happened using the close and the wick. In our example, the short body shows a small difference between the opening and closing prices. Also, the bottom wick is long, while the top wick is very short.

If you look at this on a daily time frame, this tells you that when the market opened, the sellers quickly took control and pushed the price down to these extreme lows of the day.

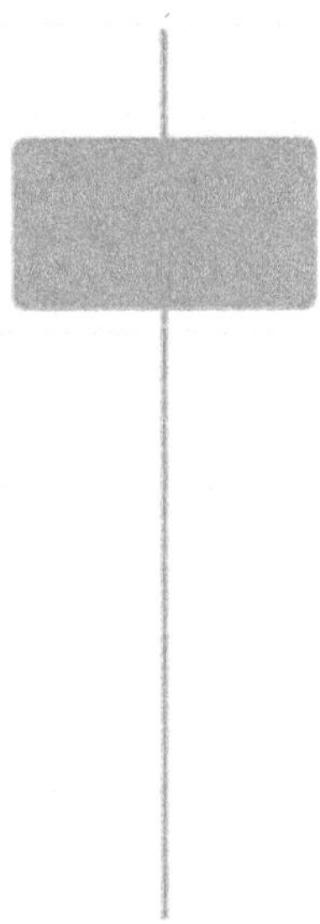

So during this point of maximum pessimism, the sellers were in control, driving the price down really low.

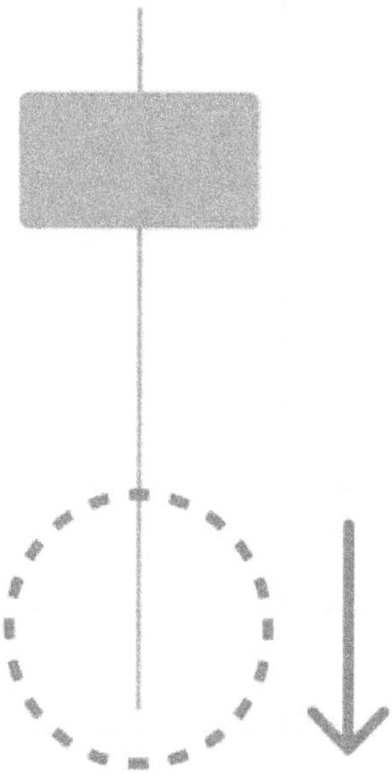

And then the buyers, cornered with their backs against the wall, suddenly found strength. They rallied, regaining control and driving the price up, eventually closing near the day's highs.

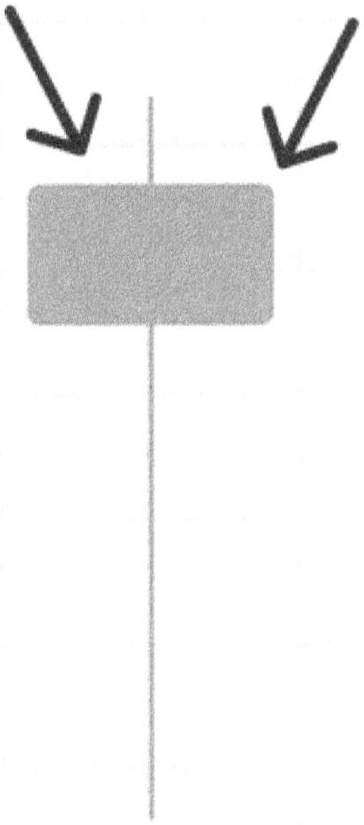

As you can see, in the early part of the day, the sellers were in control, driving the price lower. But eventually, the buyers stepped in and pushed it up, finally closing near the highest of the day. You'll see this shape pop up a lot, and traders actually have a name for it. They call it a "Hammer" - pretty fitting when you look at it, right?

The bigger picture:

Based on the candlestick we just analyzed (short body, long bottom wick, very short top wick), what does this signal about market sentiment?

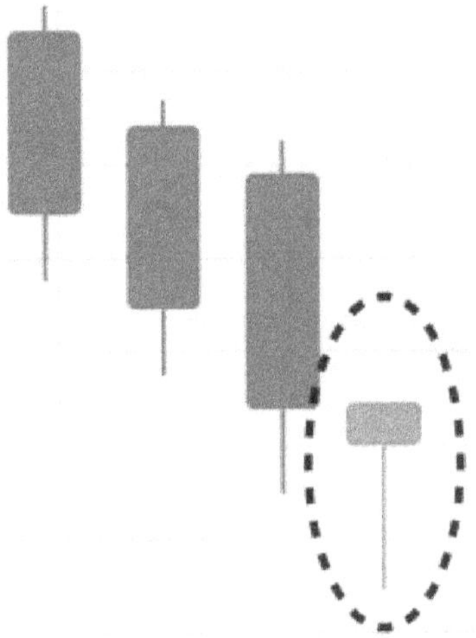

Answer: This candlestick suggests prices might rise, so it could be a good time to buy. The long lower wick means prices dropped at first, but closing near the top shows buyers pushed the price back up. This indicates strong buying pressure that may continue.

Here's how it might look on trading charts, showing the likely progression after this candlestick type.

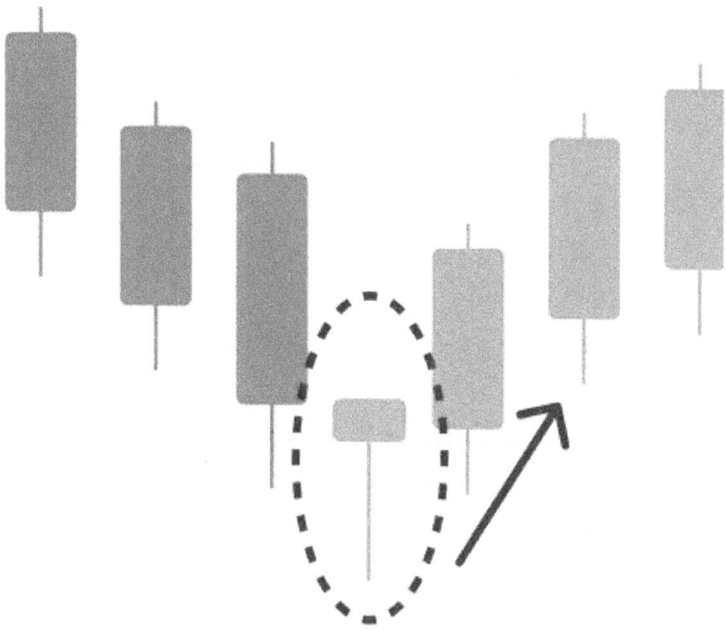

Keep an eye out for the upside-down version of this pattern too. Traders call that one a "Shooting Star". Now, you might be wondering - are these two patterns basically the same deal? Well, not quite.

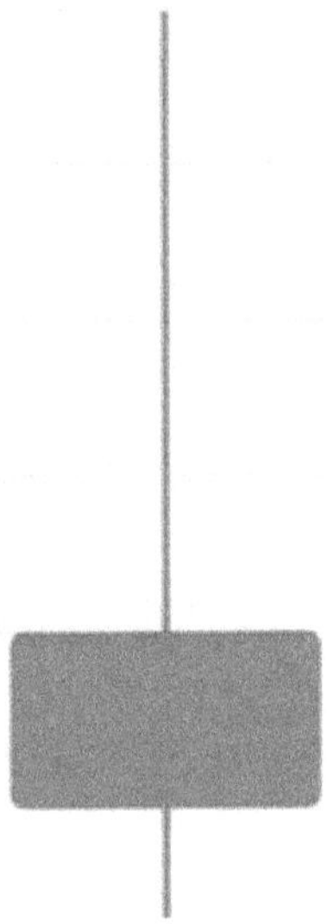

This new candle has a small lower body at the bottom and a long upper wick. This shows that during the session, buyers pushed the price up, but couldn't maintain control and the price fell close to its opening level.

This specific type is important because it indicates that despite buying pressure, sellers took over by the session's end, potentially leading to a price drop.

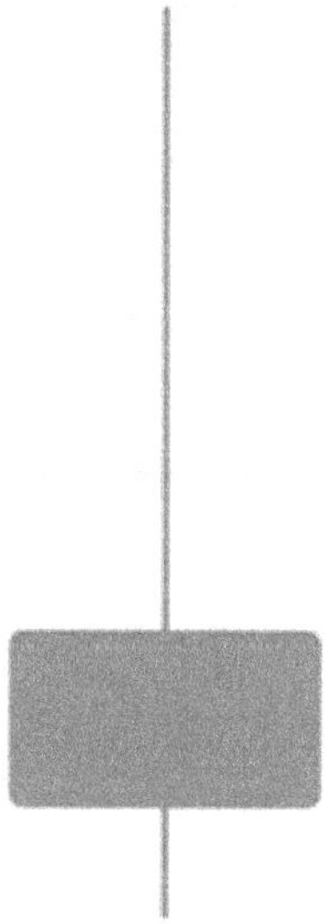

The bigger picture:

Alright, time to put your knowledge to the test! Check out this candle pattern - it's got a tiny body at the bottom and a long wick reaching for the sky. Ring any bells? Yep, that's our friend the "Shooting Star" we were just talking about. What does this specific candle type typically indicate?

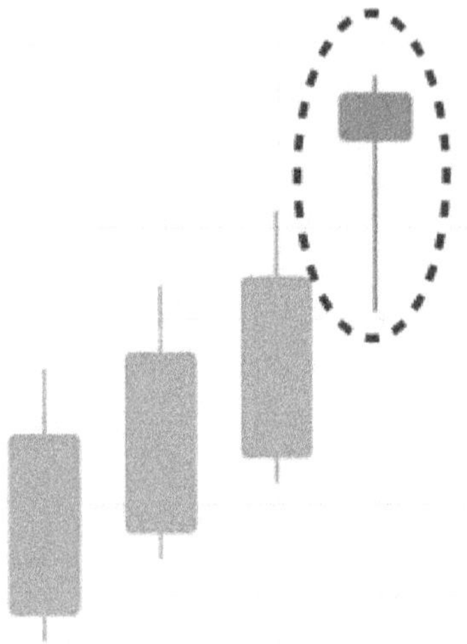

Answer: This candle suggests selling opportunities after a rise. The long upper wick shows buyers pushed the price up but lost control. The small body near the bottom indicates sellers took over, possibly leading to a price drop.

Here's how it might look on trading charts, showing the likely progression after this candlestick type.

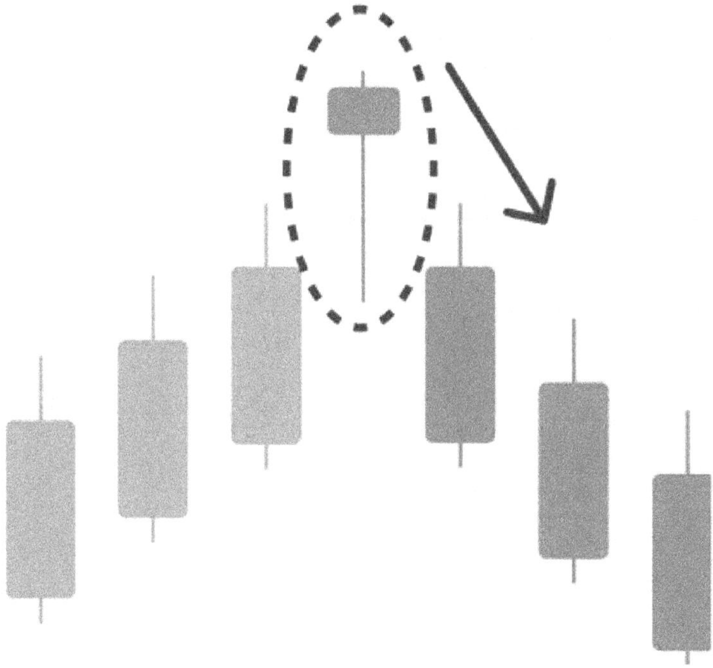

As you noticed we are no longer just looking at red and green candles and the open and close, we're now forming a story of what's been happening during each of those sessions.

Let's continue! You can also see a candle that looks like this, where the low (4) is the open (2), and the high (3) is the close (1), and there are no wicks. If it's a green candle, that's a strong buying candle, indicating the market has strong momentum to the upside.

Similarly, if the open (2) and high (3) are at the top and the close (1) and low (4) are at the bottom - forming a red candle - it indicates strong selling pressure, suggesting the market will likely continue downward after that candle closes.

Candles without wicks:

Let's test your understanding of candles without wicks. What do these candlesticks typically indicate about market momentum?

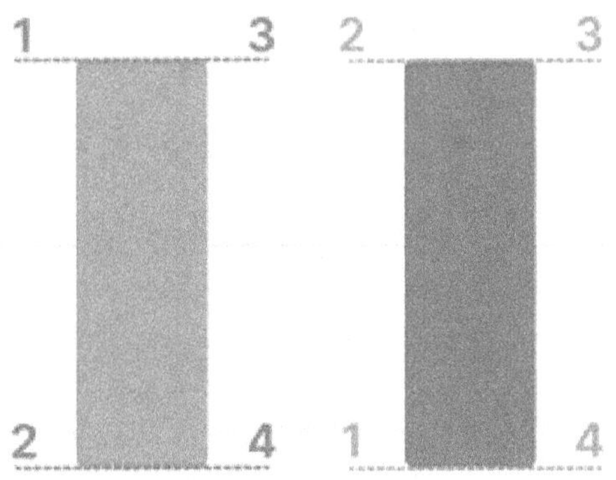

Answer: A green candle without wicks signals strong buying and likely upward movement. A red candle without wicks indicates strong selling and likely downward movement. These candles show consistent one-directional pressure.

And there you have it! Candlesticks are your window into market psychology. They're not just red and green price indicators - the relationship between wicks and bodies tells a deeper story. As you practice, you'll uncover valuable insights into market trends and potential movements. You've taken a big step in mastering technical analysis. Great job on completing this lesson!

Lesson 4: Reading Price

Let's test your knowledge!

You've done an amazing job understanding candlesticks and market dynamics! Now, it's time to put your skills to the test. Don't worry if you make mistakes - it's all part of learning.

Identify candle colors:

You are looking at two candlesticks. Candle A and Candle B. Candle A opened at $45 and closed at $50. Candle B opened at $60 and closed at $55. What are the colors of Candles A and B?

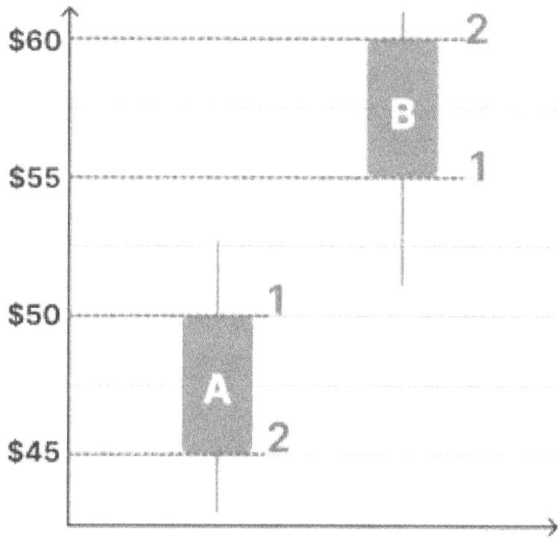

Answer: Candle A is green since it closed higher than it opened, and Candle B is red since it closed lower than it opened.

Interpreting market activity:

You are looking at a candlestick with an open price of $90, a high of $100, a low of $85, and a close of $95. What does this candlestick tell you about market activity during this period?

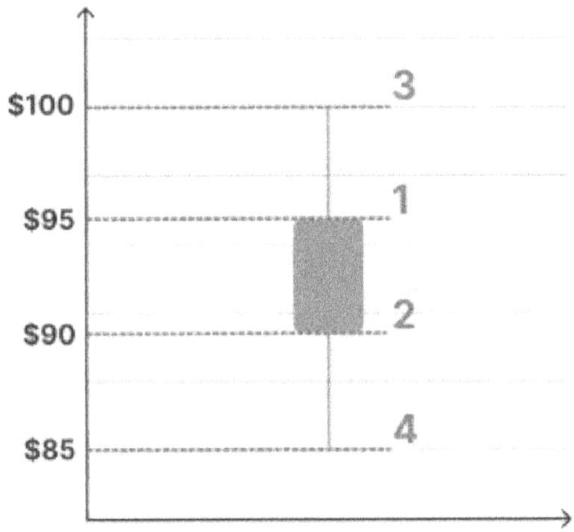

Answer: This candlestick indicates strong buying pressure since it closed higher than it opened. The market experienced some volatility, as seen in the high and low prices.

Candle prices:

You are looking at an hourly candlestick chart. What does the candle mean?

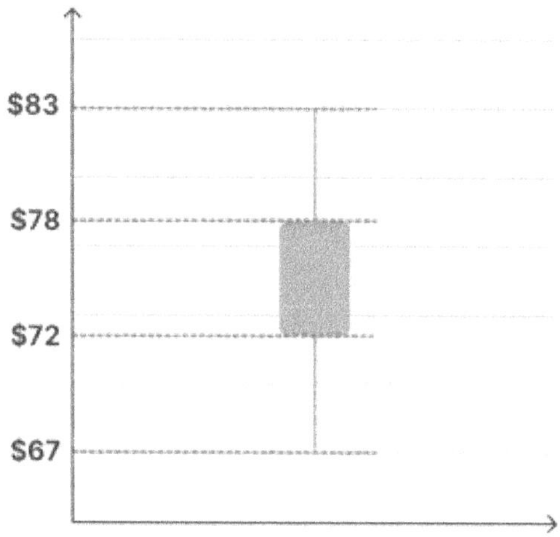

Answer: The correct answer is: Open = $72, Close = $78, High = $83, Low = $67. The candle's body represents the open and close prices, while the wicks indicate the high and low prices.

Large gap in green candle:

You can notice the large gap between the opening and closing prices in this green candlestick. What does this large gap between the opening and closing prices indicate?

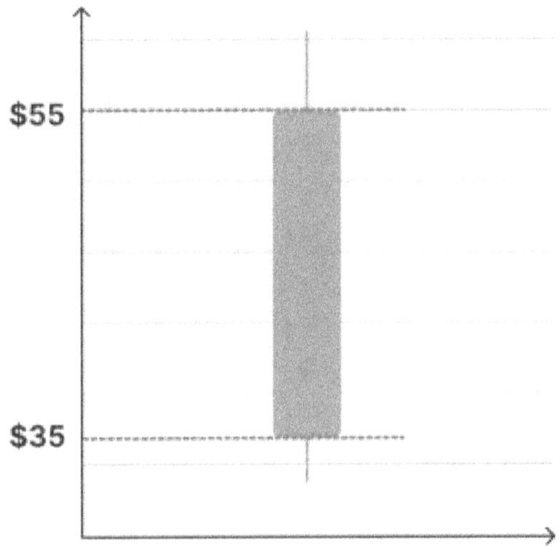

Answer: A large gap between the opening and closing prices in a green candle shows strong buying pressure, indicating a significant price increase during that period.

Large gap in red candle:

A red candlestick has an opening price of $75 and a closing price of $60, with a large gap between them. What does this large gap between the opening and closing prices tell us about market behavior?

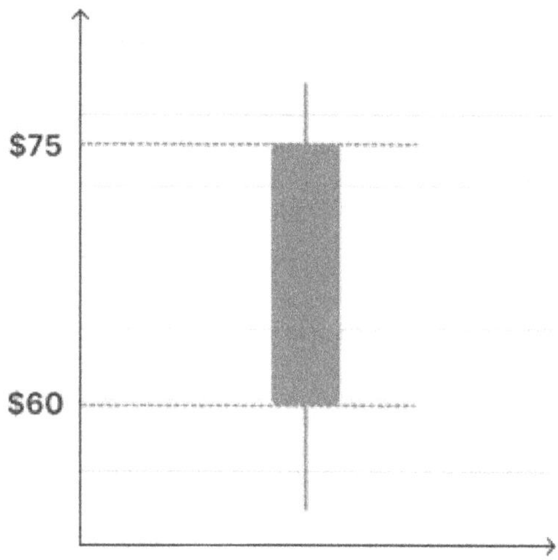

Answer: A large gap in a red candle means strong selling pressure, with the price dropping sharply from the opening ($75) to the close ($60). This signals that sellers were in control and the market experienced a strong downward move during the session.

Short body candlestick:

You see a candlestick with a short body and long wicks. The opening price is $20, the closing price is $21, and the high and low prices are far apart ($30 high, $15 low). What does this candlestick tell you about market conditions?

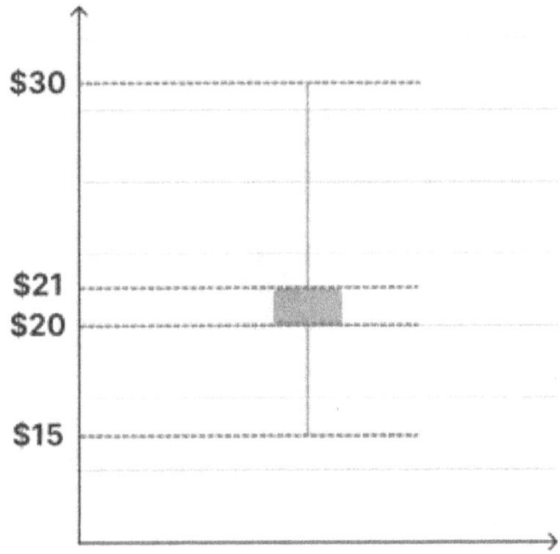

Answer: A candlestick with a short body and long wicks often shows indecision, as neither buyers nor sellers could maintain control.

S&P 500:

On March 12, 2020, during the height of the COVID-19 pandemic, the S&P 500 opened at $2,580, dropped to a low of $2,475, and closed at $2,550. What does this candlestick suggest about the market early in the session?

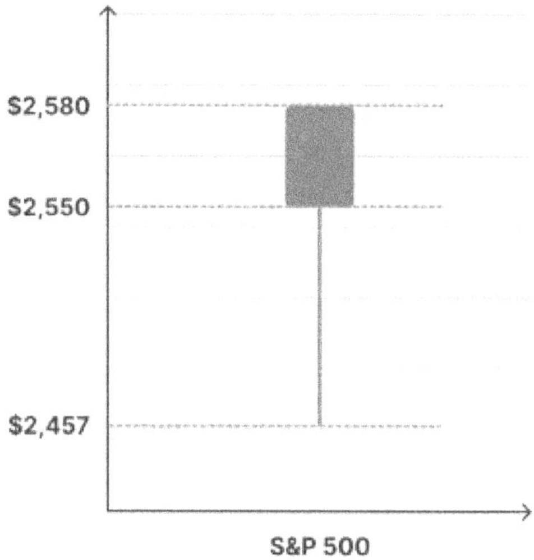

Answer: The long lower wick indicates that sellers dominated early in the session, pushing the price from $2,580 to $2,475, but buyers regained some control later, causing the price to recover to $2,550 by the close.

TSLA:

On September 1, 2020, Tesla (TSLA) opened at $490, rallied up to $502 during the session, but by the end of the day, it fell back to $475. What does this candlestick suggest about market activity?

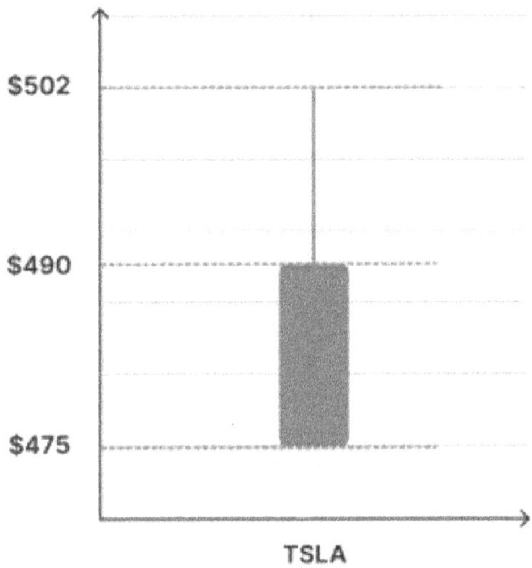

Answer: The long upper wick indicates that buyers initially pushed the price up, but sellers regained control, driving the price down from $502 to $475, close to the opening level.

AAPL:

On August 31, 2020, Apple (AAPL) opened at $127.58 and closed at $129.04 without significant pullbacks, forming a green candle without wicks. What does this candlestick indicate about market momentum?

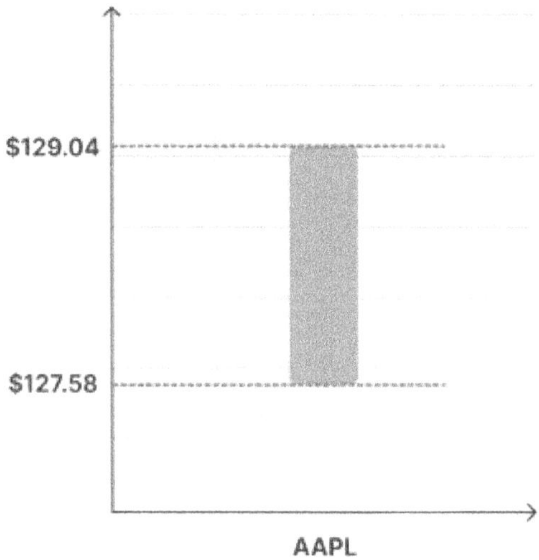

Answer: A green candle without wicks indicates strong buying pressure, as the price steadily increased from $127.58 to $129.04 without significant pullbacks during the session.

NVIDIA:

On September 3, 2020, NVIDIA (NVDA) opened at $540 and closed at $485, forming a red candle without wicks, indicating steady downward movement throughout the session. What does this candlestick suggest about the market's movement during the session?

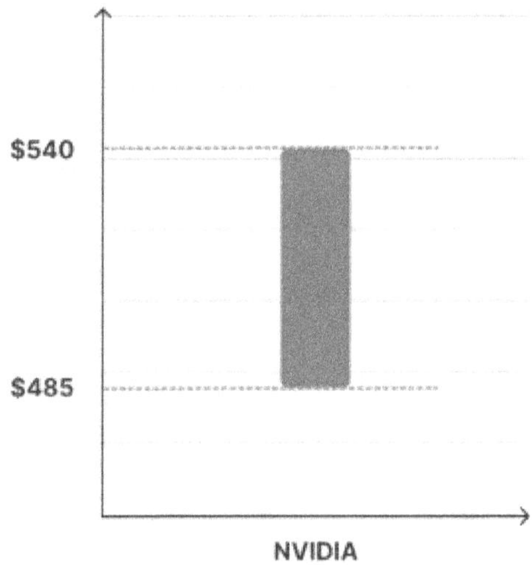

Answer: A red candle without wicks indicates strong selling pressure, as the price steadily decreased from $540 to $485 without any significant pullbacks or buying pressure during the session.

Great job! I hope you enjoyed this lesson. If you find anything complicated, don't hesitate to go back to the previous lessons. Remember, mastering technical analysis takes practice, and each candlestick tells a story that will help you make smarter trading decisions over time. Keep up the great work!

Chapter 2: Candlestick Patterns

Lesson 1: Bullish Engulfing and Bearish Engulfing

Expanding your candlestick toolkit:

So, we've covered how patterns like the Hammer and Shooting Star can reveal some key market moves. Pretty useful stuff, right? But here's the kicker - there are more patterns just like these.

In this chapter, we'll dig into the other patterns that really matter when you're in the thick of day-to-day trading. Each one is like a unique constellation, telling its own story about market sentiment and pointing to potential profit opportunities.

Before you begin, let's review the terminology one more time. Remember the body (1) of a candlestick is the colored part between the opening and closing prices.

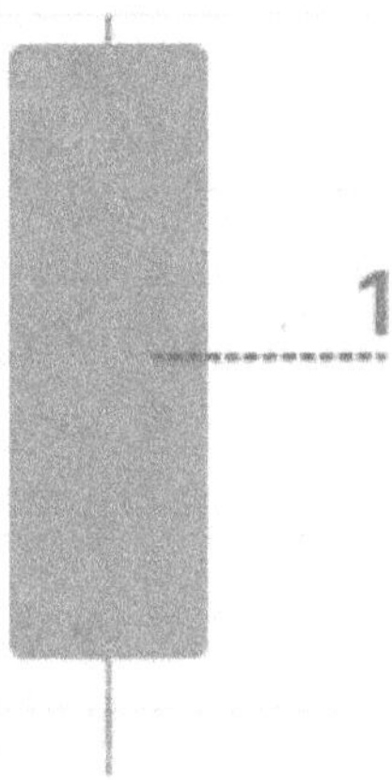

Then, there are the shadows (2), or wicks, which indicate the high and low prices during the candle's formation.

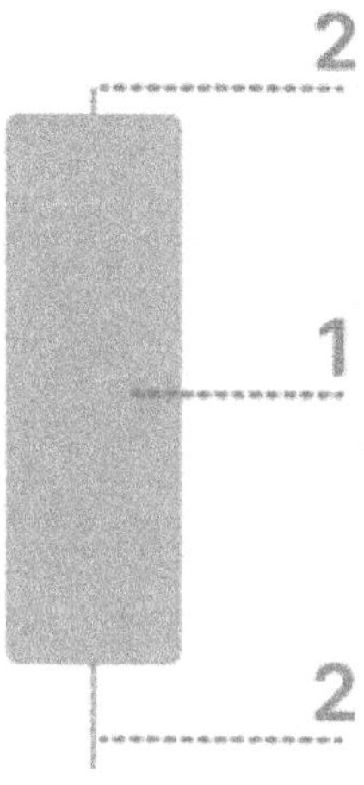

Now, we are ready to explore new patterns. These differ from the previous two because they involve combinations of two candlesticks.

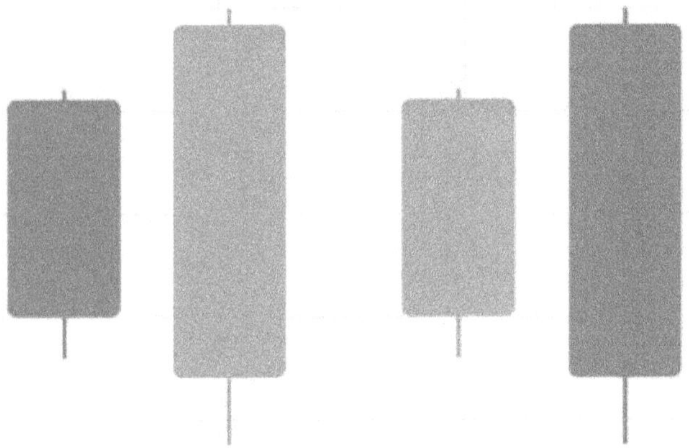

The first one is the Bullish Engulfing, which occurs over a span of two days.

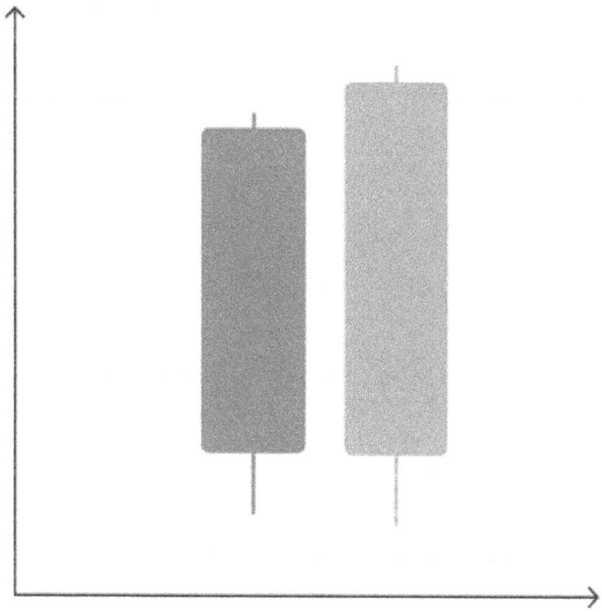

On the first day, the market closes lower, with the candlestick closing near the day's low.

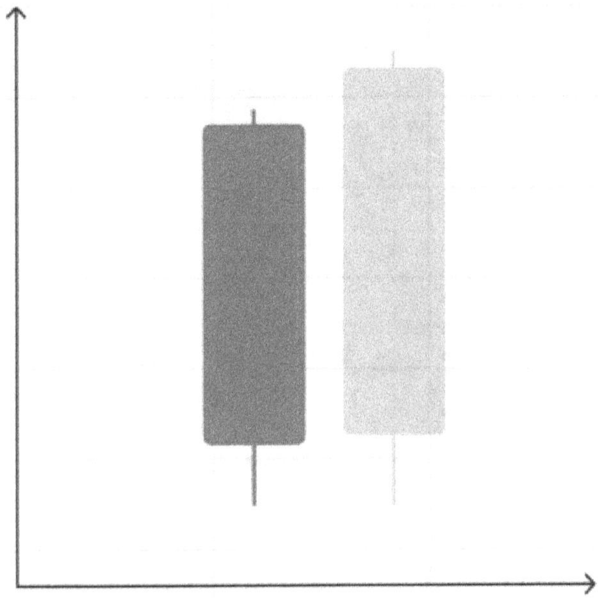

On the second day, the market opens at or below the previous close but then buyers take charge, pushing the price up to close above the previous day's open, engulfing the first day's body.

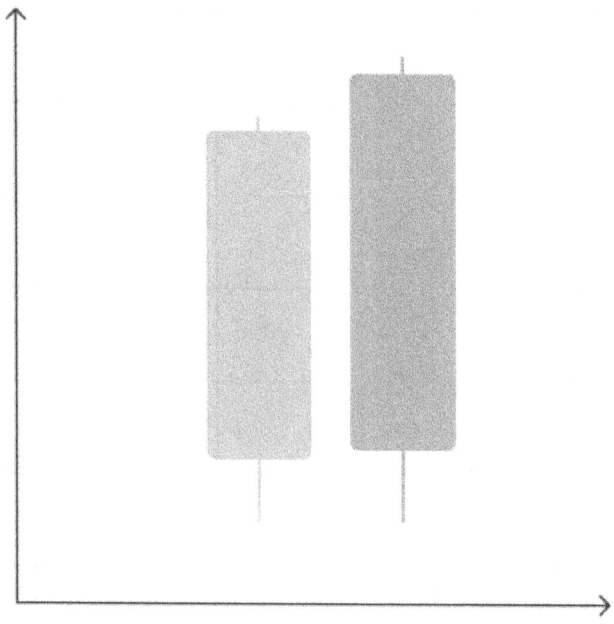

The bullish engulfing candle shows that a downtrend might be ending and suggests that more people are starting to buy when it appears at the bottom of a downtrend.

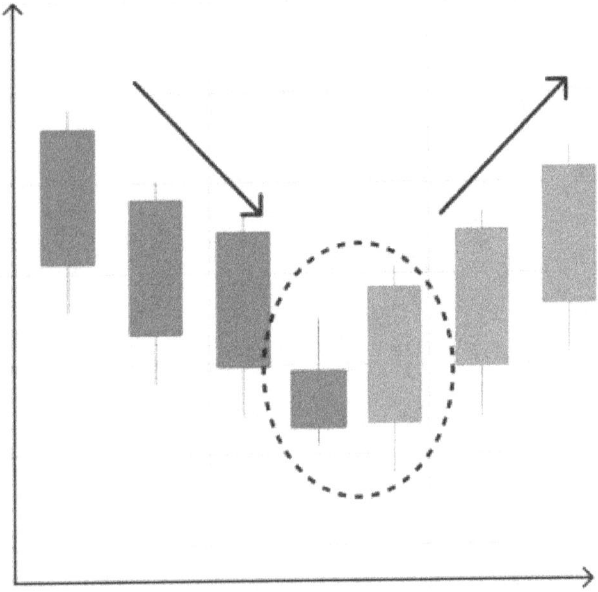

What's the Bearish Engulfing telling us?

We've just learned about the Bullish Engulfing pattern. Now, let's flip the script and think about its opposite - the Bearish Engulfing pattern. What does a Bearish Engulfing pattern typically indicate?

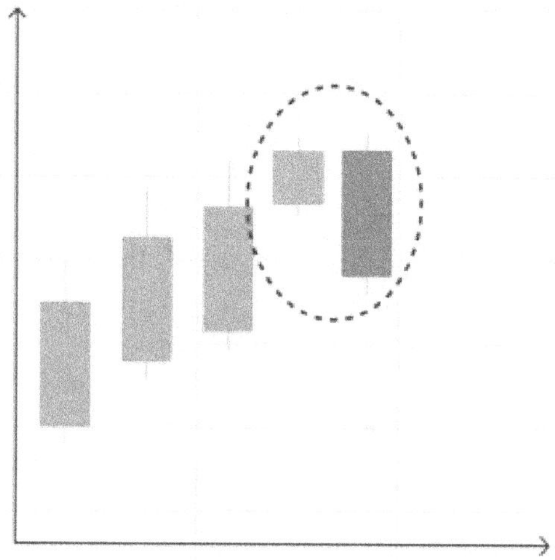

Answer: A Bearish Engulfing pattern signals a potential reversal from an uptrend to a downtrend, indicating sellers are overpowering buyers.

In the Bearish Engulfing pattern, the first day's candlestick is green, showing buyers in control and closing near the day's highs.

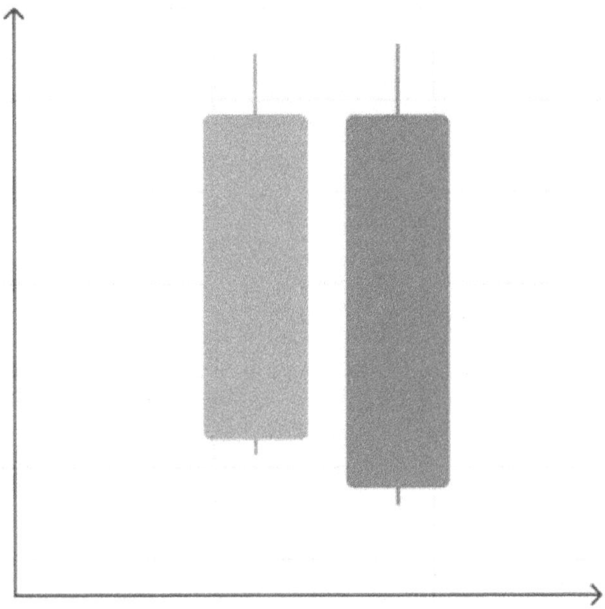

On the following day, however, the market opens at or above the previous day's close. Sellers quickly take over, driving the price down to close below the previous day's open, engulfing the first candle's body.

This shift from buyers to sellers can be a strong signal that the uptrend is losing momentum and that prices may start to fall.

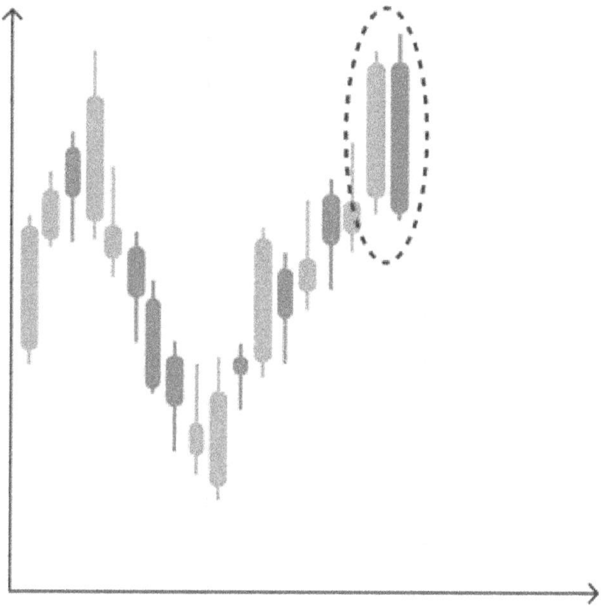

In this example, we can see that the uptrend has indeed lost its momentum and prices have started to fall.

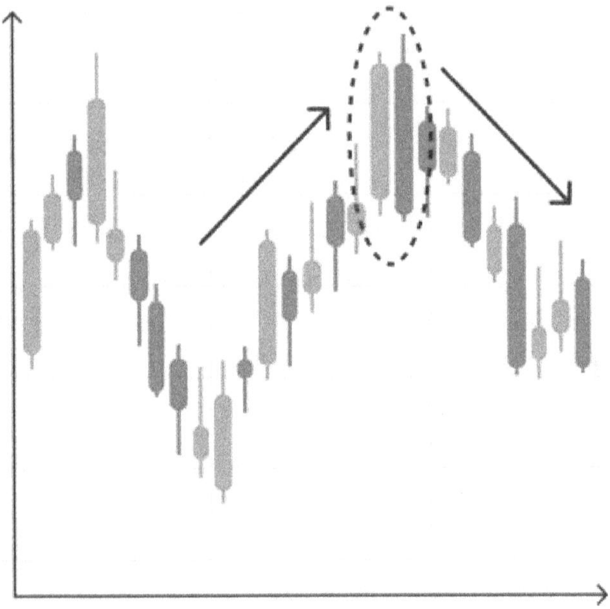

Spot the Engulfing pattern:

Alright, time to put your new knowledge to the test! Take a look at these two sets of candlesticks. Can you identify which one is showing a Bullish Engulfing pattern and which one is showing a Bearish Engulfing pattern?

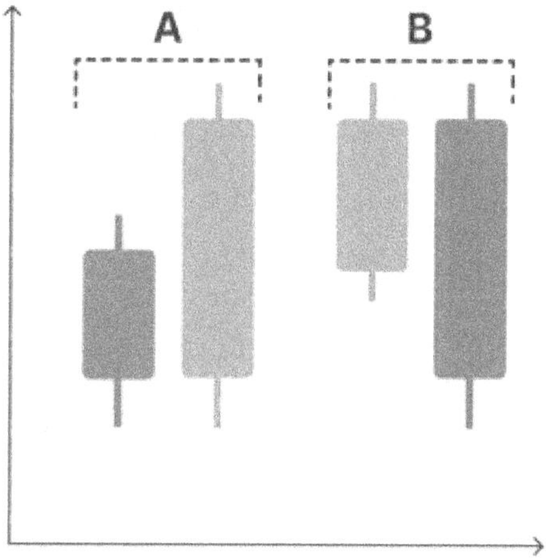

Answer: Set A shows a Bullish Engulfing pattern with a small red candle followed by a larger green one. Set B displays a Bearish Engulfing pattern, with a small green candle engulfed by a larger red one. If you guess correctly, you're getting the hang of these patterns!

As we conclude our exploration of the Bullish and Bearish Engulfing patterns, remember that the power of candlestick analysis lies not just in recognizing these patterns, but in understanding the stories they tell about market sentiment. By mastering these insights, you're better equipped to anticipate market moves and make decisions that align with your trading strategy.

Lesson 2: Doji, Gravestone Doji, and Dragonfly Doji

Understanding Doji patterns:

Now we will explore three unique candlestick patterns: the Doji, Gravestone Doji, and Dragonfly Doji. These patterns can provide valuable insights into market indecision and potential reversals.

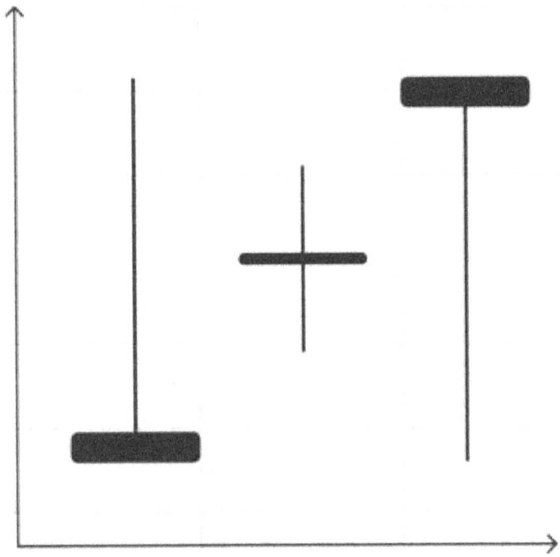

What is a Doji?

A Doji is a candlestick pattern where the opening and closing prices are the same, or very close to each other. This creates a candlestick with a very small or nonexistent body.

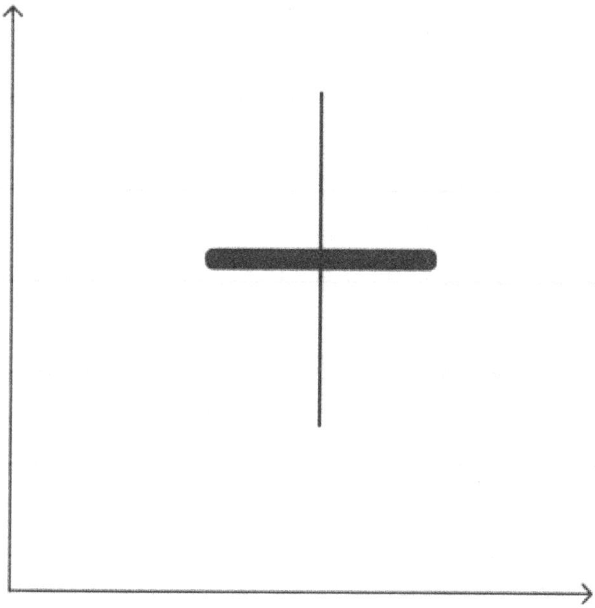

The Doji appears as a cross or a plus sign on the chart. Its distinct shape is due to the market opening and closing at the same price, despite trading higher and lower throughout the period.

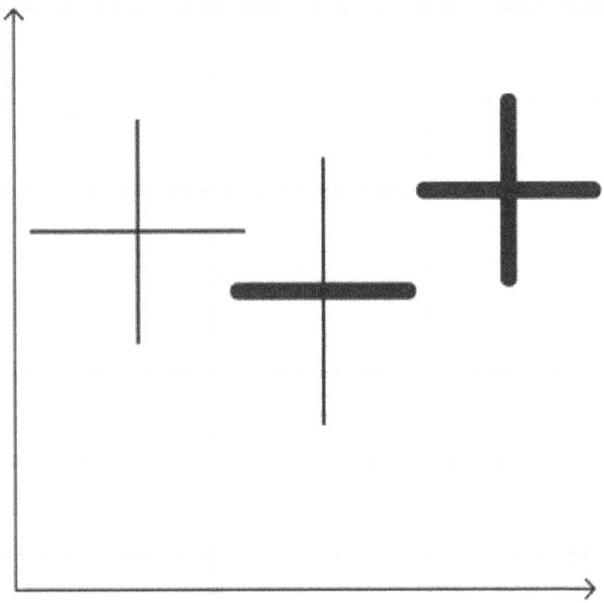

Remarkably, the open and close are at the same price level, emphasizing the market's indecision. So there is no visible body here.

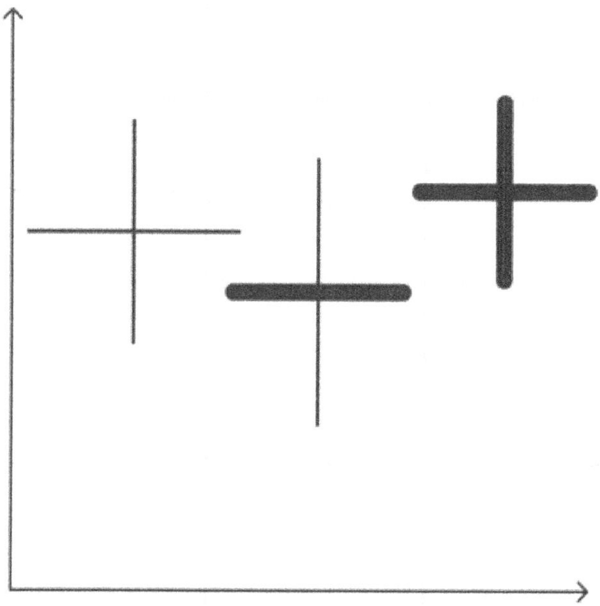

Dojis can occur in various market conditions but are most significant after a prolonged trend, where they may signal a potential reversal or a continuation of indecision.

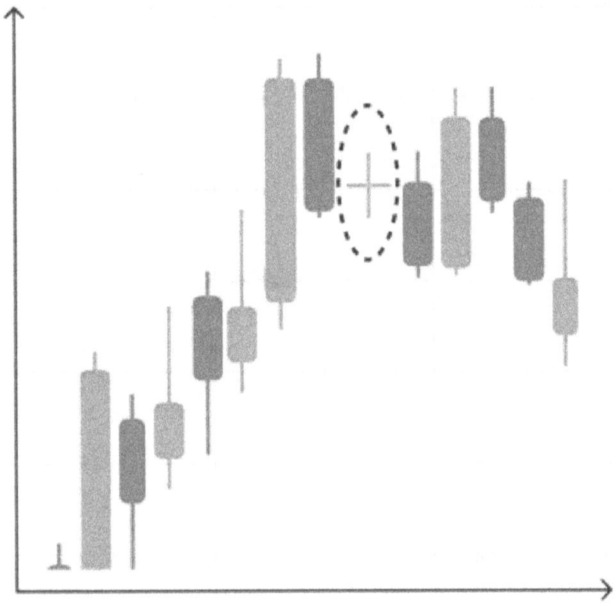

A Doji signifies a balance between buyers and sellers, indicating uncertainty or a pause in the market's momentum. It often calls for cautious interpretation, requiring confirmation from subsequent candles.

Doji in action:

You're analyzing a stock that has been in a strong uptrend for the past month. Today, you notice a Doji pattern forming. Based on this information, what would be the most appropriate action for a trader?

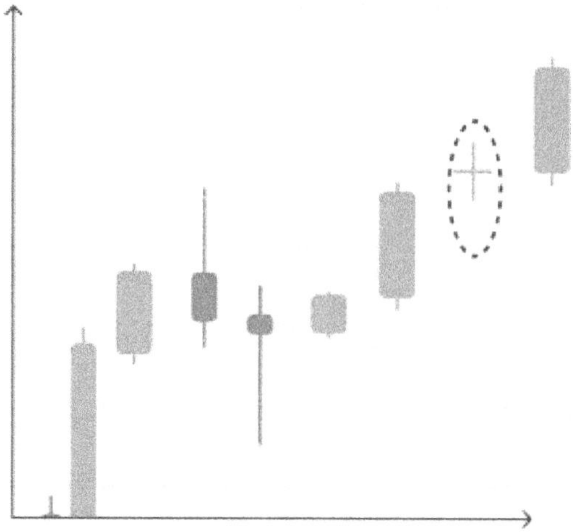

Answer: A Doji after an uptrend suggests market indecision, which could precede a reversal. However, it's not a guarantee. Setting tighter stop-losses prepares for a potential reversal while maintaining the position if the trend continues. Always look for confirmation from subsequent candlesticks.

Next we have Gravestone Doji which looks like the following:

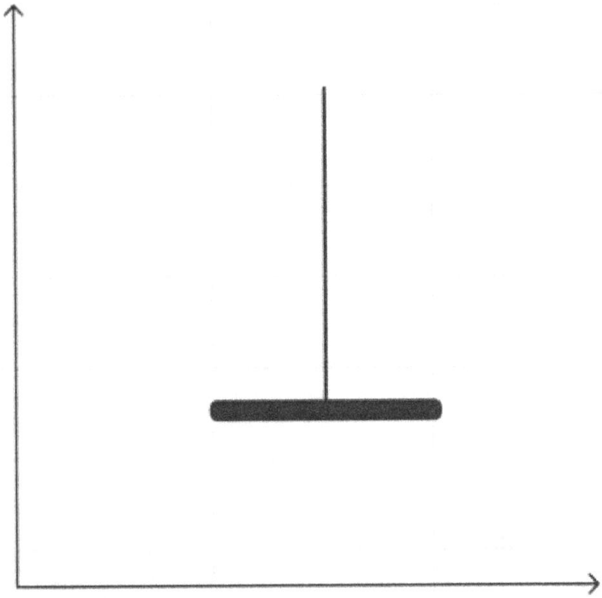

The Gravestone Doji is identified by a small or no body at the lower end, with a long upper wick. It suggests that buyers initially pushed prices higher, only for sellers to drive them back down by the close.

In terms of appearance, the Gravestone Doji looks like an inverted "T". It is particularly noteworthy at the end of an uptrend, signaling that buying pressure may be exhausting.

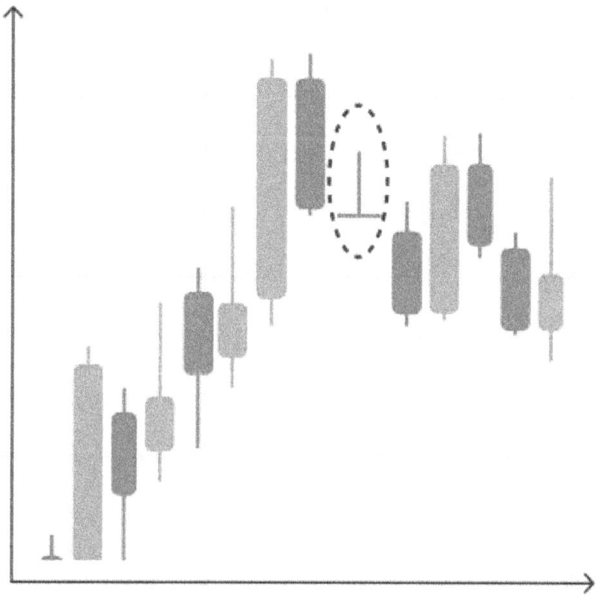

Just like the basic Doji, the Gravestone has the open and close prices at the same level, typically at the lows of the session, with the high creating the long upper shadow.

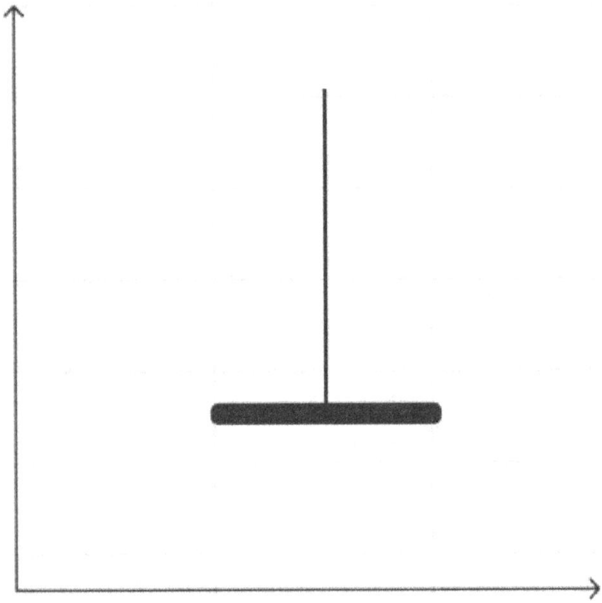

This pattern suggests that any attempt by buyers to continue the trend is met with strong selling pressure, potentially leading to a downtrend reversal. It is a warning that buyers are losing control and sellers might be taking over.

Next, we have Dragonfly Doji, which looks like the following:

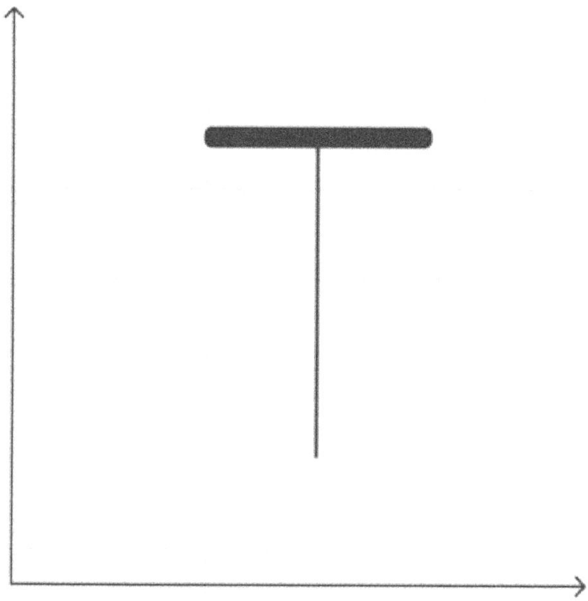

The Dragonfly Doji has a long lower wick and a small or no body at the upper end, resembling the Dragonfly it is named after. This pattern suggests that sellers dominated during the session, but buyers managed to push prices back to the open.

This pattern often forms at the bottom of downtrends and can signal a potential uptrend reversal. It indicates strong buying pressure at lower price levels.

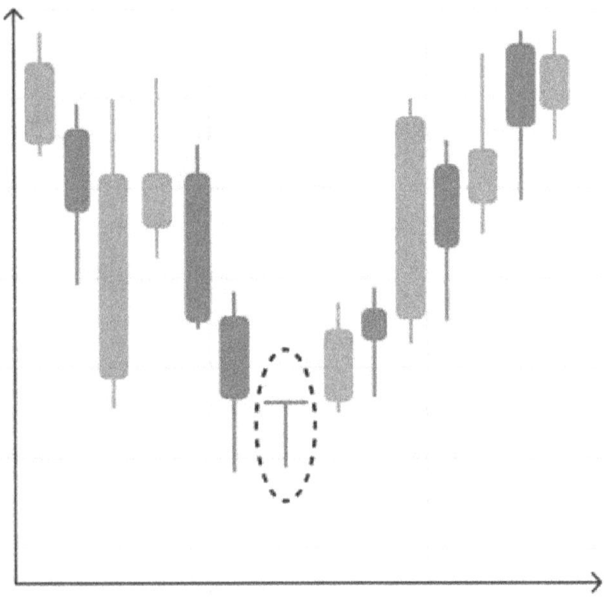

Like other Doji variations, the Dragonfly's opening and closing prices are at the same level, positioned at the high of the day, with the long lower shadow indicating rejected lower prices.

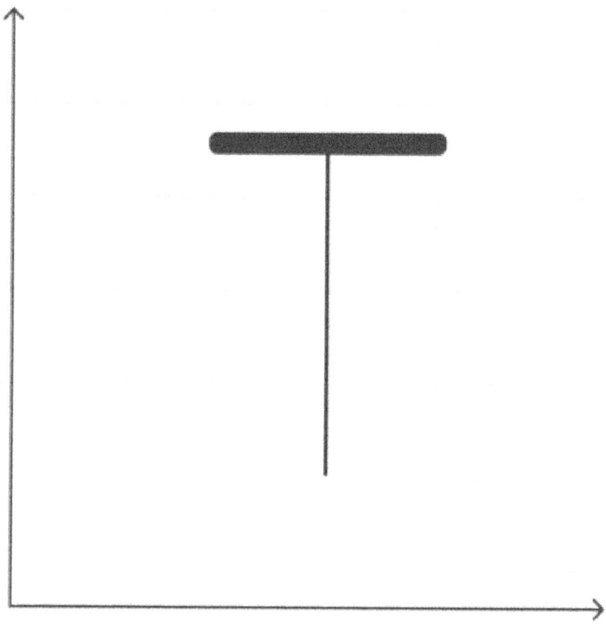

It's crucial to look for confirmation following a Dragonfly Doji, as it suggests a significant shift from selling to buying momentum that may lead to an upward trend.

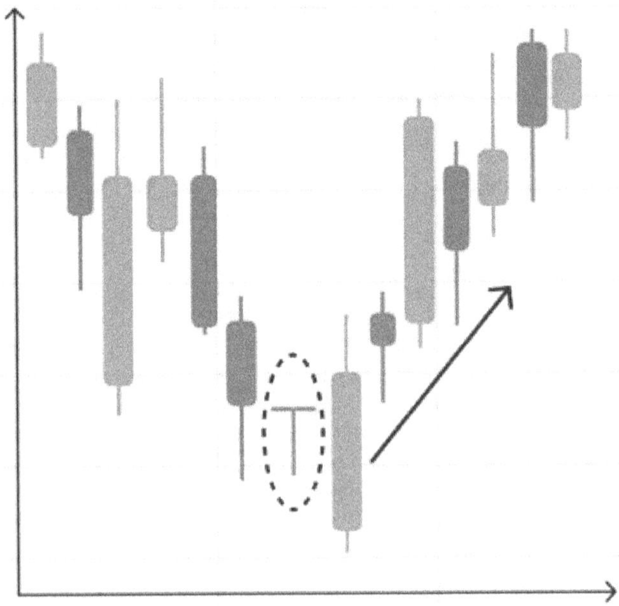

The Dragonfly Doji can signal that buying interest is strong and may outweigh selling pressure, leading to a potential uptrend.

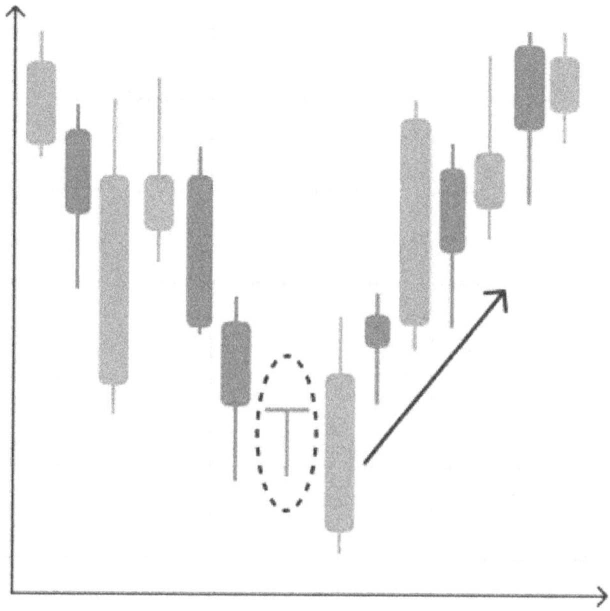

Doji patterns are characterized by having the opening and closing prices at or very close to the same level, creating a minimal or nonexistent body.

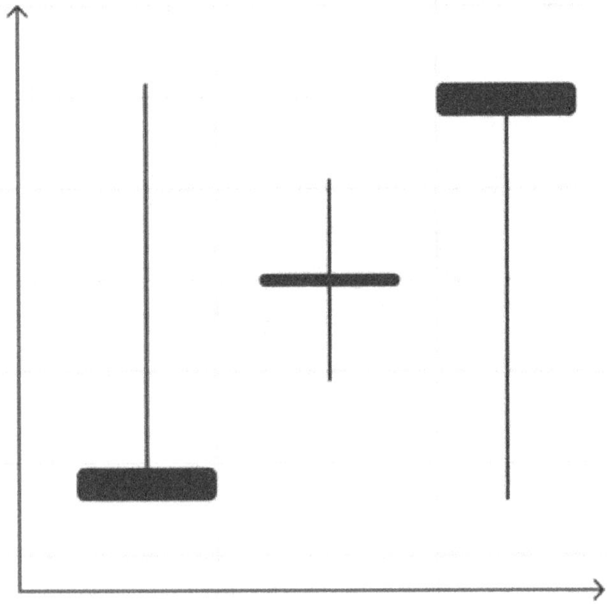

Interpreting the Dragonfly:

You're monitoring a stock that's been in a downtrend. You observe a Dragonfly Doji forming at a support level, followed by a strong bullish candle. What does this pattern suggest about market dynamics, and what might be a prudent trading strategy?

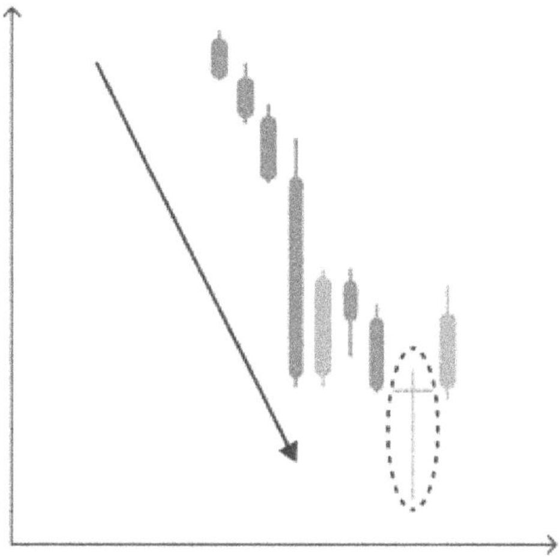

Answer: The Dragonfly Doji at support suggests a strong rejection of lower prices. The following bullish candle confirms buying pressure. A small long position with a stop-loss below the Doji's low balances the reversal opportunity with prudent risk management. Always consider the broader market context too.

The Doji and its variations offer a snapshot into moments of market equilibrium where neither sellers nor buyers have clear control. Recognizing these patterns can help traders anticipate significant shifts in market sentiment, thus aiding in making more informed trading decisions. As always, confirmation is key to validating these patterns before making any trades.

Lesson 3: Morning Star and Evening Star

Two more patterns...

Now we are ready for two patterns that signal significant shifts in market momentum: the Morning Star and Evening Star. These patterns are pivotal in identifying changes in the market direction.

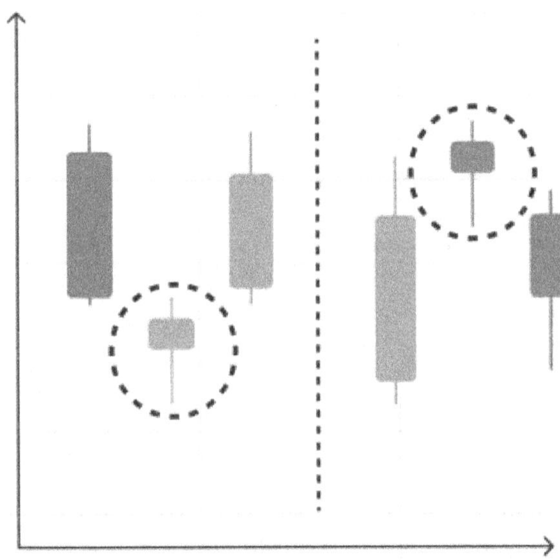

The Morning Star pattern is a three-candle formation that typically appears at the end of a downward trend.

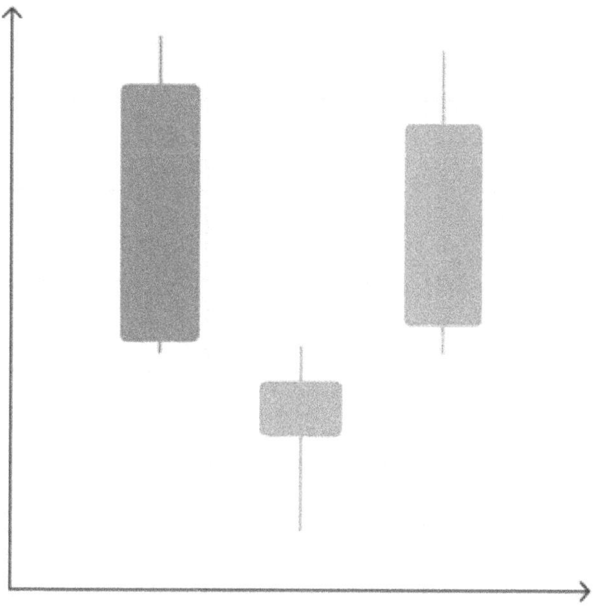

It suggests that the market could be moving from a period dominated by sellers to one where buyers are starting to take control.

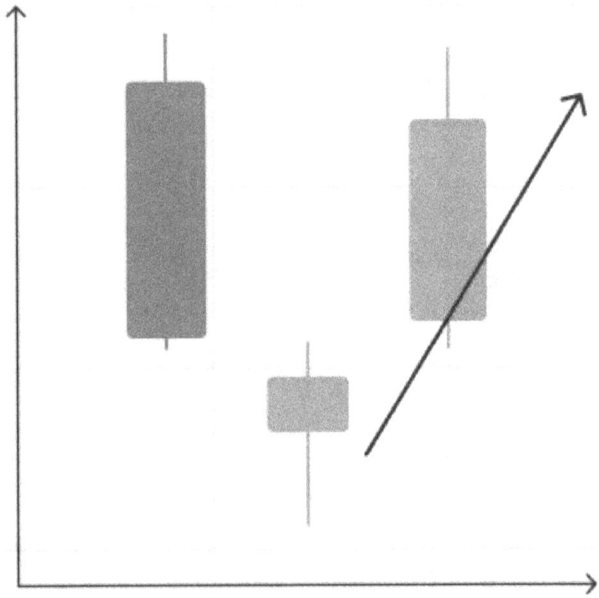

The first candle in the Morning Star formation is a long candlestick driven by sellers, indicating that prices are closing at a low. This reflects strong selling pressure but sets the stage for a possible shift.

The second candle is smaller and can either be a downward or upward candle, usually gapping lower than the first candle. It shows market indecision and is the pivotal point for the potential reversal.

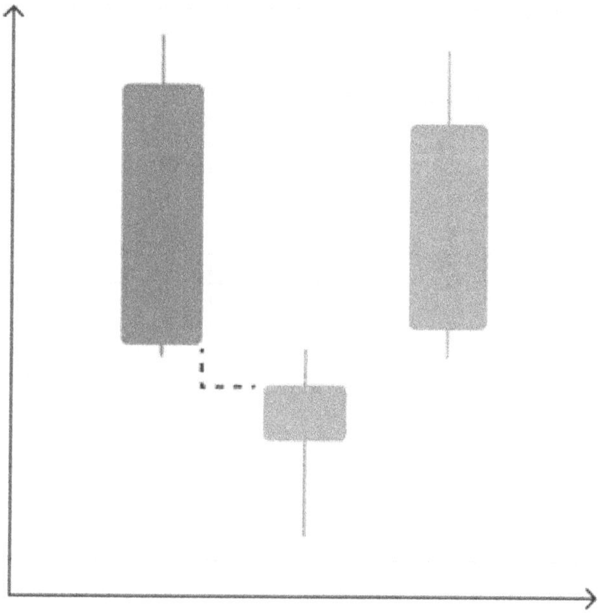

The third candle is where the buyers come into full force, typically a long candle that closes well into the first candle's body. This strong closing by buyers signals a shift in market control.

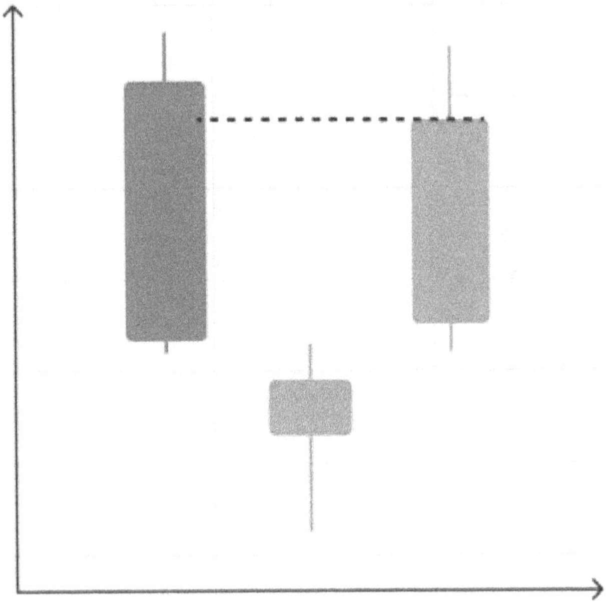

Together, these three candles resemble a morning sunrise, symbolizing the dawn of buyer dominance after a dark period controlled by sellers.

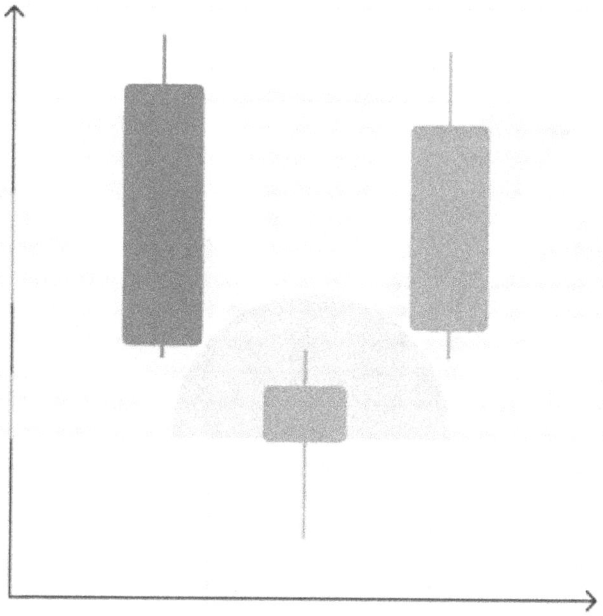

The Morning Star is seen as a signal for potential upward movement, as buyers have successfully pushed back against the previous selling pressure, suggesting a bullish outlook.

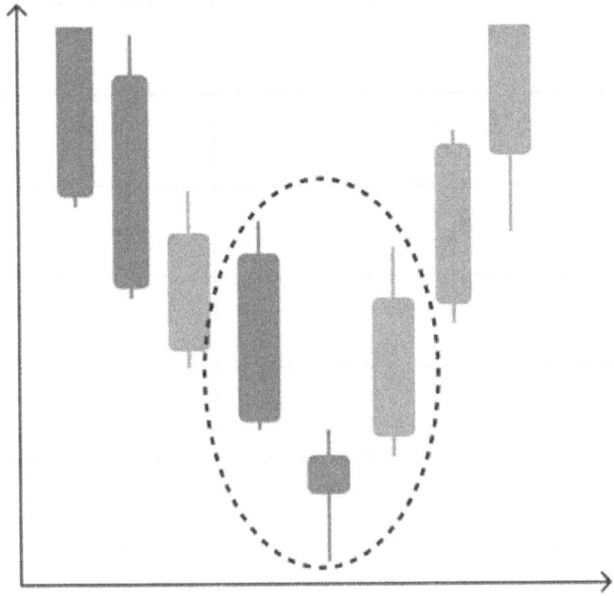

Traders often look for additional confirmation following a Morning Star pattern to ensure the upward trend has solid support and isn't just a temporary rally.

Then we have the Evening Star pattern is the mirror opposite of the Morning Star and typically appears at the end of an upward trend, signaling a transition from buyer to seller control.

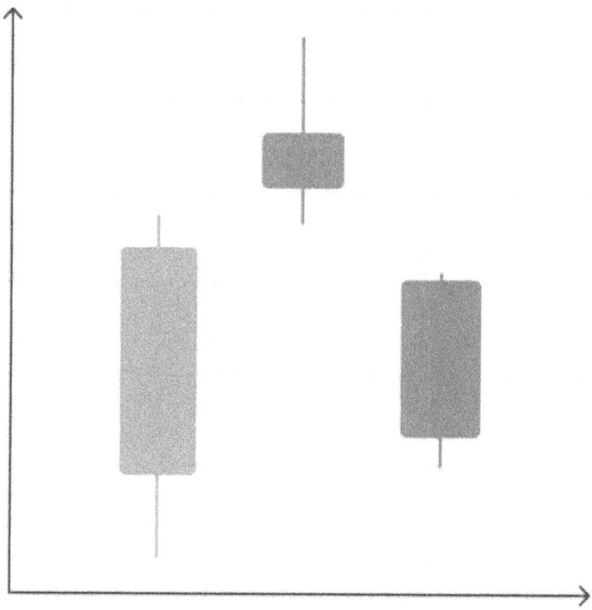

The first candle in the Evening Star formation is large and driven by buyers, closing at a high and indicating strong buying pressure.

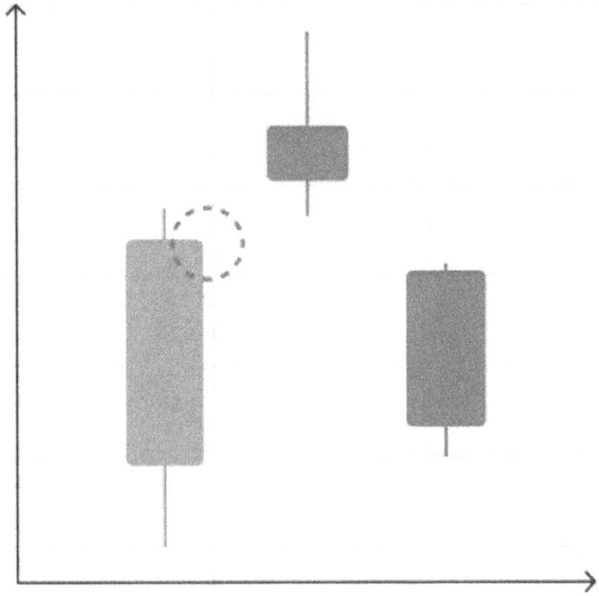

The second candle is smaller and represents market indecision; it could open higher than the first candle, suggesting initial continued buyer enthusiasm but closes without significant gains.

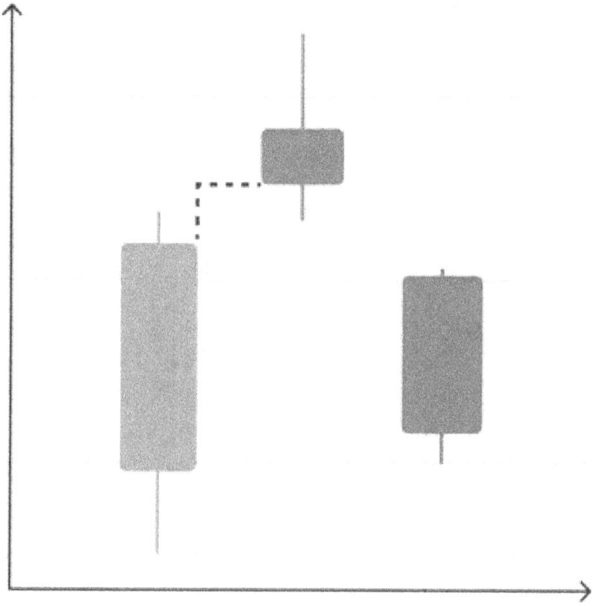

The third candle is key - it opens lower than the second and is a long candle driven by sellers, closing well into the first candle's body. This action signals that sellers are taking back control.

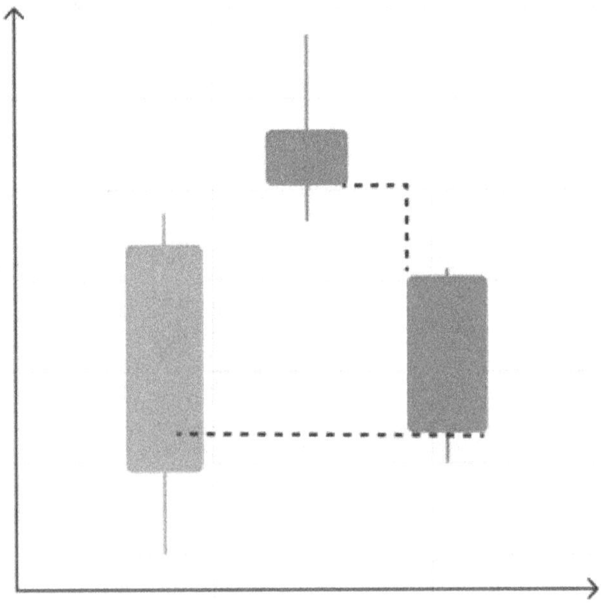

This formation resembles an evening twilight, where the darkness of seller dominance begins to close in after a period of daylight controlled by buyers.

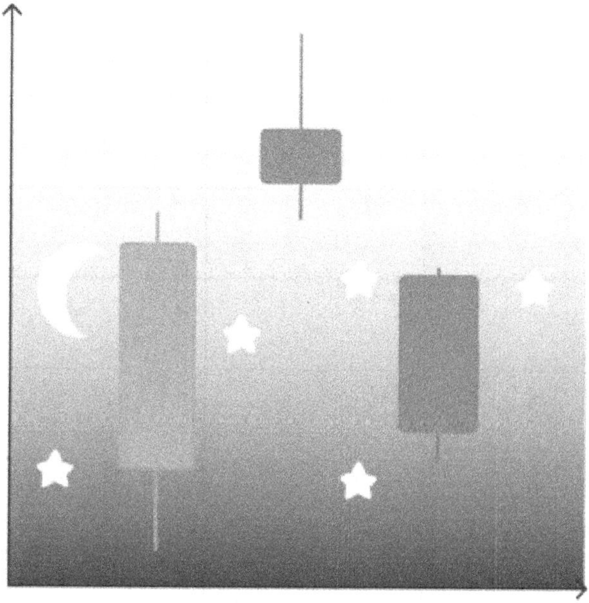

An Evening Star pattern suggests that the price might start to move downward as the sellers overcome the buyers, pointing to falling prices.

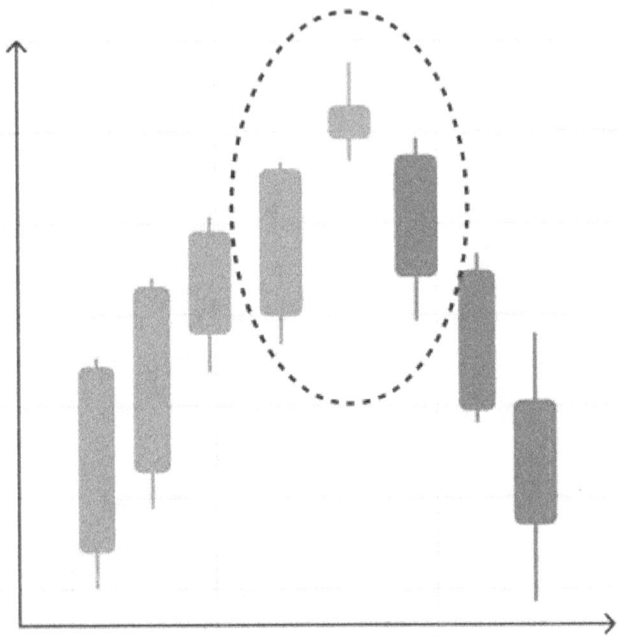

Decoding star patterns:

You're analyzing a stock that has been in a strong downtrend. You notice a potential Morning Star pattern forming over the last three days. As a trader, what would be the most prudent course of action based on this pattern?

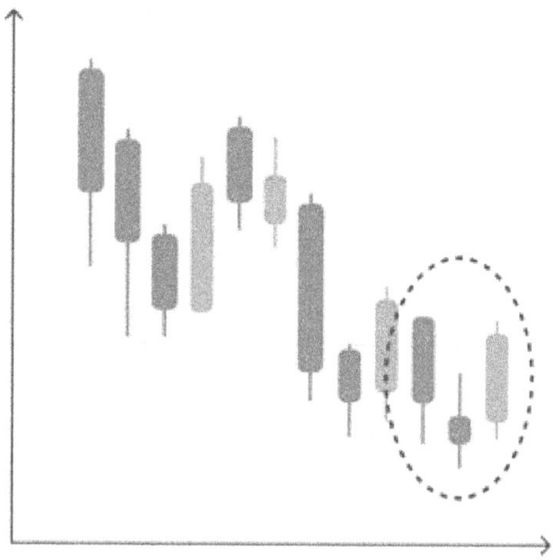

Answer: The Morning Star pattern at the end of a downtrend is a potentially strong reversal signal, but it's wise to seek additional confirmation. Opening a small long position allows you to capitalize on the potential reversal while managing risk with a stop-loss. This balanced approach respects the signal while maintaining prudent risk management.

It's helpful to know that while the Evening Star pattern provides a strategic exit point for traders with long positions, the Morning Star pattern is generally considered a strategic entry point for initiating long positions, not an exit point.

Both the Morning Star and Evening Star patterns are important for traders as they signal significant shifts in market sentiment. Recognizing these patterns can provide strategic entry and exit points, helping to optimize trading outcomes. As with all candlestick patterns, confirmation is essential to validate these signals and to plan trades effectively.

Chapter 3: Opportunity Confluence

Lesson 1: Identifying Market Conditions

Understanding market conditions:

Reading chart prices is a good start, but it's not enough to make money trading. We'll now focus on recognizing trading opportunities, starting with identifying market conditions. This knowledge forms the basis for making informed trading decisions.

There are four main market conditions we need to be aware of: bullish, bearish, ranging, and choppy/indecisive. Let's explore each of these in detail.

First, let's look at a bullish market. In a bullish market, prices generally move from the bottom left to the top right of the chart. This indicates an upward trend.

You might be wondering, "What does bullish mean?" The term bullish comes from the way a bull attacks - by thrusting its horns upward. In financial markets, it represents optimism and an upward price movement.

The opposite of a bullish market is a bearish market. Here, prices move from the top left to the bottom right, showing a downward trend.

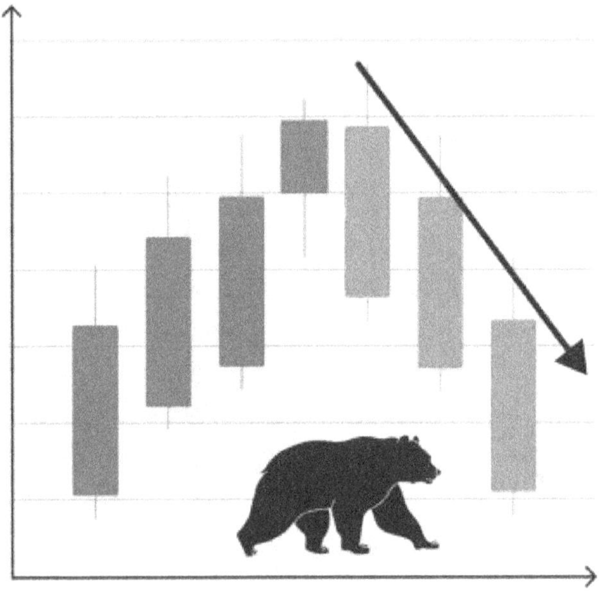

Where does the bearish term come from?

We've learned that bullish represents optimism and upward price movement, coming from how a bull attacks by thrusting its horns upward. But about the opposite term, bearish? Why do you think bearish represents a downward price movement in financial markets?

Answer: Bearish comes from how bears attack by swiping downward with their paws. This downward motion symbolizes falling prices or a declining market, contrasting with the upward thrust of bulls.

There is also a ranging market that moves sideways. It's neither consistently bullish nor bearish. Prices oscillate between upper and lower boundaries.

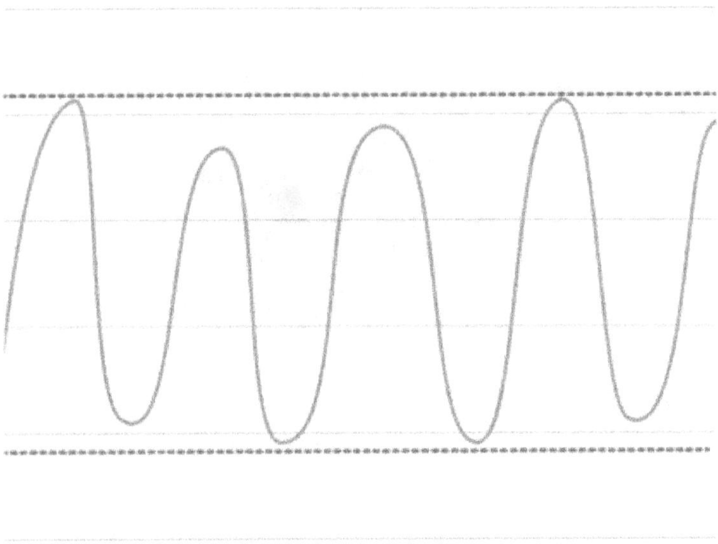

Finally, we have choppy or indecisive markets. These are erratic, with frequent breakouts and breakdowns. It's best to avoid trading in these conditions as they lack a clear edge.

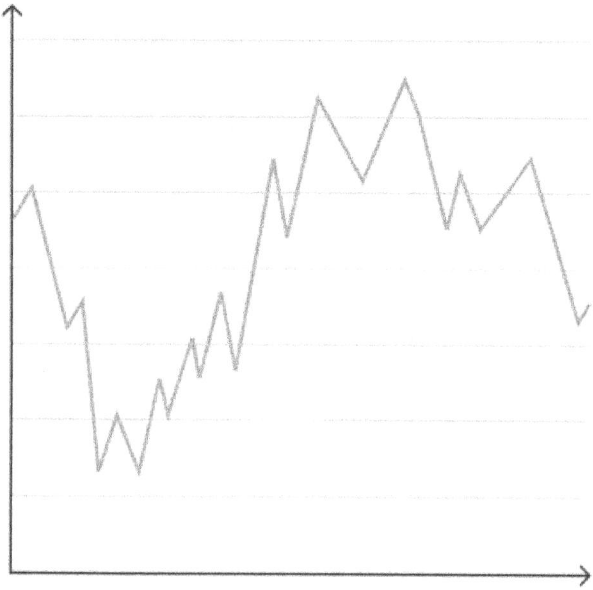

Now, let's look at some examples. Remember, actual charts might look messier than our simplified ones, but the principles remain the same.

Here's an example of a bullish market in USD/JPY (Dollar-Yen). Notice how the overall trend moves from bottom left to top right, despite some fluctuations.

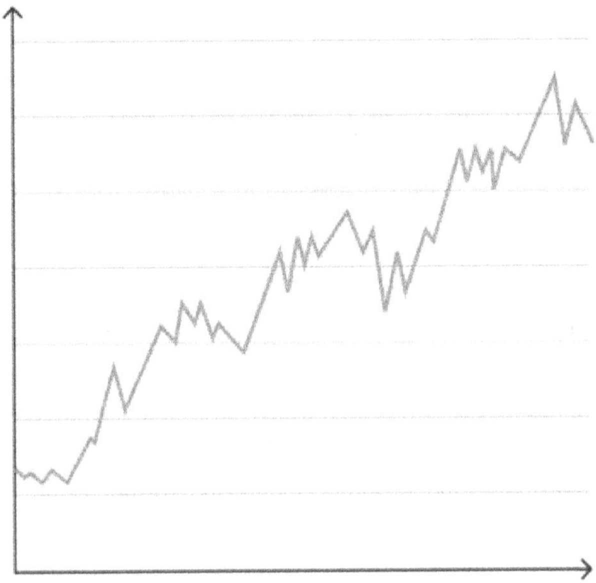

Identify market conditions: example 1

Now it's your turn to apply what you've learned. Take a look at this Pound-Dollar chart and identify the market condition. What market condition does this chart represent?

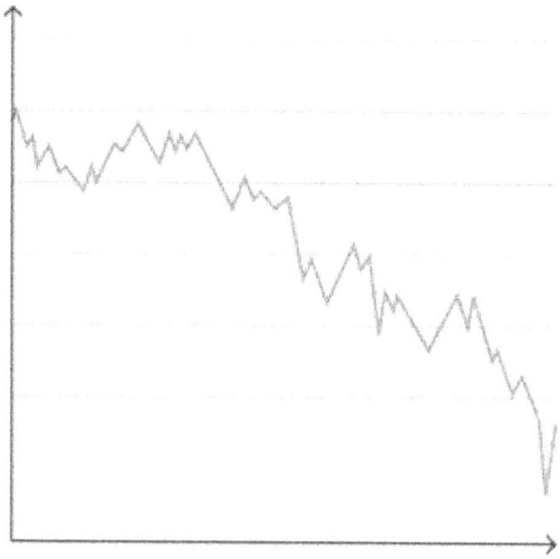

Answer: This is a bearish market. The overall trend moves from top left to bottom right, showing a clear downward trend despite some fluctuations.

Identifying market conditions: example 2

Let's try another one. Which market condition does this chart illustrate?

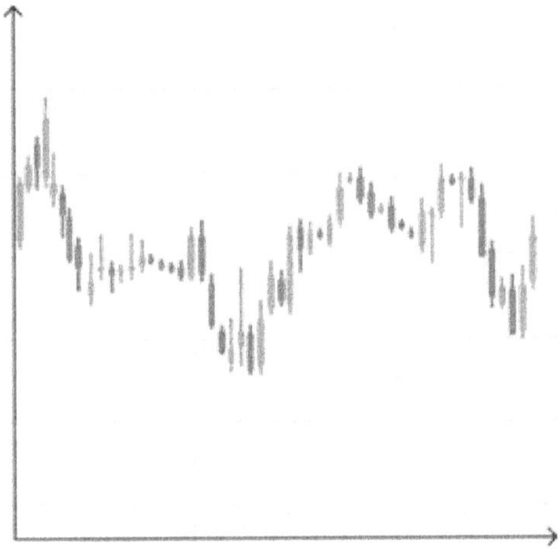

Answer: This is a ranging market. Notice how the price oscillates between clear upper and lower boundaries, moving sideways rather than showing a consistent upward or downward trend.

Identifying market conditions: example 3

Examine this chart carefully. What type of market condition does this chart display?

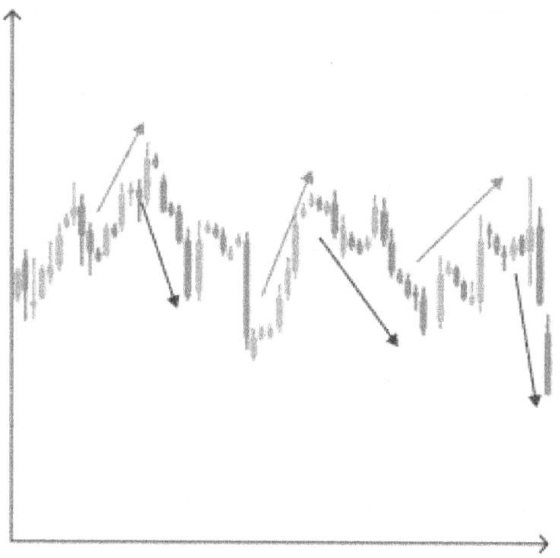

Answer: This is a choppy or indecisive market. Notice the erratic price movement with frequent breakouts and breakdowns. Remember, these conditions are best avoided as they lack a clear edge for trading.

Remember, identifying market conditions is super important for successful trading. It helps you choose appropriate strategies and avoid unfavorable market environments.

Great job! You've now learned to identify the four main market conditions and understand what "bullish" and "bearish" mean. In our next lesson, we'll explore how to use this knowledge to spot potential trading opportunities. Keep practicing your market condition identification skills!

Lesson 2: Understanding Market Phases

Understanding market phases:

So, now you know how to identify the market condition. The next step is to understand the market phase. This knowledge will help you spot better trading opportunities and avoid common pitfalls.

In any trending market, whether bullish or bearish, we can identify two main phases: the run and the pullback. Let's explore these using a real-world example!

Here's our Dollar-Yen chart from earlier. Remember, we identified this as a bullish market. Now, let's break it down into phases.

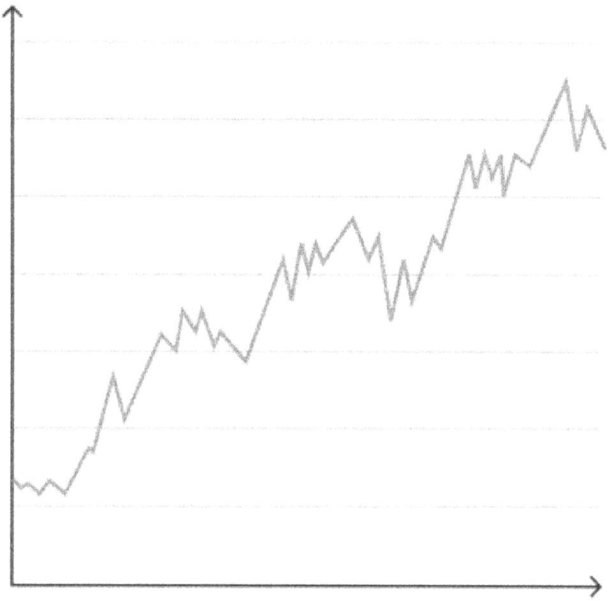

The first phase we see is what we call "the run" or "the extension". This is when the price moves strongly in the direction of the trend - in this case, upwards.

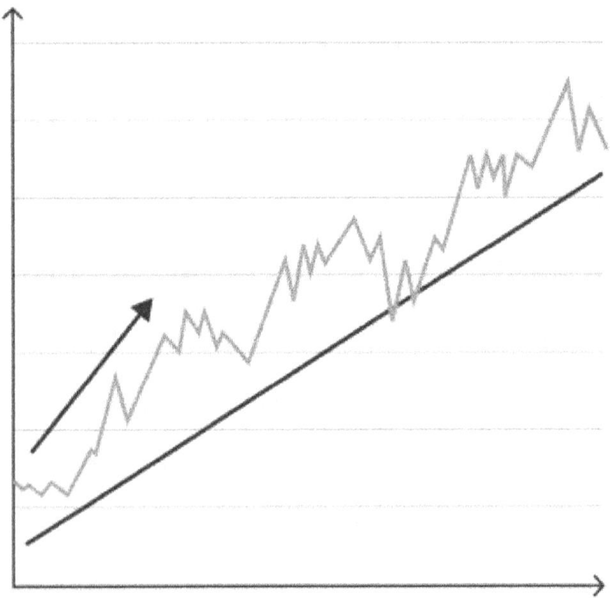

Following the run, we see a pullback. This is a temporary reversal or correction in the opposite direction of the main trend.

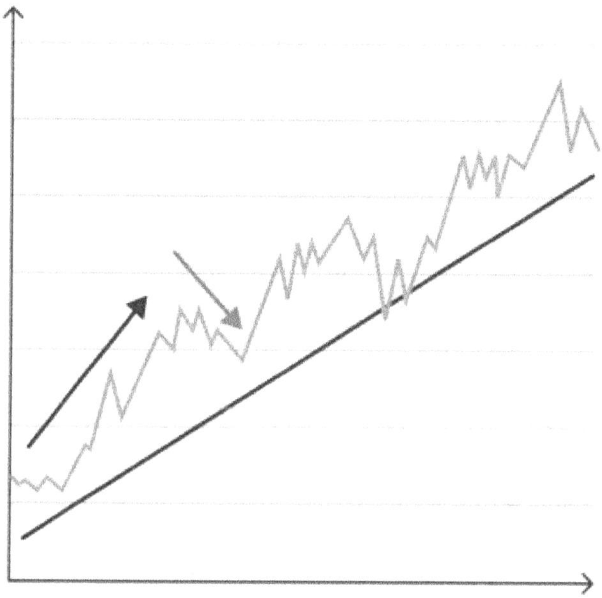

This pattern of run and pullback repeats throughout the trend. Each provides different trading opportunities depending on your strategy.

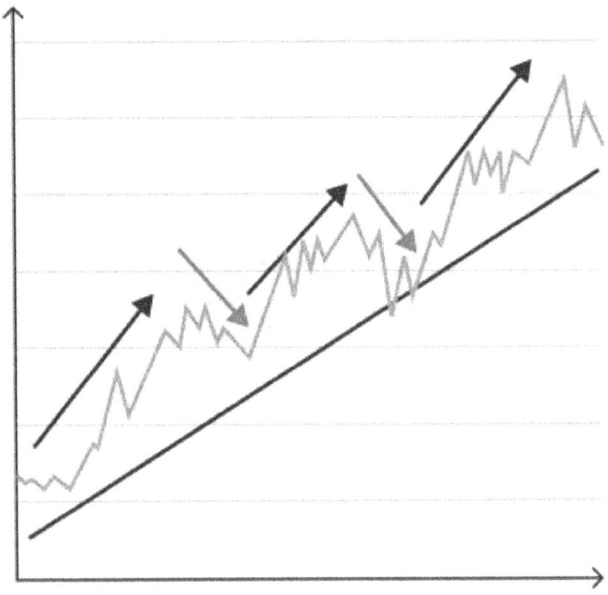

The run phase is the extension in the direction of the trend. It's when the market is making new highs (in a bullish trend) or new lows (in a bearish trend).

The pullback phase is the retracement or correction. It's a temporary move against the main trend, often seen as the market "taking a breather" before continuing.

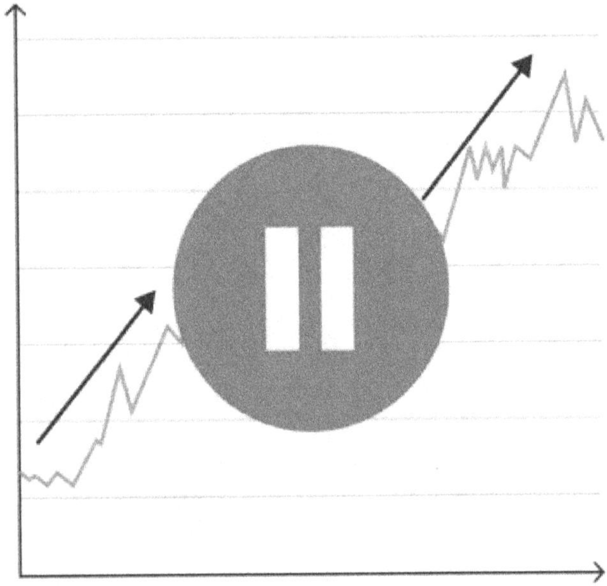

Identifying run phases:

Let's test your understanding of the run phase. Look at this chart and identify the run phases. How many clear run phases can you identify in this chart?

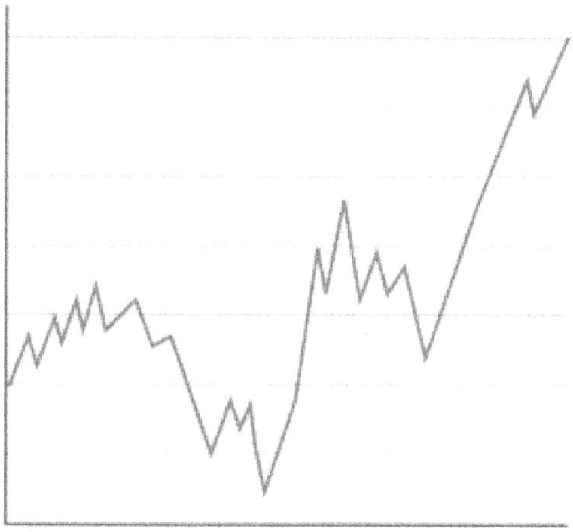

Answer: There are 2 clear run phases. These are the periods when the price is moving strongly in the direction of the overall bullish trend, making new highs.

Let's look at a bearish example to reinforce these concepts. Here's our Pound-Dollar chart from earlier.

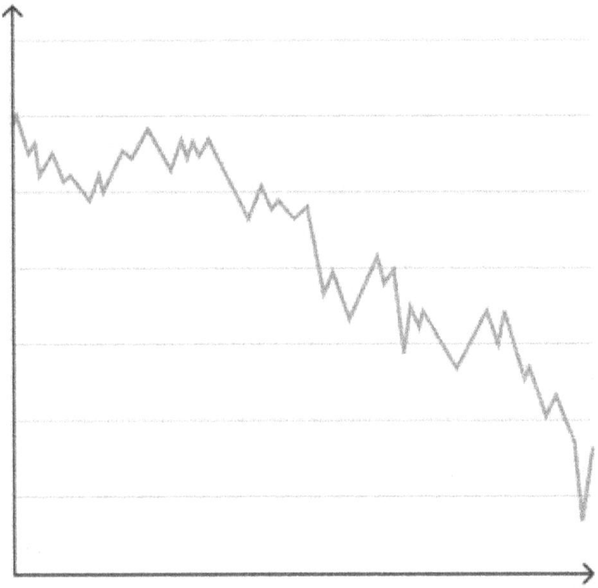

In this bearish trend, we still see the same phases, just in the opposite direction. The run is downward, and the pullback is upward.

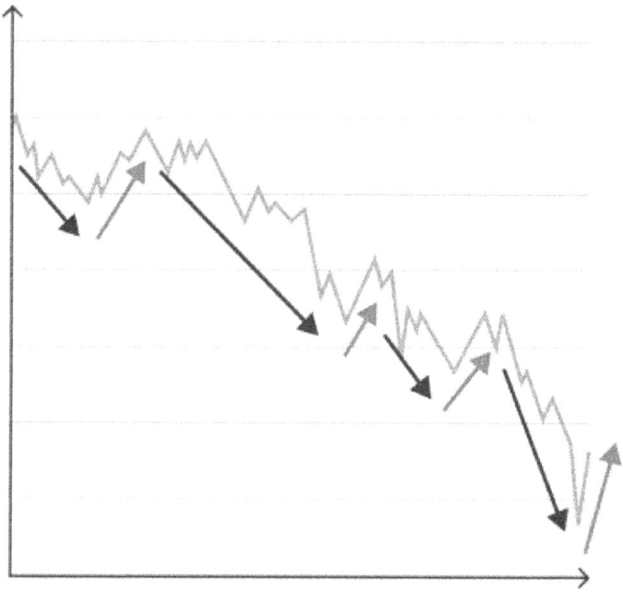

Identifying pullback phases:

Now, let's focus on identifying pullback phases. Examine this bearish chart carefully. How many distinct pullback phases can you spot in this chart?

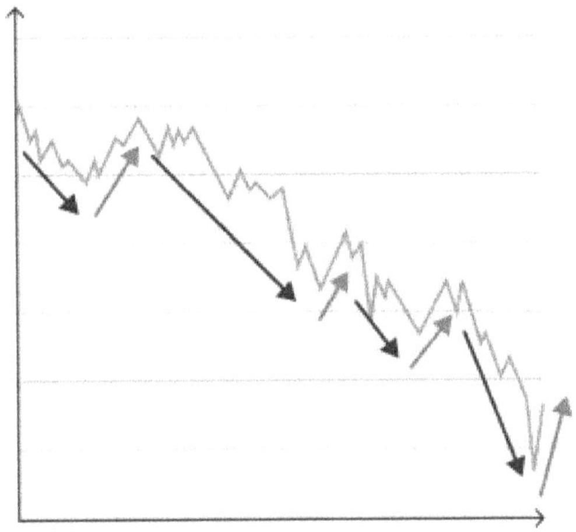

Answer: There are 4 distinct pullback phases. These represent periods when the price temporarily moves upward, counter to the overall bearish trend.

Identifying these phases is crucial for timing your trades. As a rule, you don't want to buy in the middle of a run - that's a common mistake many beginners make.

Instead, skilled traders often look to enter during the pullback phase, aiming to get the best possible price before the next run begins.

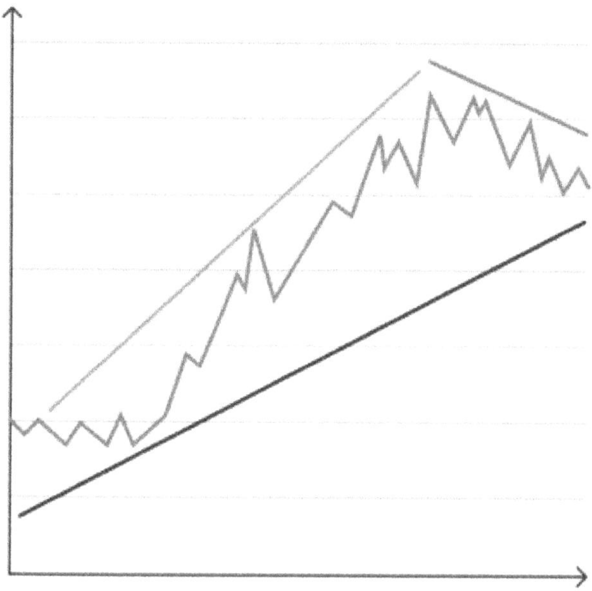

Remember, it's impossible to consistently catch the exact bottom of every pullback or the top of every run. That's not our goal as traders.

Our job is to get in at a good price during the pullback and exit at a good price during the run. This maximizes our potential profit while managing risk.

Identifying current market phase:

Let's test your understanding one more time. Look at this chart and identify the current market phase. What phase is the market currently in?

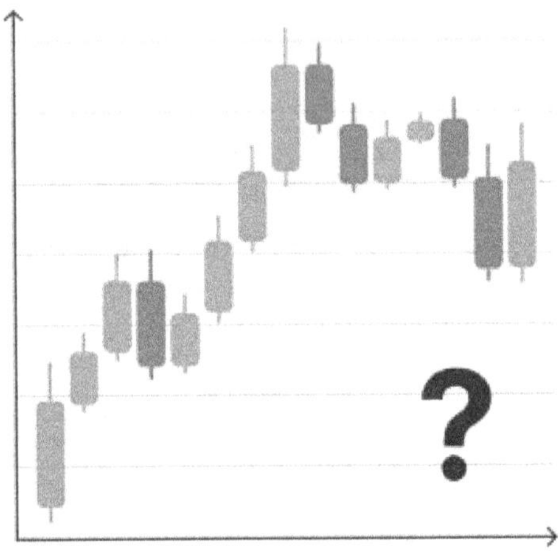

Answer: The market is in a pullback phase. The price is temporarily moving against the main trend, which could present a potential entry opportunity if you're trading with the trend.

Great job! You've now learned to identify market phases within trends. In our next lesson, we'll explore how to use this knowledge along with other tools to pinpoint high-probability trading opportunities. Keep practicing your phase identification skills!

Lesson 3: Identifying Support and Resistance

What do support and resistance mean?

Now that we can identify market conditions and phases, let's explore another powerful concept: support and resistance. This will help us pinpoint high-probability trading opportunities.

Support and resistance are key levels on a chart where the price tends to pause or reverse. They're like invisible barriers that can influence price movement.

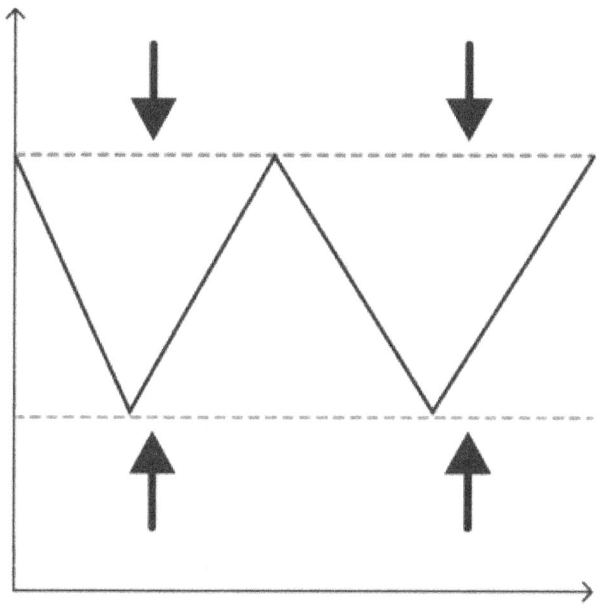

Let's look at resistance first. Resistance acts like a ceiling, temporarily stopping the price from moving higher. It's where selling pressure overcomes buying pressure.

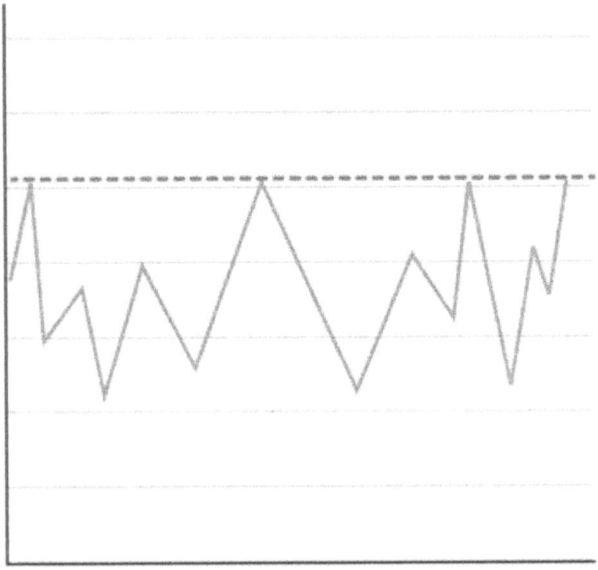

Support, on the other hand, acts like a floor. It's a level where buying pressure overcomes selling pressure, preventing the price from falling further.

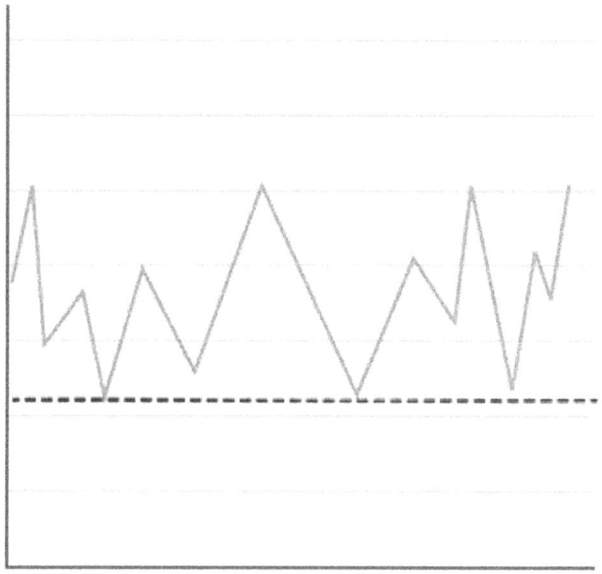

Here's something interesting: in a trending market, previous resistance often becomes new support. This is a key concept for identifying potential entry points.

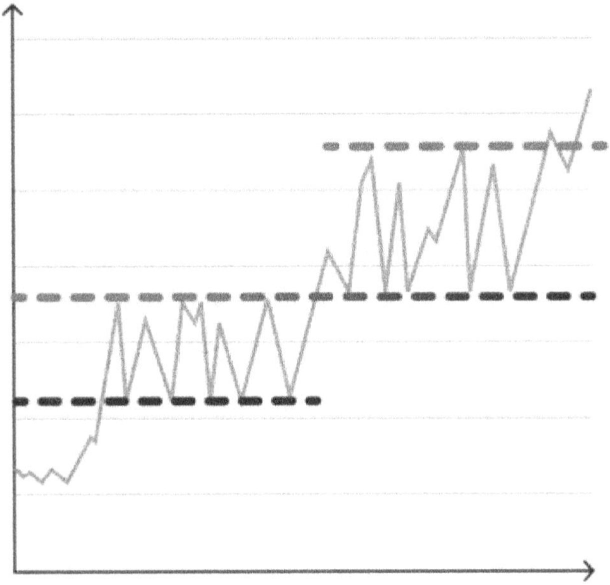

Let's look at a this example. In this bullish trend, can you see how the previous resistance level is now acting as support during the pullback?

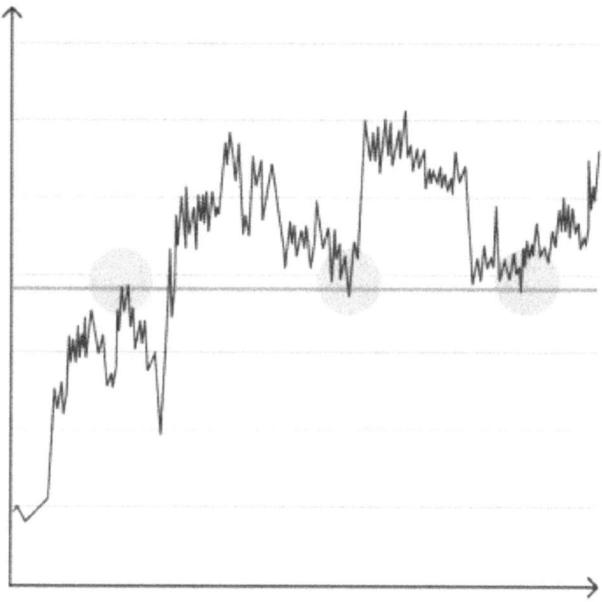

Identifying support and resistance:

Look at this chart and identify the key support and resistance levels. How many clear support or resistance levels can you identify?

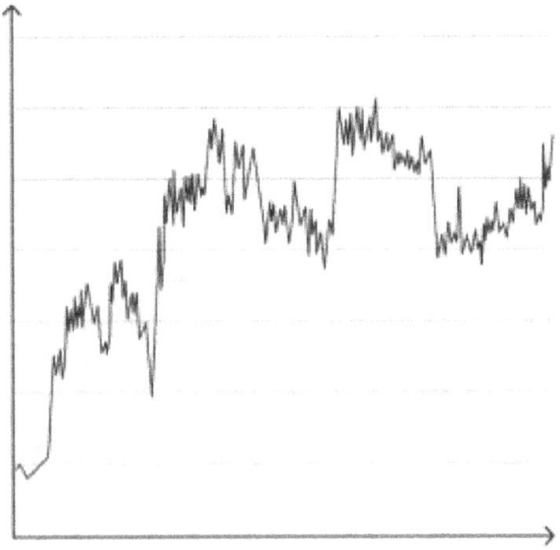

Answer: There is one key support and resistance level. This is an area where the price has consistently reversed, serving as a barrier to further movement.

Now, let's put it all together. We've identified our market condition (bullish), our market phase (pullback), and now we're using support and resistance to pinpoint a potential entry.

This combination of factors gives us a higher probability setup. We're not just guessing - we're using multiple pieces of evidence to make an informed decision.

Remember, trading is about probabilities, not certainties. We're looking for situations where the odds are in our favor, based on recurring patterns in the market.

A trading strategy is essentially a set of rules built around these high-probability patterns. When traded consistently, this approach can lead to profitability over time.

Applying support and resistance:

Let's test your understanding. In this bullish trend, where would be a good potential entry point based on support and resistance? Where's the most promising entry point based on support and resistance?

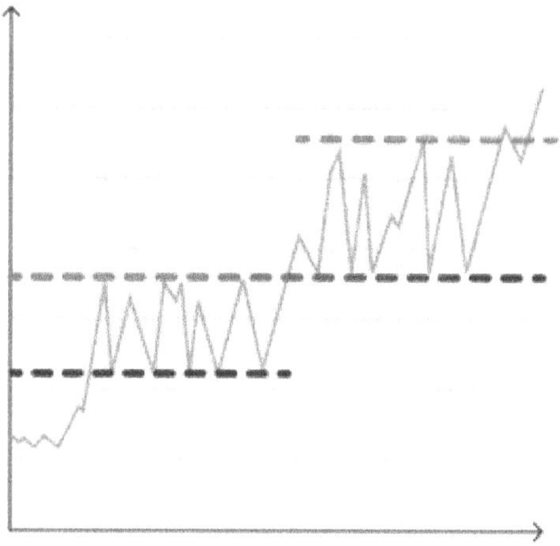

Answer: In an uptrend, the support level is the most promising entry point. It's where buyers are likely to step in, potentially ending the pullback and resuming the uptrend.

But we're not done yet! While support and resistance are powerful tools, we want even more confirmation. In our next lesson, we'll explore how to analyze price behavior when it reaches these key levels.

Remember, successful trading isn't about predicting the future with certainty. It's about identifying situations where the odds are in your favor and managing your risk effectively.

Great job! You've now added support and resistance to your trading toolkit. Keep practicing identifying these levels - they're crucial for spotting high-probability trading opportunities.

Chapter 4: Angular Analysis of Entry Points

Lesson 1: Angular Support and Resistance

Angular support and resistance:

As we delve deeper into technical analysis, it's crucial to recognize that markets are rarely as simple as straight horizontal lines. In reality, trends move at angles, and understanding these angular movements can give us a significant edge.

In this lesson, we're expanding our analysis toolkit with a powerful concept: angular support and resistance. This often-overlooked technique will elevate your ability to identify high-probability trade setups and anticipate market turns with greater accuracy.

Remember, we're trying to think like as many other traders as possible to pinpoint areas with a high probability of price reaction. Angular support and resistance help us do just that, especially in trending markets.

Let's examine a downward trend. We've got our familiar phases - the run, the pullback, another run, and another pullback. But there's more to this story than meets the eye.

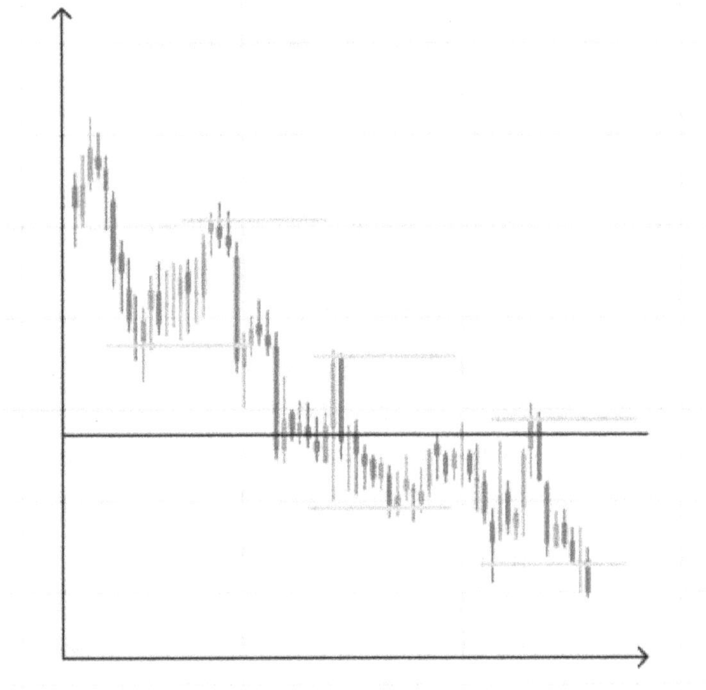

Notice how previous support becomes resistance? That's a concept we're familiar with. But watch what happens when we connect the closing prices of the pullback candles.

This line forms what we call angular resistance - a diagonal ceiling that price tends to respect during its downward journey. It's like an invisible force guiding the market's path.

When markets are truly trending, they often respect these angular levels with surprising consistency. It's not an exact science, but it's a powerful tool in our analytical arsenal.

The real power comes when we align angular support and resistance with everything else we've learned - market conditions, phases, and horizontal support and resistance. This combination uncovers setups with seriously high probability.

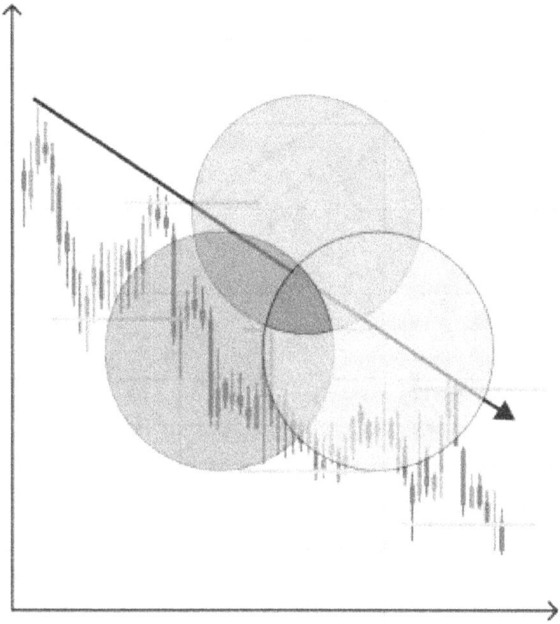

Identifying angular resistance:

Let's put this into practice. Analyze this chart and identify the primary angular resistance level. Which line best represents the angular resistance in this downtrend?

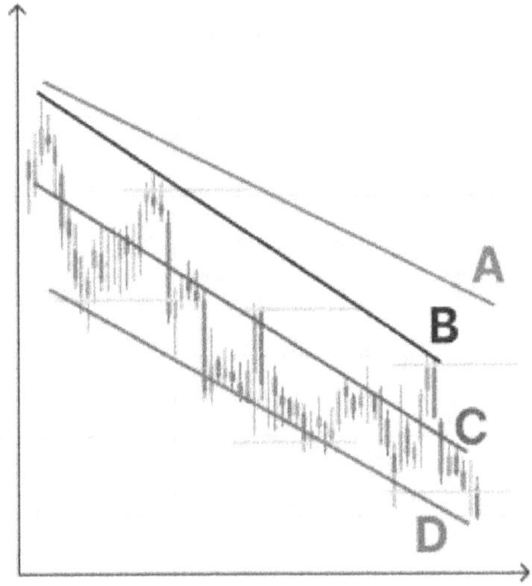

Answer: Line B correctly represents the angular resistance. By connecting the closing prices of the pullback candles, we can see how the price consistently respects this diagonal level throughout the downtrend.

Now, let's look at angular support in a downtrend. The concept is the same, but we're looking at a sinking floor that price tends to bounce off during pullbacks.

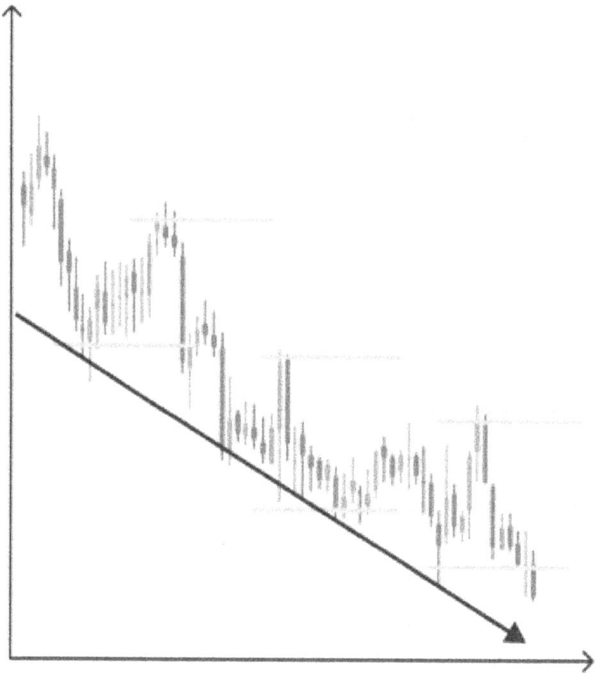

Applying angular support:

Study this uptrend chart carefully. Where would be the most optimal entry point for a long trade?

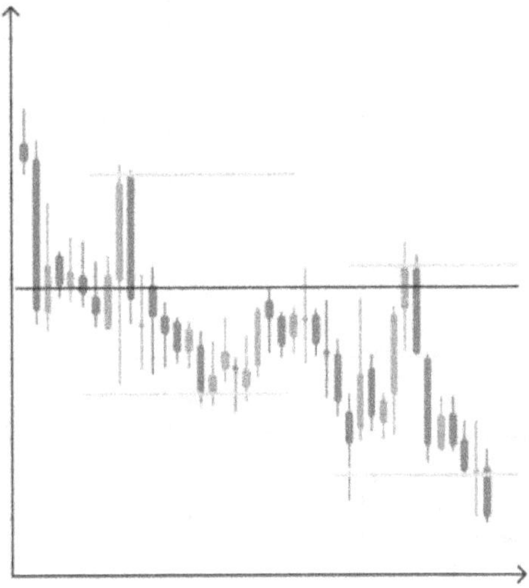

Answer: The intersection of angular and horizontal support creates a potentially strong entry point. This confluence of factors increases the probability of a favorable price reaction.

It's crucial to remember that angular support and resistance levels are not about finding perfect touch points. We're looking for areas of respect. The power lies in combining this with other forms of analysis we've learned.

As we progress through this chapter, we'll explore how angular support and resistance interact with price action patterns and candlestick formations. This will further refine our ability to identify high-probability trade setups.

Remember, mastering angular support and resistance is a key step in developing a comprehensive trading strategy. It provides a dynamic perspective on market structure that complements our existing analysis tools. In our next lesson, we'll delve into price action and deceleration patterns, building on the foundation we've established here.

Lesson 2: Price Action and Deceleration

Advanced price action analysis:

Welcome to our next lesson! We're going to dive deeper into price action, focusing on how to read the market's "story" and identify high-probability entry points.

Remember, we're not just looking at individual candles or patterns in isolation. We're combining multiple factors to build a comprehensive view of the market.

Let's start by revisiting the concept of momentum. In a trend, we often see strong momentum candles in the direction of the trend.

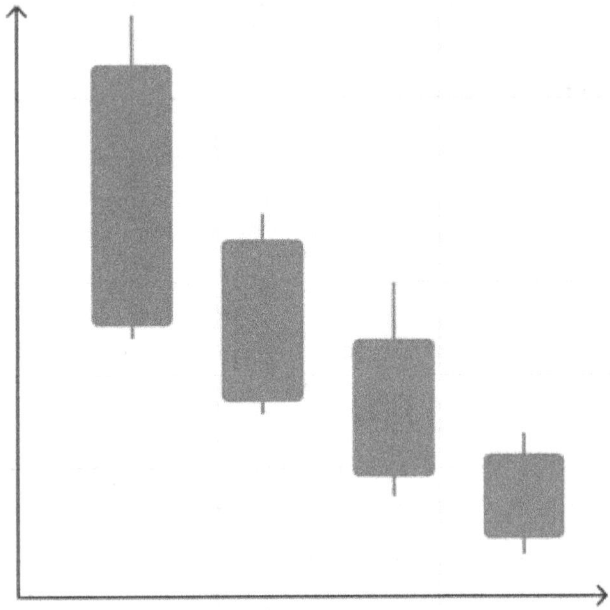

However, trends don't last forever. We need to be able to identify when a trend might be losing steam. This is where deceleration comes into play.

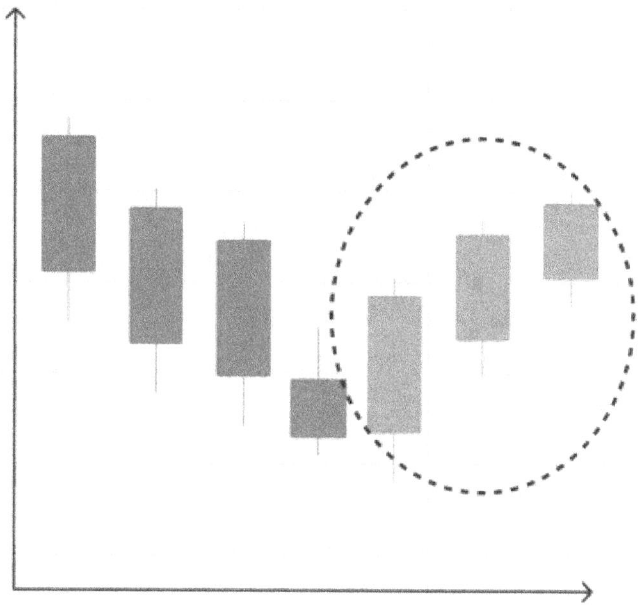

Deceleration often manifests as a series of candles with progressively smaller bodies. This suggests the dominant trend is weakening.

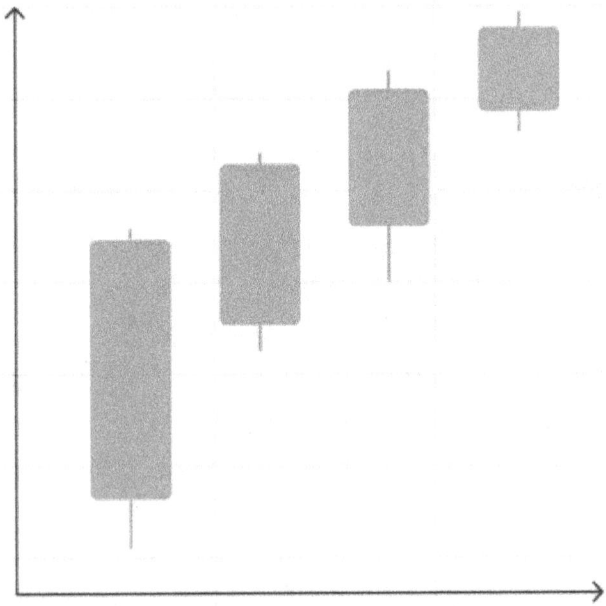

Let's look at this example. Here's a chart of AUD/NZD. We can see a clear downtrend with runs and pullbacks.

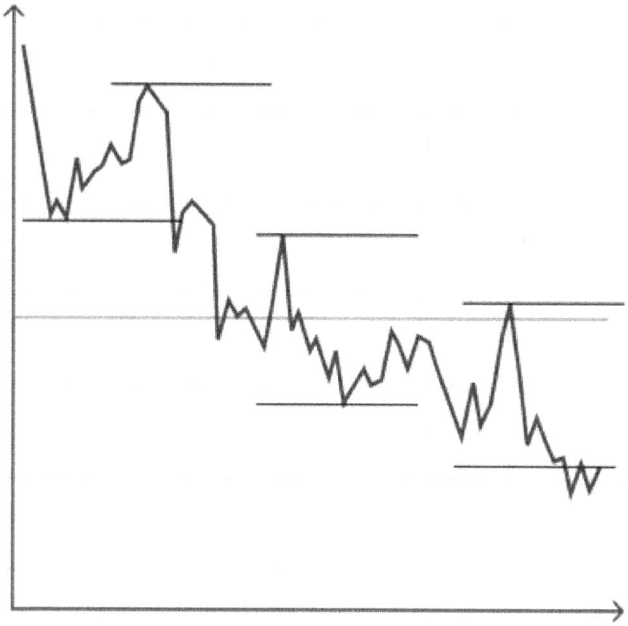

Notice how we have previous structure support becoming resistance. We also have angular resistance forming.

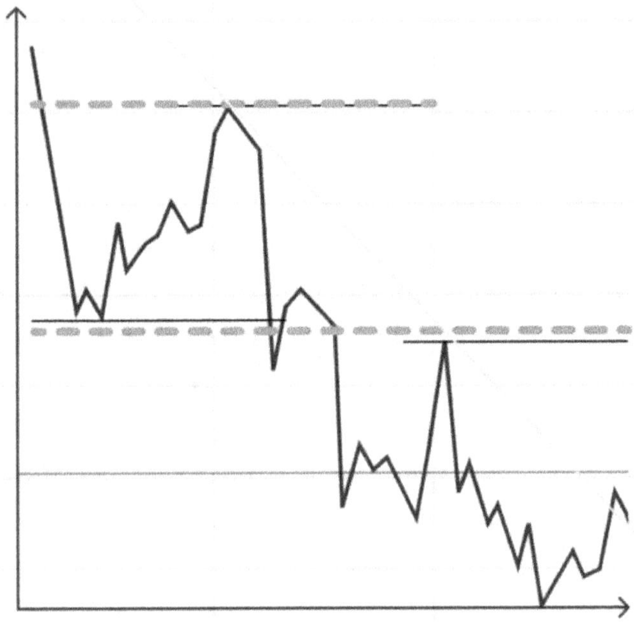

Now, let's zoom in on this pullback phase. This is where we can really start to read the price action story.

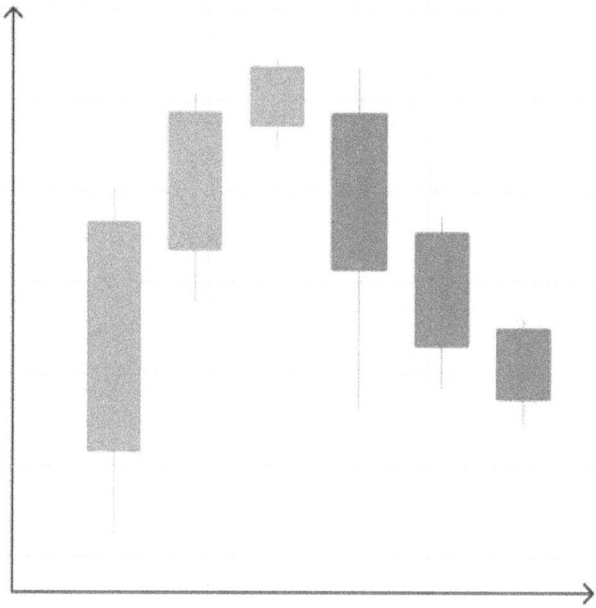

We start with a strong bullish candle, followed by several more bullish candles. But have you noticed anything about these candles?

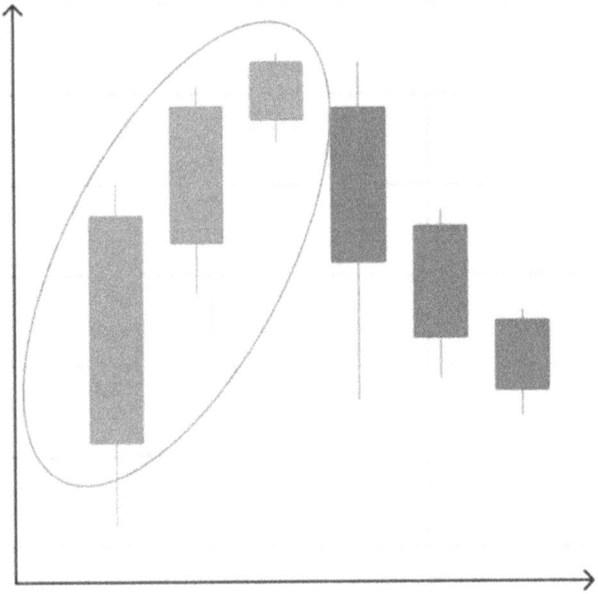

They're getting progressively smaller. This is our first clue of deceleration. The bullish momentum is weakening.

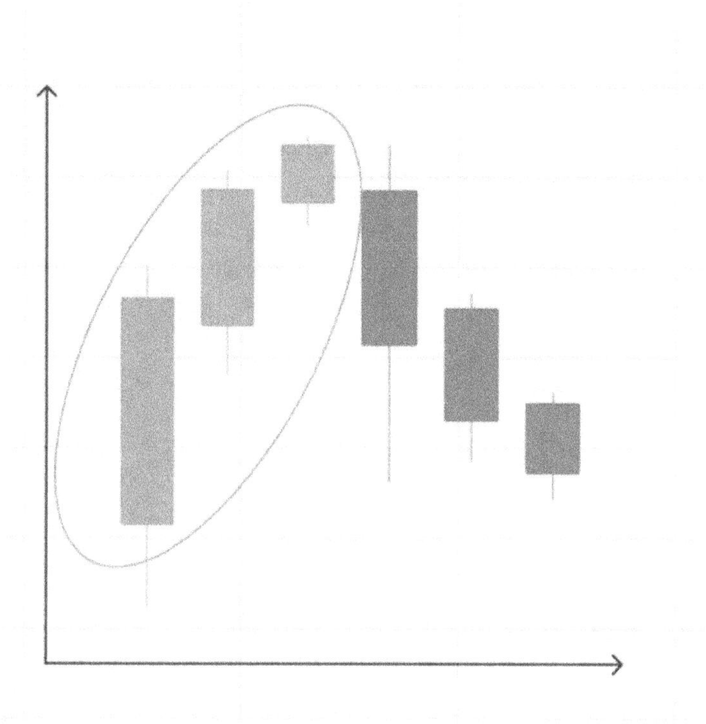

Identifying deceleration:

Based on what we've discussed, can you identify where deceleration begins in this chart? At which point does deceleration become evident?

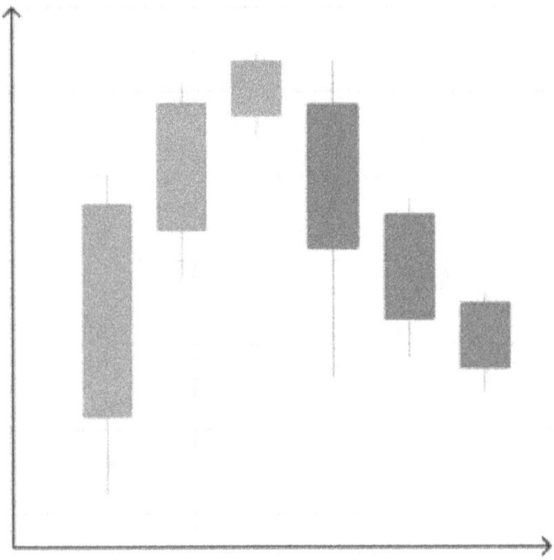

Answer: Deceleration becomes evident when the candle bodies start getting smaller. This suggests the current move is losing momentum.

Now, let's talk about specific candlestick patterns. We've seen this high-test candle, also known as a shooting star. It's particularly significant given its location.

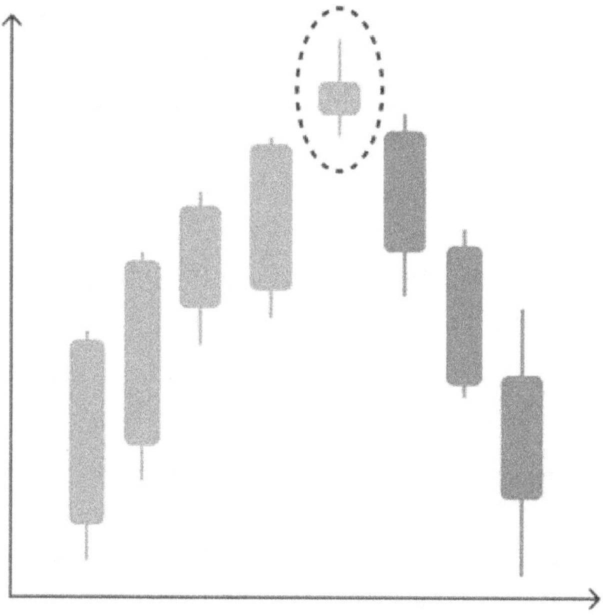

Remember, these patterns occur throughout the chart. Their significance comes from their context. Here, it's at a resistance level during a pullback in a downtrend.

We've also discussed Doji candles before. These represent indecision and can be powerful when they appear at key levels.

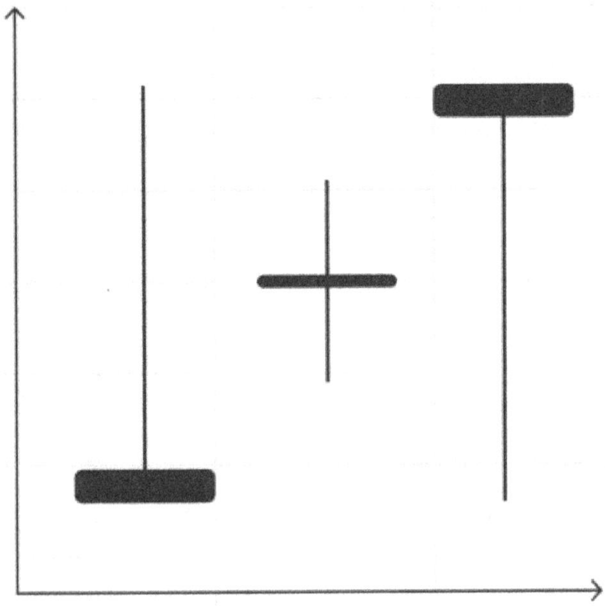

Again, the key is not just identifying these patterns, but understanding their context within the larger market structure.

Before we wrap up this lesson, let's take all the elements we've discussed - market condition, phases, support/resistance, and price action patterns - and see how they work together in practice.

This is where everything comes together to form a complete market analysis. By layering all these factors, we create a comprehensive view of the market, helping us identify high-probability entry points with a favorable risk-to-reward ratio.

For example, in this chart, we see a bearish market condition, a pullback phase, support and resistance (both horizontal and angular), deceleration in price action, and the appearance of key candlestick patterns like the shooting star.

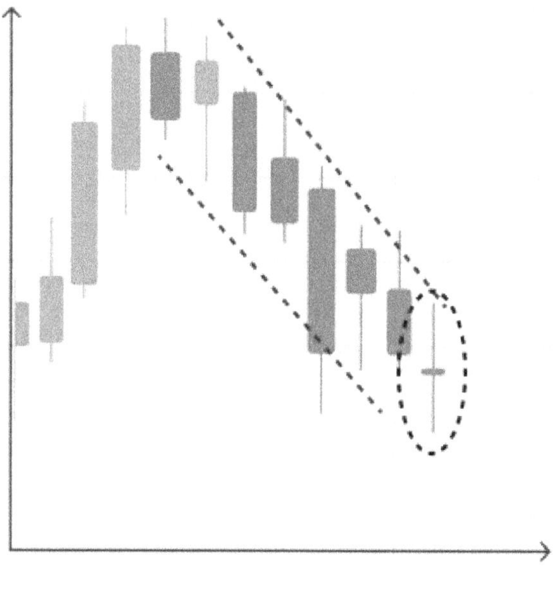

This combination of factors helps us identify high-probability entry points. Remember, we're not trying to perfectly time the market, but to find the best possible entries based on multiple confirming factors.

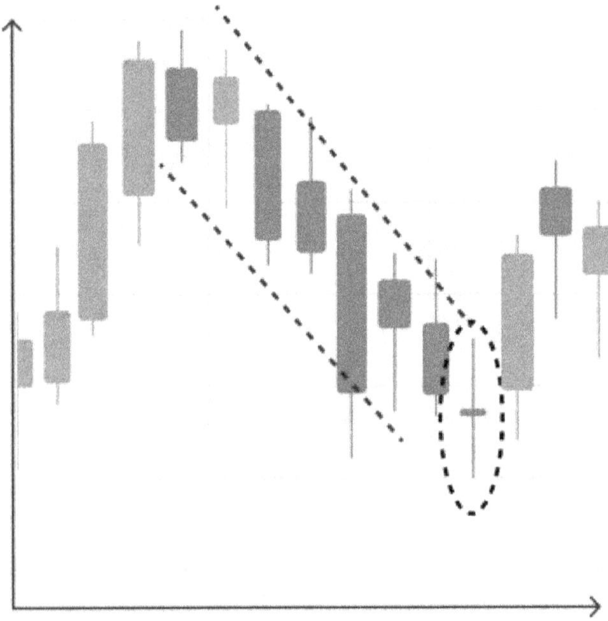

Wrapping up, you've learned how to identify deceleration in price action and understand its significance in the context of market trends. Remember, this skill takes practice to master. Keep analyzing charts and you'll soon be spotting these patterns with ease. In our next lesson, we'll explore how to use this information to plan your trades effectively.

Lesson 3: Indicators and Trade Execution

Indicators and trade execution:

In this lesson, you will learn how indicators can enhance your analysis and how to use this information to execute trades effectively.

We've already covered market conditions, phases, support/ resistance, and price action patterns. Now, let's introduce indicators as additional filters for confirmation.

Two popular indicators are Fibonacci retracements and exponential moving averages. For now, we'll focus on Fibonacci retracements as an example.

The Fibonacci retracement tool is often used to identify potential reversal levels during a pullback. It's based on mathematical ratios found in nature.

You can find these in the drawing or analysis section of any modern charting software. To use them, select the Fibonacci tool, then click and drag from a significant low to a high (or vice versa) on your chart. The software will automatically display Fibonacci levels (23.6%, 38.2%, 61.8%) which can help identify potential support, resistance, or price targets.

Two key levels to watch are the 38.2% and 61.8% retracements. The 38.2% level often indicates a stronger trend, while 61.8% suggests a deeper retracement.

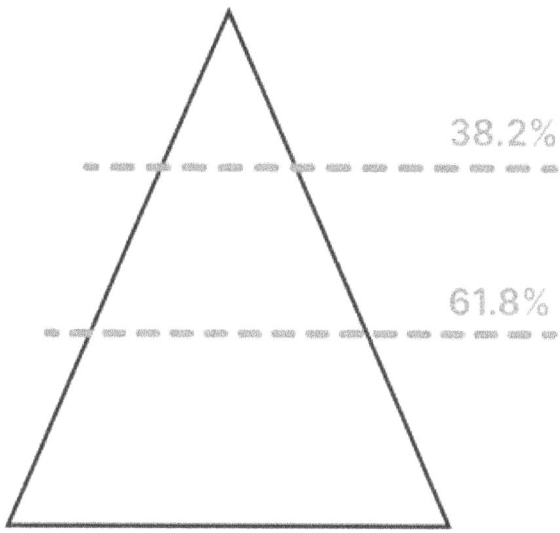

Let's add this to our analysis. We now have horizontal and angular support/resistance, our market phase (pullback), and a Fibonacci level all aligning in one zone.

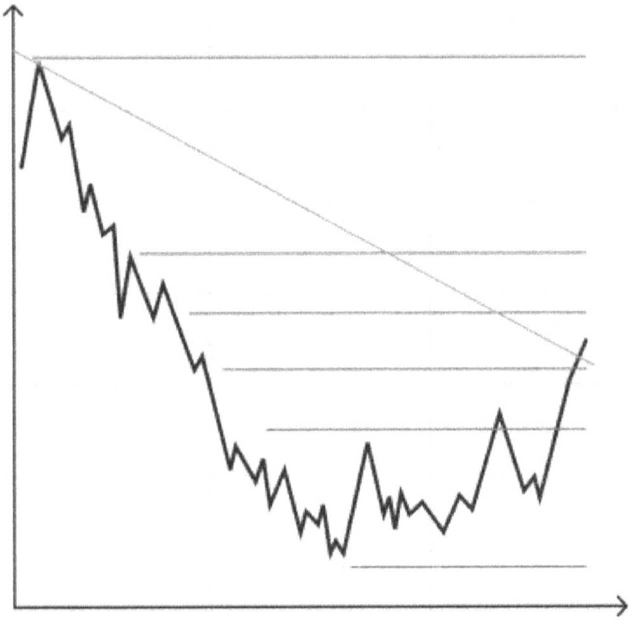

Another factor to consider is psychological levels. These are round numbers like 1.1000 or numbers ending in 50, which often act as support or resistance.

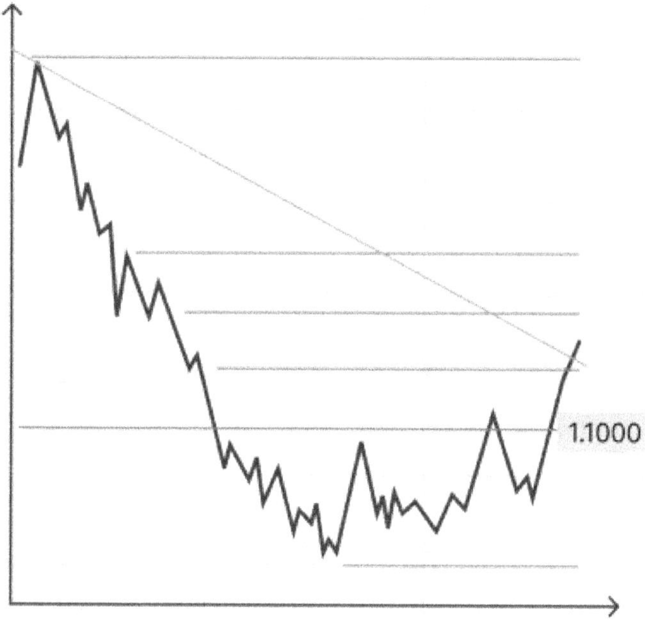

These levels are significant because many traders place orders around them, leading to increased market activity and potential reversals.

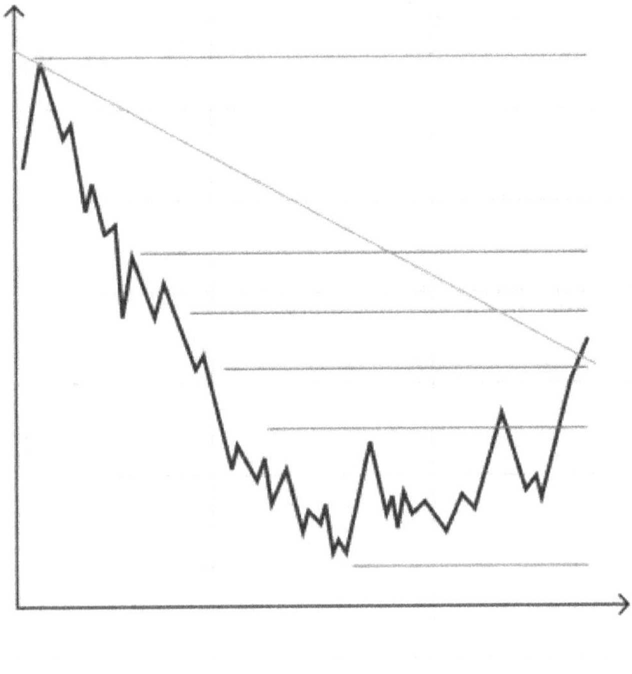

Identifying confluence:

Looking at this chart, how many confirming factors can you identify for a potential trade setup? How many confirming factors are present in this setup?

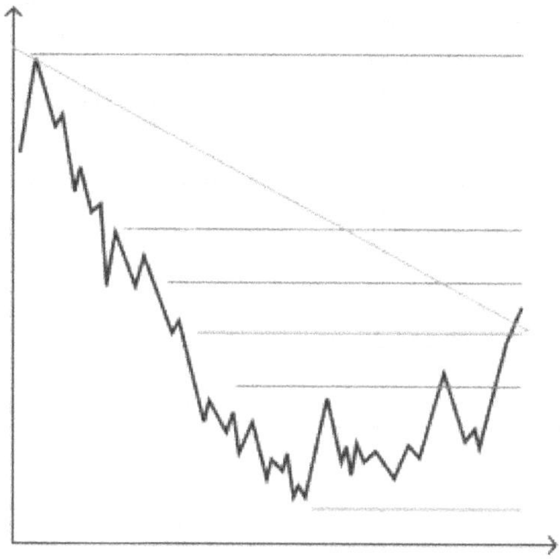

Answer: There should be 3 confirming factors! Consider all the elements we've discussed, including market structure, Fibonacci levels, and psychological numbers.

Now that we've identified a high-probability setup, it's time to think about trade execution. We're looking for a specific candlestick formation as our final entry signal.

In this case, we have a high-test candle (or Shooting Star) forming at our confluence zone. This becomes our signal to prepare for a trade entry.

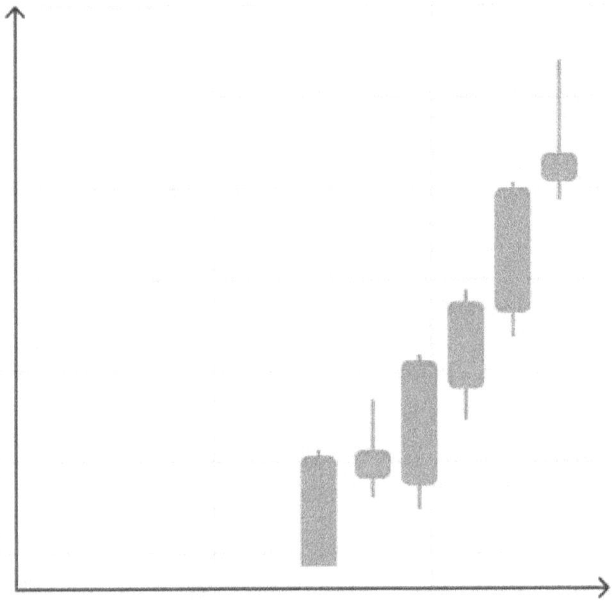

For a short trade, we might place a sell-stop order just below the low of this signal candle. This means we'll enter the trade if the price moves below this level.

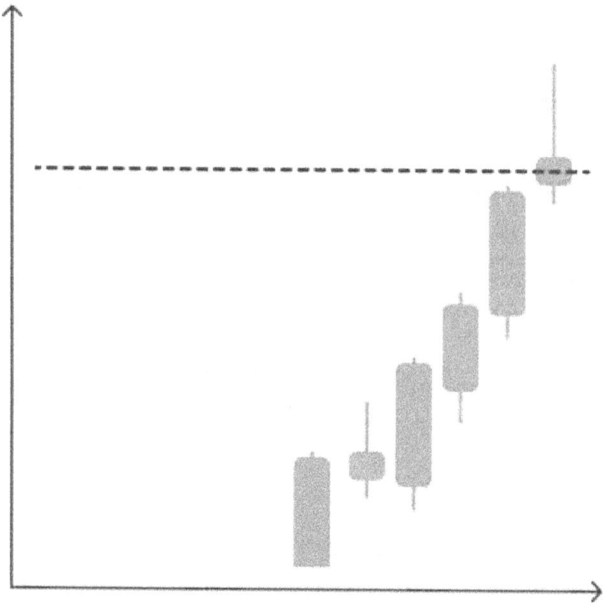

We also need to consider our stop loss - the point at which we'll exit the trade if it moves against us. A common placement is just above the high of the signal candle.

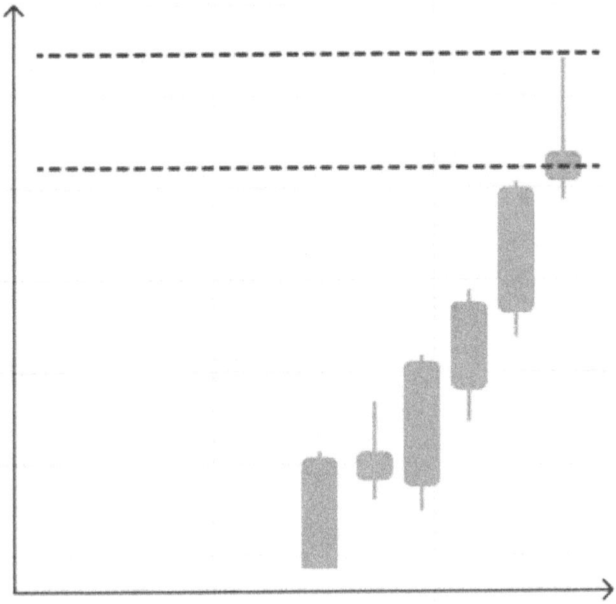

Our profit target could be set at a previous low or another support level. This gives us a favorable risk-to-reward ratio for our trade.

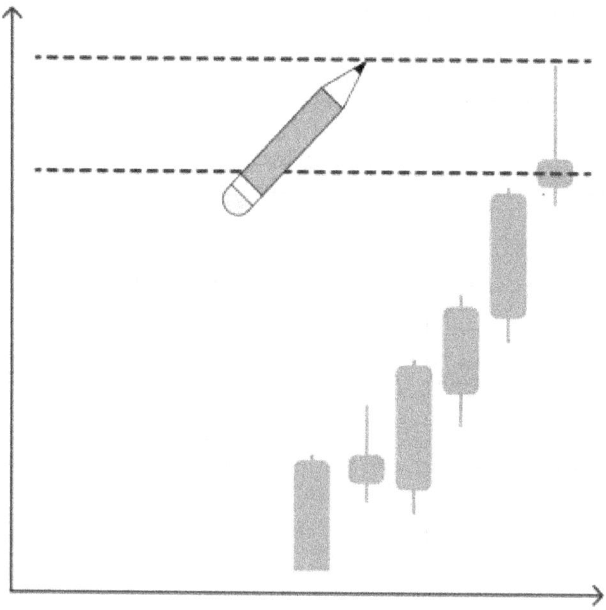

In this example, we see the trade triggered and moving in our favor. Note the "three-bar reversal" pattern: a lower low and lower close than the previous candle.

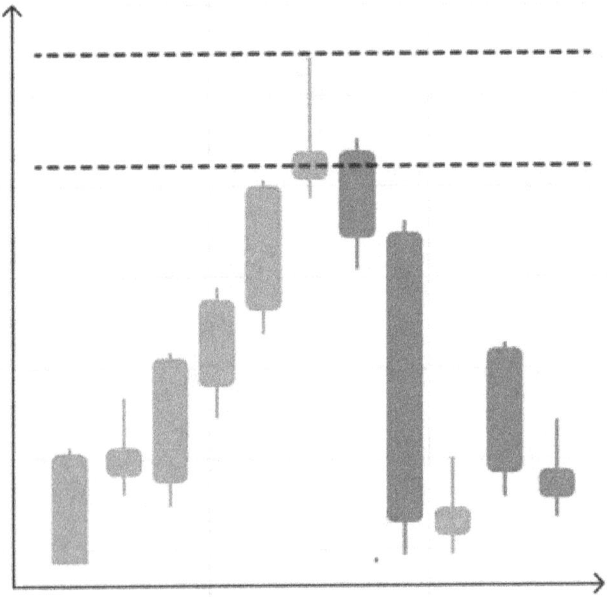

Even if you missed the initial entry, a second rejection at this level could provide another entry opportunity with additional confirmation.

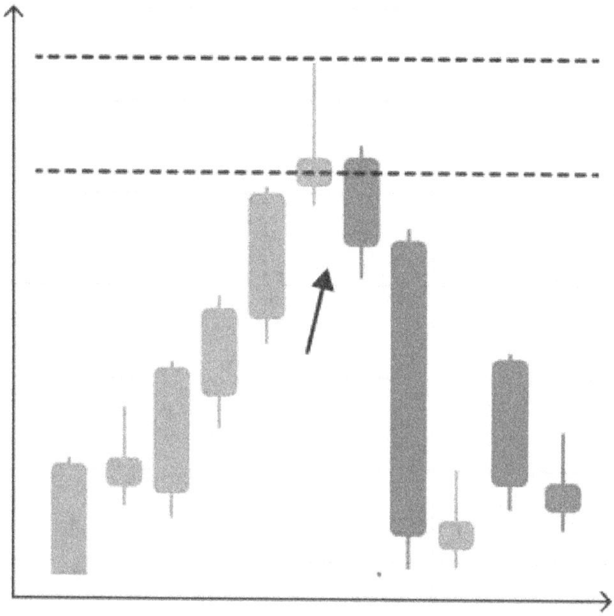

Trade management:

Based on this chart, what would be the most appropriate action at this point in the trade? What's the best course of action here?

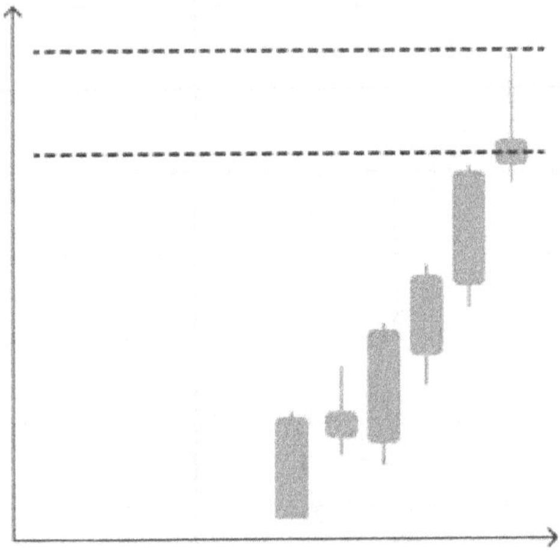

Answer: Taking partial profits secures some gains, while moving the stop to breakeven eliminates the risk of a loss. This allows the remainder of the position to potentially capture more profit.

Congratulations on finishing the "Technical Analysis Basics" section! You've learned how to read charts, recognize patterns, and understand market trends. Now you can confidently spot key price levels and make smarter trading decisions.

SECTION 3: TRADING DECISIONS

This section teaches how to make informed trading decisions using a trading simulator. It covers market analysis, combining technical and fundamental data, entry and exit strategies, and portfolio risk management.

The section provides hands-on experience with real market scenarios while eliminating financial risk through simulation.

Received skills:

MARKET ANALYSIS

PORTFOLIO MANAGEMENT

TRAIDING STRATEGY

What will you learn from this section:

- Chart Reading and Analysis: You'll master reading different chart types and timeframes to identify market trends and potential trading opportunities.

- Entry and Exit Strategy: The course teaches you how to identify optimal entry and exit points using both technical and fundamental data, helping you make more informed trading decisions.

- Risk Management: You'll learn to manage portfolio risk through proper position sizing, sector diversification, and regular portfolio rebalancing to maintain healthy risk levels.

Chapter 1: Understanding Market Dynamics

Lesson 1: Reading The Market

Trading practice with a stock stimulator :

There are several stock stimulator apps available for Android and iOS devices which you can download to practice stock analysis and trading. Let's explore how a stock simulator helps us understand market movements.

Most stock simulator apps let you track market prices and practice trading without using real money.

Please download an app such as Stock Market Simulator (developer: LineCentury) before continuing our lesson.

First, you'll need to select an asset. Let's start by examining the S&P 500 index.

Disclaimer: All stock data presented is for educational purposes only and may not reflect current market values.

Once you've selected an asset, you can view its current price and price history. The simulator can either show prices in line charts or candlestick views.

Test your price reading skills:

Looking at the S&P 500 chart below, let's check if you can read current market prices accurately. What is the current price of S&P

500 shown in the image?

Answer: $4,783.45 is the correct current price, as shown at the rightmost point of the chart where the line ends.

A price chart of a stock simulator usually offers different timeframes for analysis: 1 day, 1 week, 2 weeks, 1 month, and 3 months, etc. Each timeframe can reveal different market patterns.

Identify the trend:

Look at the 3-month S&P 500 chart below and analyze the overall trend. What is the dominant trend shown in this 3-month period?

Answer: The chart shows an upward trend, with the price moving from $4,200 to $4,780 over the 3-month period, despite some short-term fluctuations.

Switching between line and candlestick views helps us understand price movements differently. Line charts show continuous price movement, while candlesticks show price ranges within specific periods.

Compare chart types:

Looking at the same day in different chart types, which provides more price information? What additional information does the candlestick chart provide?

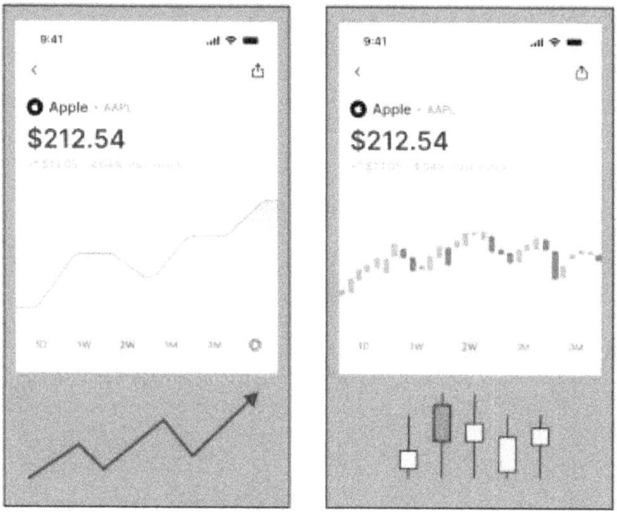

Answer: Each candlestick shows four price points: opening, high, low, and closing prices, while the line chart only shows closing prices.

Compare market views:

Examine these two charts of the same asset in different timeframes below. One is 1-day, another is 1-month view. Which timeframe shows a clearer upward trend?

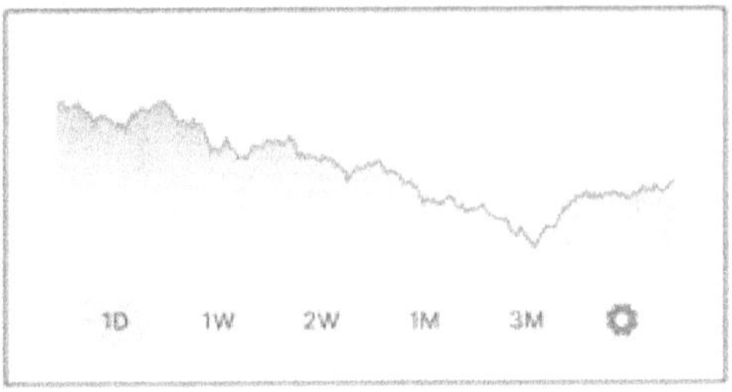

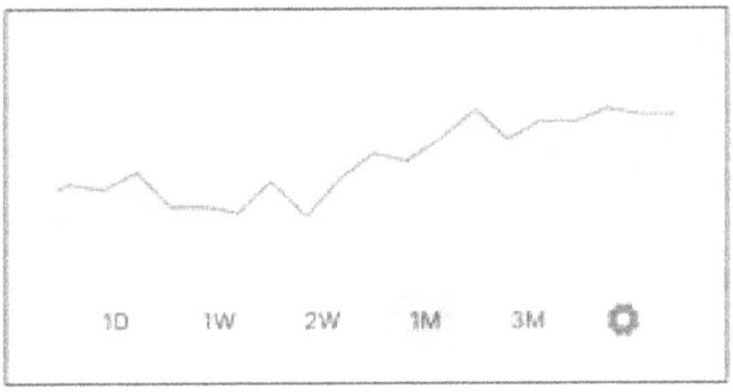

Answer: The 1-month view shows a clear upward trend, while the 1-day view shows more price fluctuations. This demonstrates why analyzing multiple timeframes is important for understanding market movement.

Understanding how to read different chart types and timeframes is essential for market analysis. In our next lesson, we'll explore how to use this information for making trading decisions.

Lesson 2: When to Use Fundamental Data?

Making informed trading decisions:

Let's explore how combining price charts with fundamental data can enhance our trading decisions. Today, we'll analyze Apple Inc. (AAPL) to understand this approach.

Disclaimer again: All data presented is for educational purposes only and may not reflect current market values.

While price charts tell us "what" is happening in the market, fundamental analysis helps us understand "why." Let's examine AAPL through both lenses.

Currently, Apple's stock is trading at $175. Before making any trading decisions, let's consider some key fundamental factors that could affect its price.

Apple recently announced their quarterly earnings: revenue grew by 8%, iPhone sales increased by 6%, and they expanded their services revenue by 15%.

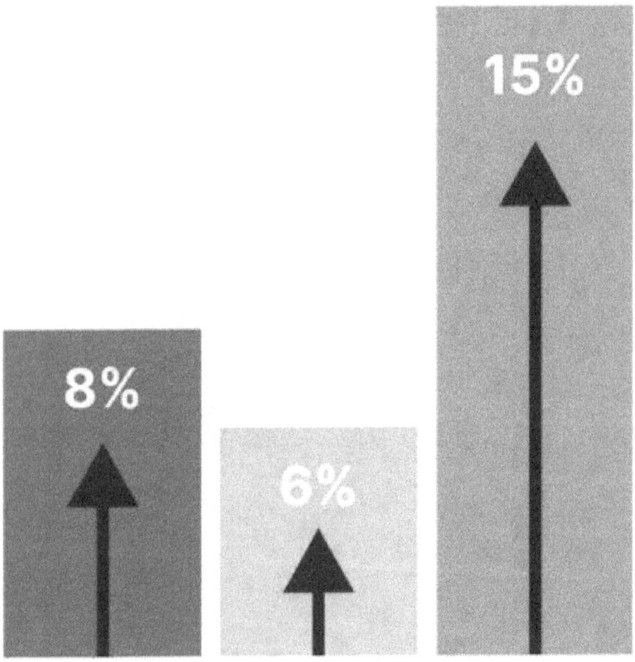

Connect the dots:

Looking at the fundamental data and the price chart, what would you expect to happen to Apple's stock price? Which scenario is most likely based on this information?

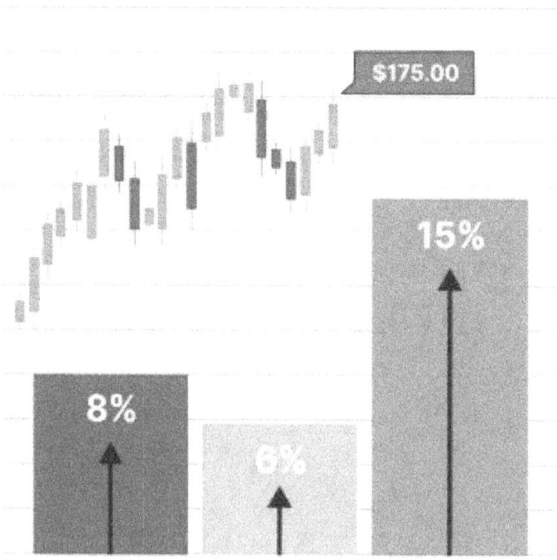

Answer: A price increase is the most likely scenario because growing revenue, increasing sales, and expanding services revenue indicate strong company performance that attracts investors.

Let's switch to the price chart view in the stock stimulator app. Looking at the 1-month timeline, we can see how the market reacted to this news.

Notice the price movement following the earnings announcement. The market's reaction confirms our fundamental analysis, but timing our entry is crucial.

Practice case analysis:

Now examine the 3-month chart. A significant dip occurred in Apple's stock price before the recent rise. What's the most likely

explanation for this dip in Apple's stock price prior to the earnings announcement?

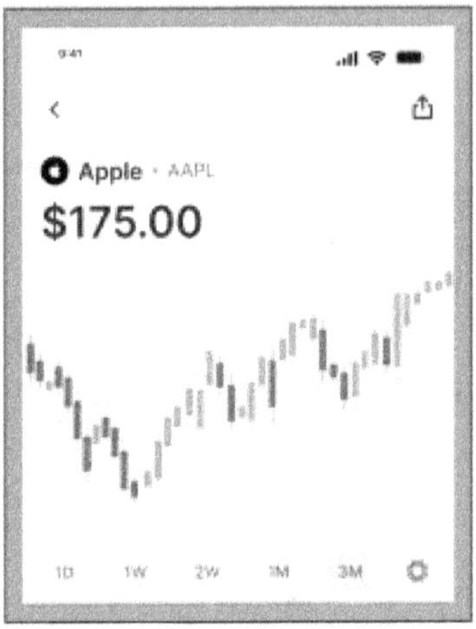

Answer: The dip was likely due to investor concerns about the upcoming earnings report. Fears that Apple might miss expectations can lead investors to sell, causing the price to drop. The rise after positive earnings shows these concerns were unfounded.

Let's practice combining price analysis with another fundamental factor: market sentiment. When major tech companies announce new products, it often affects their stock price.

Real-world application:

Apple just announced a new product launch. The stock is currently consolidating. Based on historical patterns, when would be the optimal time to enter a trade?

Answer: Entering before the launch is optimal because markets typically price in positive expectations ahead of major events, leading to price increases before the actual announcement.

Before making any trading decision, always cross-reference your chart analysis with fundamental data. This dual approach helps validate your trading thesis. In our next lesson, we'll explore specific entry and exit strategies using both fundamental and technical analysis. Until then, practice analyzing other stocks using price charts of a stock simulator and publicly available fundamental data.

Chapter 2: Entering and Exiting Trades

Lesson 1: Spotting Trading Opportunities

Entry and exit strategies for different markets:

Today we'll practice identifying optimal entry and exit points using Tesla stock as our example. Let's learn to spot opportunities in trending and ranging markets.

Using a stock simulator, set the TSLA chart to a 3-month view. First, we'll identify the overall market direction - an essential step before planning any trade.

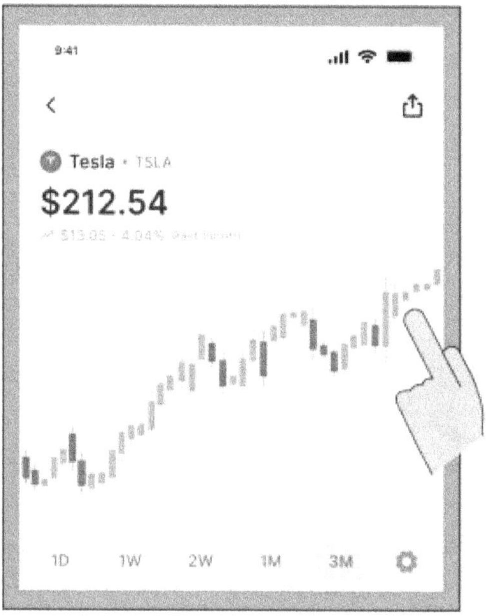

Identify market condition:

Looking at Tesla's 3-month chart, let's determine the market condition. What type of market is shown in the chart?

Answer: A strong uptrend is evident from the series of higher highs and higher lows, suggesting trend-following strategies might be more appropriate.

In a strong uptrend, one effective strategy is to enter during temporary price pullbacks. Switch to the 1-month view to identify these opportunities.

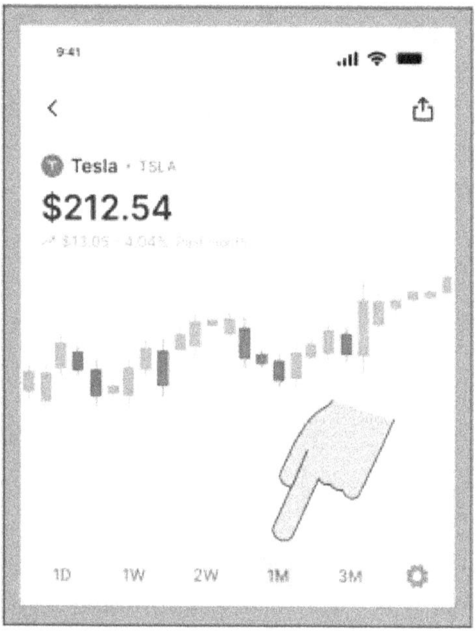

Spot entry opportunities:

Looking at the recent pullback in Tesla's price, identify the potential entry point. When would be the optimal time to enter a long position?

Answer: Entering after price stabilizes provides confirmation that the pullback might be over while still offering a good risk-reward ratio for the trend continuation. Trying to catch the exact bottom is risky, and entering at previous highs or during falls lacks confirmation of trend continuation.

Now switch to candlestick view. Candlesticks can provide additional insight into market sentiment during potential entry points.

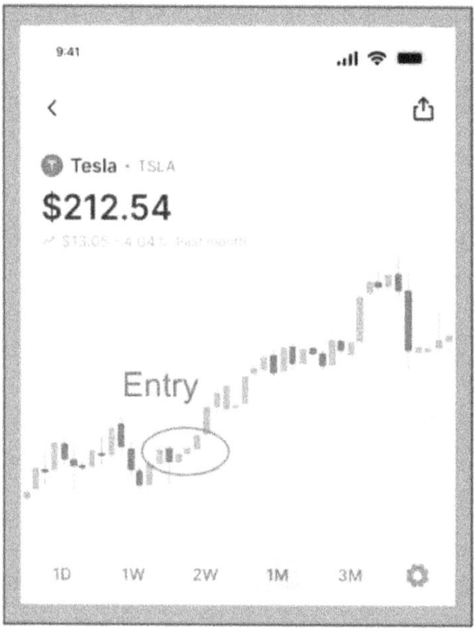

Now, exit points are just as crucial as entries. In trending markets, consider taking profits when price shows signs of momentum loss or reversal patterns.

Exit strategy practice:

Examine the candlestick pattern at the recent high. What indicates a potential exit point? Which sign suggests it might be time to exit the uptrend?

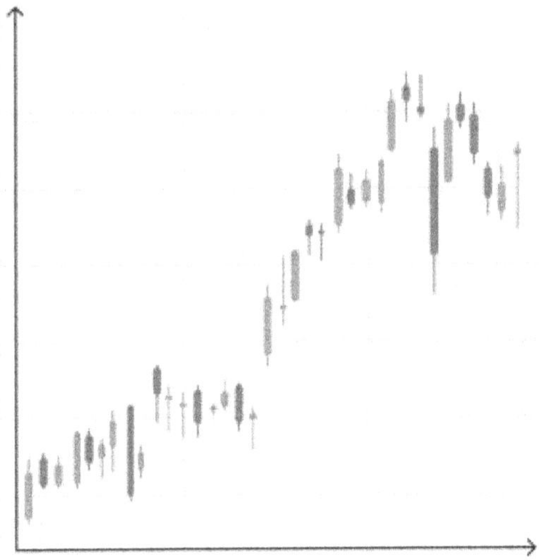

Answer: Larger down candlesticks after an extended rise often indicate shifting momentum and potential trend exhaustion, suggesting it's time to consider exiting. Small candlesticks and normal fluctuations don't necessarily indicate trend exhaustion, while increased range alone isn't a reliable exit signal.

Let's switch to a 2-week view to practice identifying shorter-term opportunities. Notice how the same principles apply on smaller timeframes.

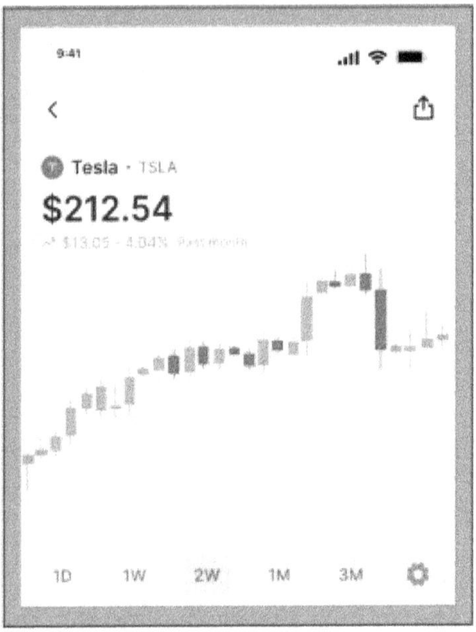

Apply your knowledge:

Study the 2-week chart showing a recent price movement. Where would you place your entry for a trend-following trade?

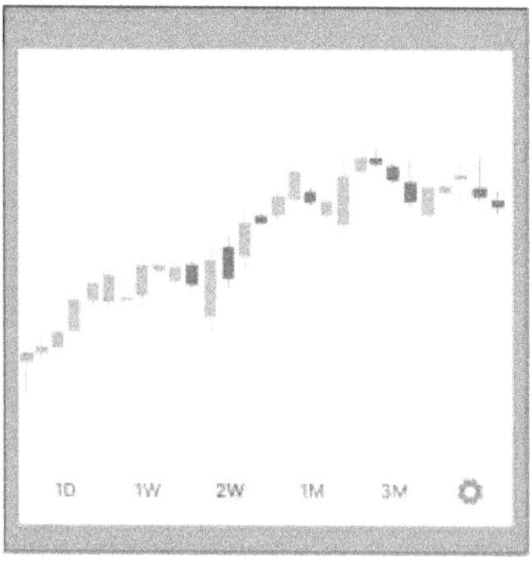

Answer: Entering after a consolidation provides a safer entry point with trend confirmation while still offering a favorable risk-reward ratio. Entering at exact lows, during sharp drops, or at peaks increases risk and reduces probability of success.

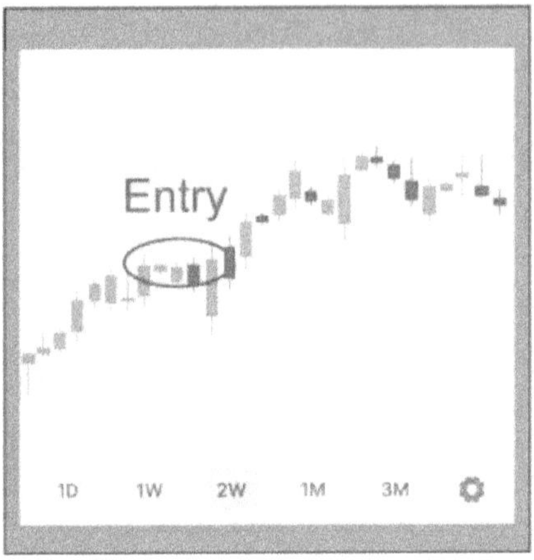

That's it! Remember: successful trading requires patience to wait for proper entry and exit setups. In our next lesson, we'll explore how to manage risk once you've entered a trade.

Lesson 2: Protecting Your Capital

Managing risk through portfolio tracking:

Let's learn to use a portfolio page for risk management. We'll practice with a sample portfolio containing Microsoft, Google, and Meta shares.

Disclaimer: All data presented is for educational purposes only and may not reflect current market values.

Your portfolio overview screen shows current positions:

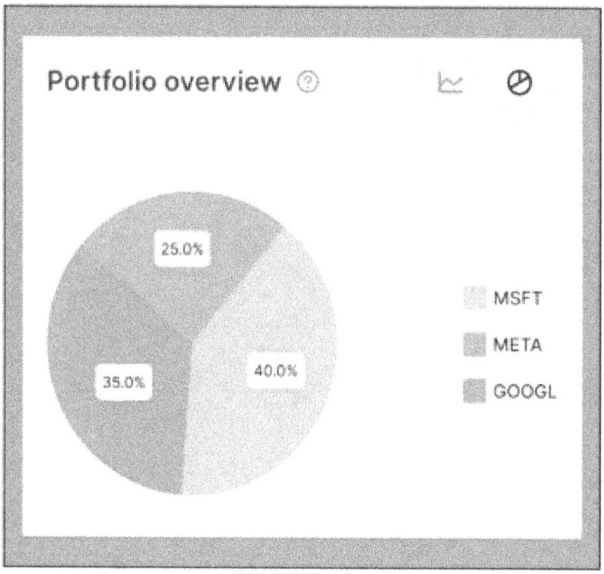

When one position exceeds 25-30% of your portfolio value, it creates increased risk if that asset underperforms. Consider rebalancing to reduce concentration risk.

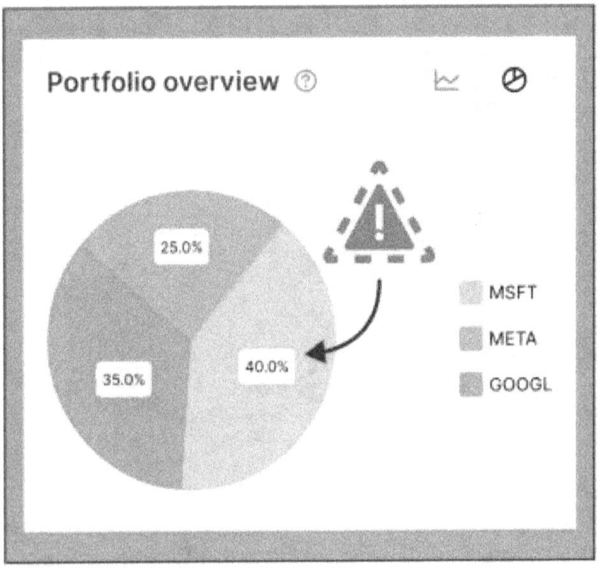

Let's check individual position performance. The portfolio page shows:

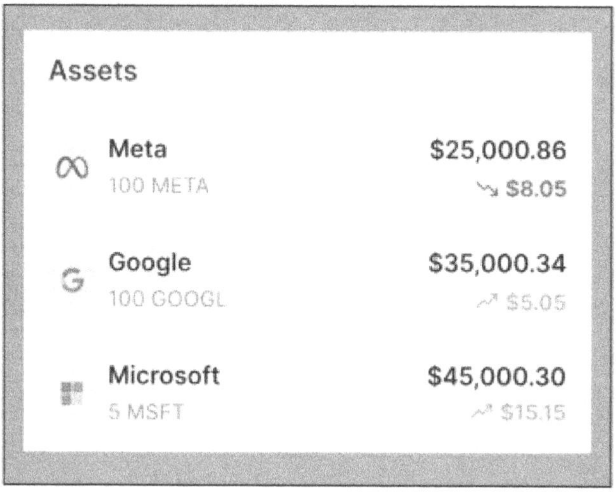

Portfolio rebalancing decision:

Given the current returns and

allocations, what action should be taken? Which rebalancing action would best manage risk?

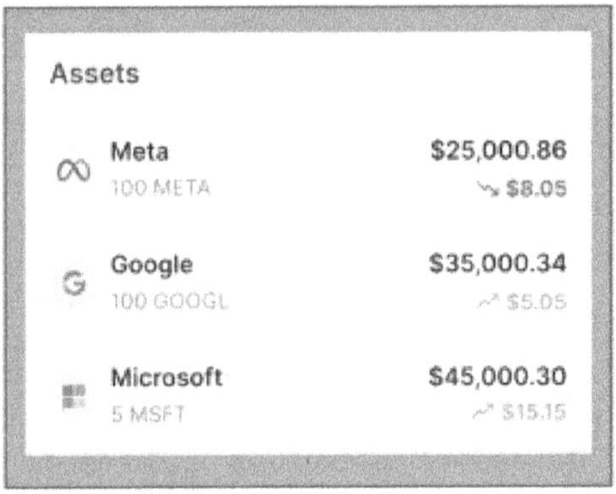

Answer: Reducing the overweight winning position (MSFT) and increasing the smaller, underperforming position (META) helps maintain balanced risk while potentially buying low and selling high. Increasing concentrated positions or making no changes leaves portfolio risk high. Selling all losing positions isn't optimal for diversification.

The portfolio page also shows your total portfolio value trend over time. A steep increase might indicate increasing risk.

Rapid growth might indicate excessive risk-taking or portfolio concentration. Check individual position sizes and consider rebalancing even during strong performance periods.

Risk assessment scenario:

Your portfolio shows these metrics:

- Total Value: $10,000.
- Largest Position: $4,000 (MSFT).

- Daily Value Change: +8%.

Which aspect presents the highest risk?

Answer: A single position size of 40% presents the highest risk as it creates vulnerability to individual stock movements, potentially affecting the entire portfolio significantly. Portfolio value, daily changes, and position count are less concerning than extreme concentration in one position.

Portfolio adjustment practice:

META position shows -8% return but only 25% portfolio allocation. What's the most appropriate risk management action?

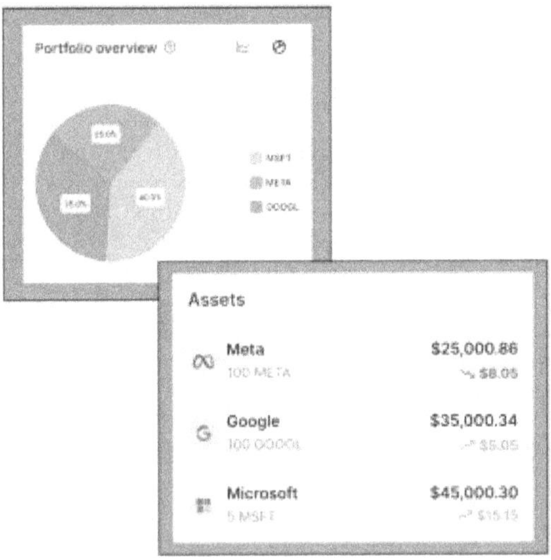

Answer: Gradually increasing the position to target allocation helps maintain diversification while potentially improving average entry price, managing risk through systematic position building.

Understanding portfolio metrics helps make better risk management decisions. In our next lesson, we'll learn how to develop a complete trading strategy using these risk management principles.

Chapter 3: Portfolio Management

Lesson 1: Following Your Trading Rules

Creating a trading strategy:

Today we'll develop and test a simple trading strategy using TechCorp (TC), an imaginary company created for educational purposes. Let's learn how to create and follow clear trading rules.

A good trading strategy has clear rules for three elements: when to enter, how much to invest, and when to exit. Successful strategies maintain consistent rules to avoid emotional decisions. Frequent rule changes lead to random trading and poor results. Let's examine TechCorp's price movement.

Let's create our first rule: we'll buy when a stock makes three consecutive higher daily closes. Looking at TechCorp's chart, let's identify this pattern.

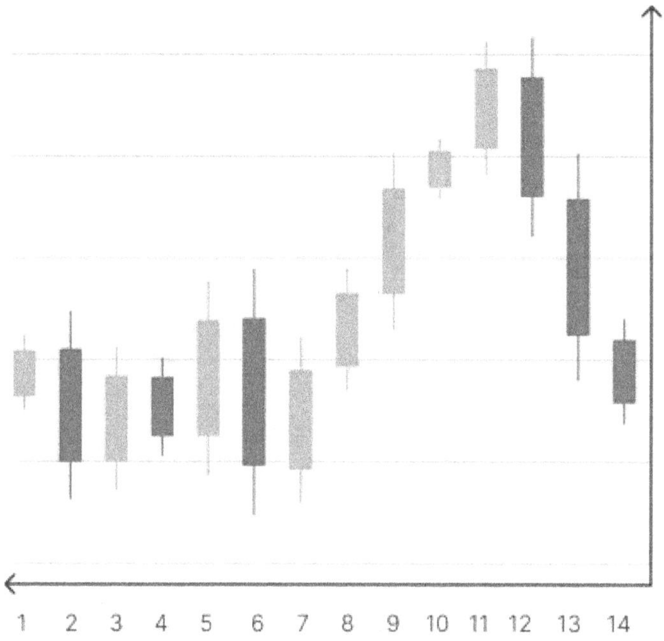

Entry point identification:

Looking at TechCorp's recent price action, where do you see our entry signal? Which sequence shows three consecutive higher closes?

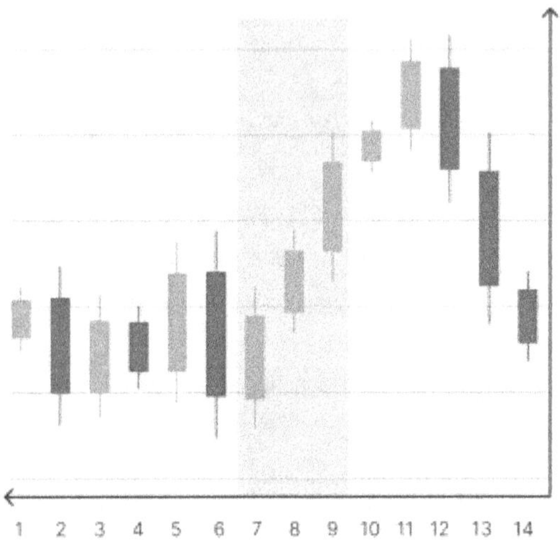

Answer: Days 3-5 show mixed closes, while 12-14 show a downward pattern. The correct sequence appears on days 7-9. Days 7-9 show clear consecutive higher closes, providing our entry signal on day 9.

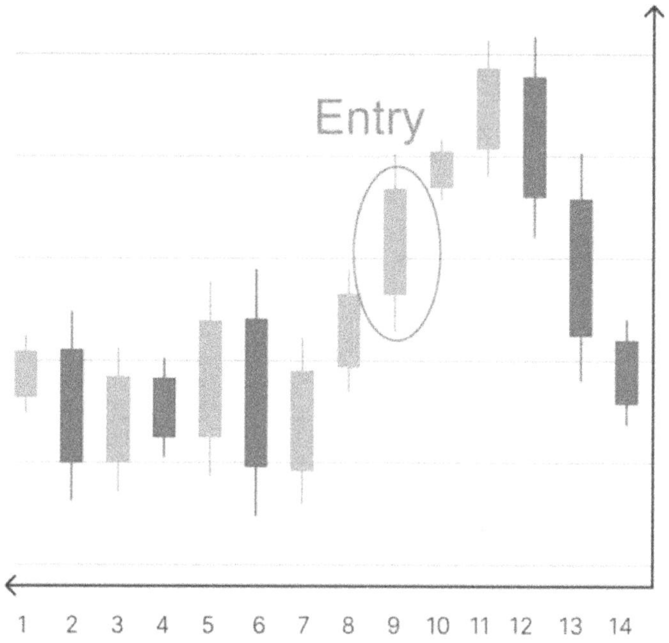

For position sizing, we'll use the 2% rule: no single position should risk more than 2% of our portfolio. Let's calculate our TechCorp position size.

Calculate position size:

Your portfolio value is $100,000. TechCorp's price is $137. How many TechCorp shares should you buy following our 2% rule?

Answer: 14 shares at $137 equals $1,918, which is very close to our 2% limit ($2,000) of the portfolio value.

Our exit rule is simple: sell if the stock closes lower for two consecutive days. Let's find this pattern on TechCorp's chart.

Find the exit point:

Examining TechCorp's price action after our entry at Day 9, locate our exit signal. Where should we exit following our rule?

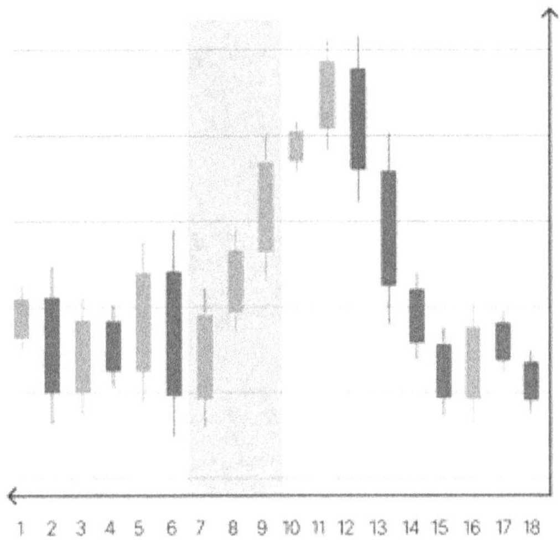

Answer: Only Days 14-15 show the required pattern of consecutive lower closes. Other points don't match our exit criteria. Days 14-15 show two consecutive lower closes, triggering our exit rule. We can place our exit on Day 15.

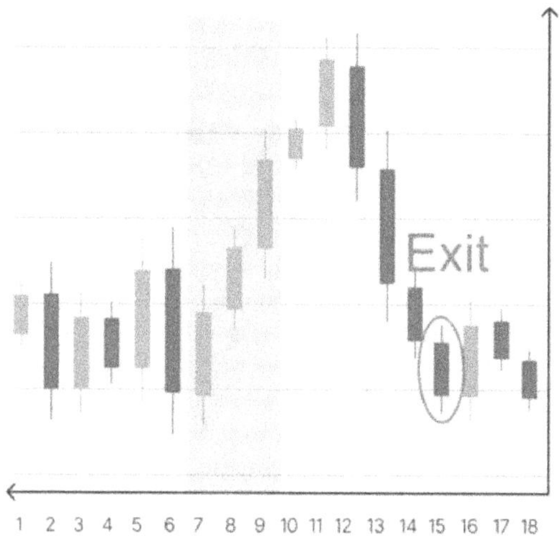

Now let's practice applying these same rules to InfoStream. We'll use the same entry, position sizing, and exit rules we developed with TechCorp.

Apply entry rules:

Study InfoStream's price movement and apply our entry rule. Which sequence provides our entry signal?

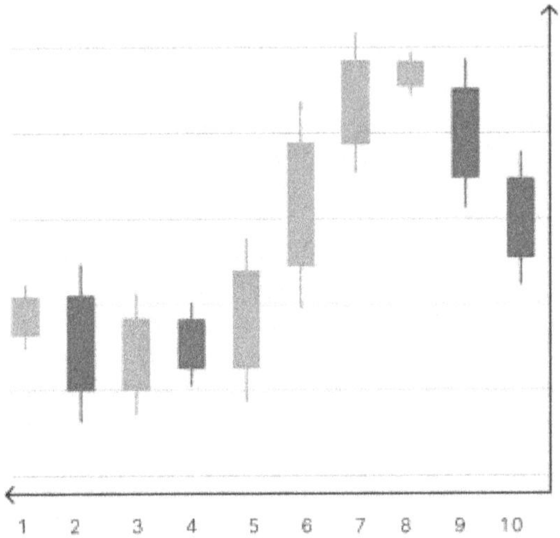

Answer: Days 2-4 show mixed movement. Days 8-10 show a downtrend. A clear upward sequence appears only on Days 4-6. Days 4-6 show higher closes, matching our entry criteria perfectly. Thus we can make an entry on Day 6.

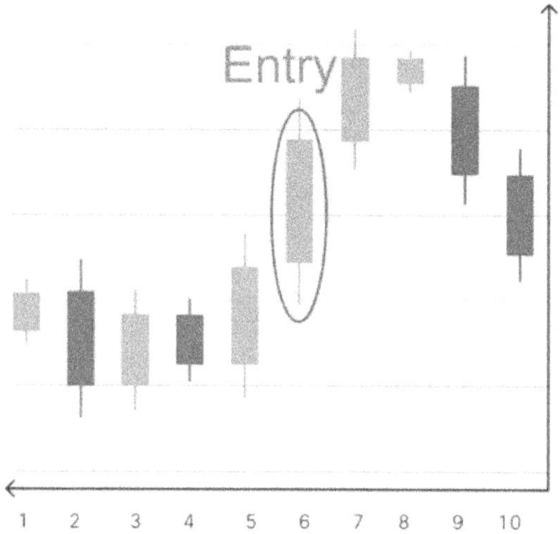

Position sizing practice:

Portfolio value remains $100,000. InfoStream's price is $490 at our entry point. Calculate the correct position size.

Answer: 4 shares at $490 equals $1,960, staying within our 2% risk limit of $2,000.

Congratulations! You've learned to develop and apply a complete trading strategy. Remember: success comes from consistently following your rules, proper position sizing, and disciplined exits. In our next lesson, we'll explore portfolio management.

Lesson 2: Managing Multiple Positions

Managing a complete portfolio:

Let's master portfolio management using portfolio tracking features. We'll analyze a diversified portfolio of top tech and retail stocks.

Your current portfolio allocation:

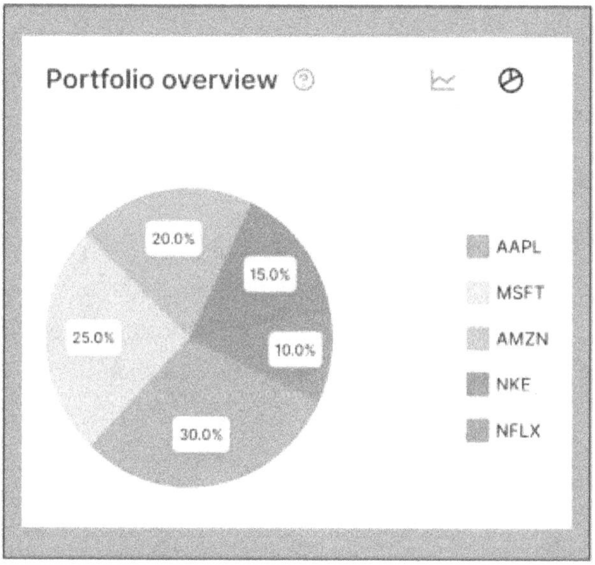

Portfolio allocations should reflect both risk management and strategic opportunities. Equal allocation isn't always optimal for achieving investment goals.

Let's examine your portfolio's sector exposure:

Technology: 55% (AAPL, MSFT)

Retail/Consumer: 35% (AMZN, NKE)

Entertainment: 10% (NFLX)

Sector concentration risk:

Looking at your sector allocation, what's the primary risk concern?

Technology: 55% (AAPL, MSFT)

Retail/Consumer: 35% (AMZN, NKE)

Entertainment: 10% (NFLX)

Which aspect needs immediate attention?

Answer: High technology concentration (55%) creates significant sector risk. If tech sector faces challenges, over half of your portfolio could be affected simultaneously. Low exposure in one sector or moderate exposure in others presents less risk than having over 50% in a single sector.

Your portfolio performance over the last month:

AAPL: +5%

MSFT: +7%

AMZN: -3%

NKE: +2%

NFLX: -4%

Performance-based rebalancing:

Given these returns, which rebalancing action makes most sense?

AAPL: +5%

MSFT: +7%

AMZN: -3%

NKE: +2%

NFLX: - 4%

What should be your first portfolio adjustment?

Answer: Reducing the outperforming, overweight position (MSFT) and adding to underperforming, underweight position (NFLX) helps maintain balanced risk while potentially buying low and selling high. Selling losing positions or increasing winners often leads to poor long-term results. No action means missing rebalancing opportunities.

Portfolio volatility assessment:

Your portfolio shows 15% technology sector gains but 20% increased volatility. Which action best addresses increased volatility?

Answer: Reducing oversized positions while maintaining some exposure helps manage volatility while keeping participation in sector growth. Extreme reactions like selling all positions or doubling exposure typically increase risk. Ignoring volatility can lead to larger drawdowns.

Successful portfolio management requires daily attention to four main aspects of your portfolio performance. Using your portfolio page, watch how your total value changes, monitor each position's current size, check sector distribution, and track returns on your entry prices.

Portfolio health check:

Your largest position has grown to 35% of portfolio value. What's the appropriate management action?

Answer: Letting overweight positions grow or adding to them increases concentration risk. Complete liquidation is an overreaction. Trimming back to target allocation maintains your risk management framework while locking in some profits.

Congratulations! You've completed the Trading Decisions section! You now understand how to analyze markets, manage risk, develop strategies, and maintain a balanced portfolio of your assets. Keep practicing these skills in your simulated trading - remember, consistency and discipline are key to trading success.

SECTION 4: TRADING CONCEPTS

This comprehensive section delves into advanced trading concepts, focusing on lot sizes, leverage, margin, and goal setting in forex trading. It provides practical insights into risk management, overcoming common trading challenges, and developing effective trading strategies. The section is designed to equip traders with the knowledge and skills needed to navigate the complexities of the forex market and make informed trading decisions.

Received skills:

RISK MANAGEMENT

LEVERAGE ANALYSIS

GOAL SETTING

What will you learn from this section:

- Lot Sizing and Leverage: You'll gain a deep understanding of how lot sizes and leverage impact your trading, allowing you to make more informed decisions about position sizing and risk management.

- SMART Goal Setting: The course teaches you how to set Specific, Measurable, Achievable, Relevant, and Time-bound (SMART) trading goals, aligning your expectations with market realities and your personal circumstances.

- Overcoming Trading Challenges: You'll learn strategies to address common trading pitfalls such as emotional trading, overtrading, and poor risk management, helping you to develop a more disciplined and systematic approach to trading.

Chapter 1: Lots, Leverage, and Margin

Lesson 1: Understanding Lot Sizes

In our first lesson, we'll explore a fundamental concept in trading: Lot Sizes. Understanding lot sizes is crucial for managing your trades effectively.

We'll use the EUR/USD pair as our example throughout this lesson. It's a familiar pair that will help us understand lot sizes in a practical context.

In forex, a "lot" refers to the size of your trade. It's a standardized unit that helps traders and brokers communicate trade sizes efficiently. There are three main lot sizes in forex trading:

1. Standard Lot: 100,000 units of the base currency

1. Mini Lot: 10,000 units of the base currency
2. Micro Lot: 1,000 units of the base currency

Using our EUR/USD example, a standard lot would mean trading 100,000 Euros. This is a significant amount and is typically used by more experienced traders or those with larger accounts.

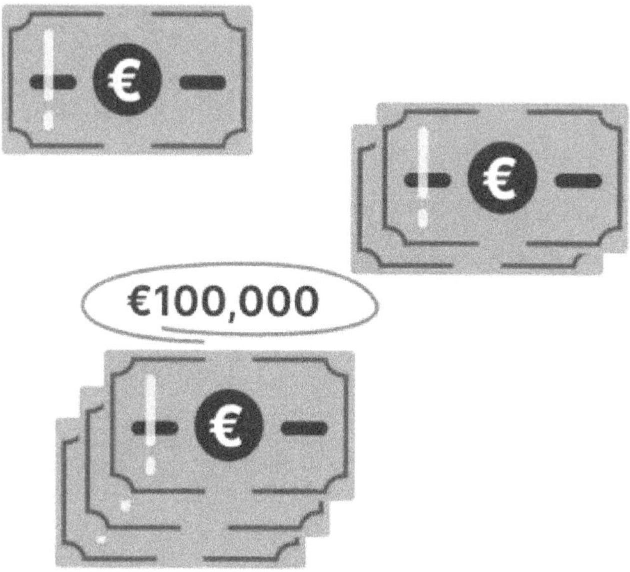

A mini lot in EUR/USD would be 10,000 Euros. This size offers a balance between meaningful position sizes and manageable risk for many intermediate traders.

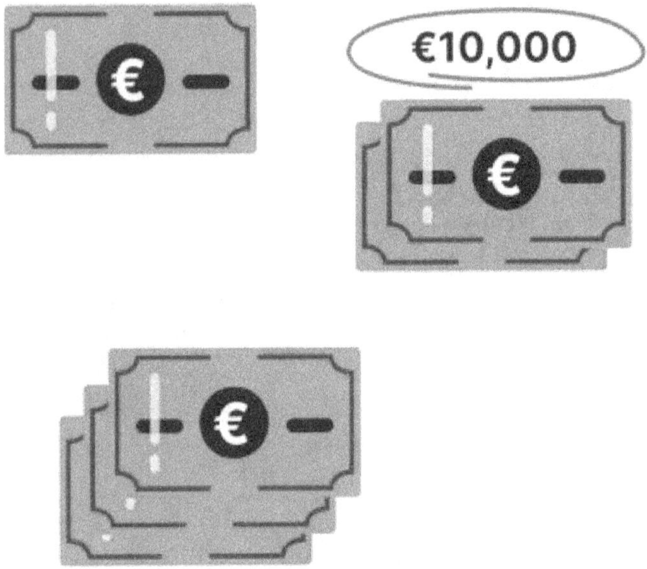

A micro lot represents 1,000 Euros in our EUR/USD example. This smaller size is often used by beginners or for testing new strategies, as it allows for better risk control.

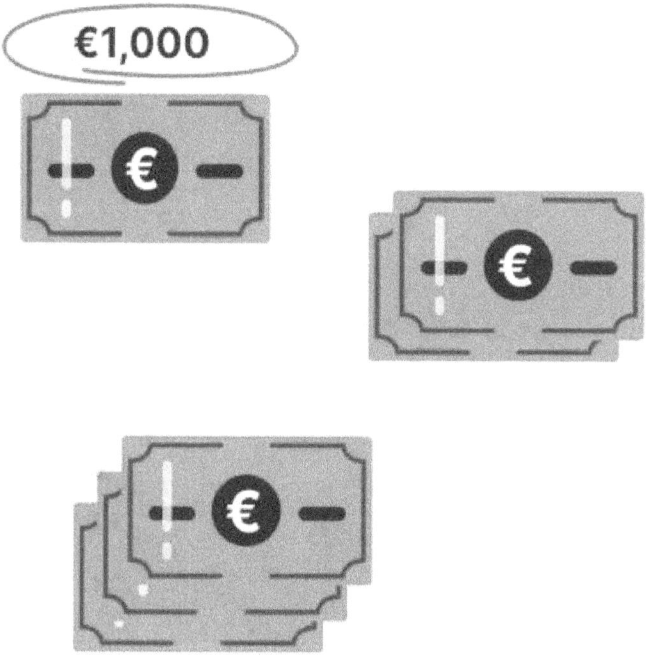

Lot sizes directly impact your potential profits and losses. The larger the lot size, the more each pip movement affects your account balance.

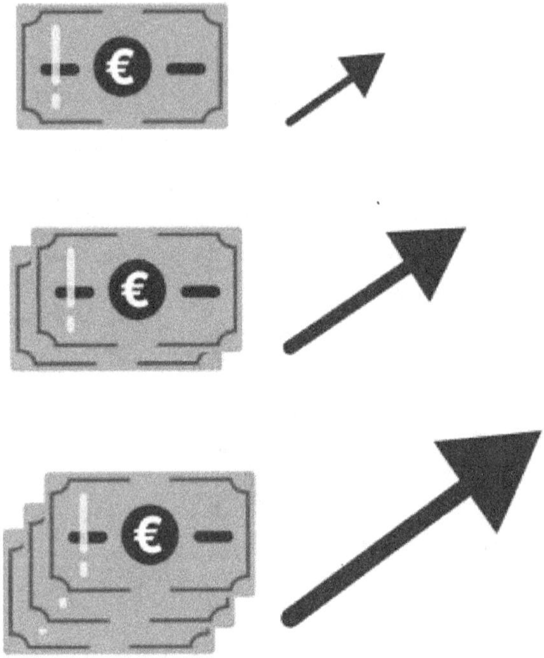

For example, a 10-pip move in EUR/ USD would have these approximate impacts:

- Standard Lot: $100 change
- Mini Lot: $10 change
- Micro Lot: $1 change

This demonstrates how lot sizes can amplify or reduce the impact of market movements on your account.

Choose the most appropriate lot size:

Let's test your understanding of lot sizes. Which lot size suits a $1,000 account best?

Answer: A micro lot is indeed the most appropriate for a $1,000 account. It allows for better risk management, giving you more flexibility to enter trades without risking a large portion of your account on a single position. This aligns well with sound risk management principles. While mini or standard lots might seem appealing for potentially larger profits, they expose a $1,000 account to too much risk. A micro lot allows for better risk management, giving you more flexibility to enter trades without risking a large portion of your account on a single position.

When trading a micro lot of EUR/ USD, each pip movement is worth approximately $0.10. This means a 100-pip move would result in a $10 change in your account. With a $1,000 account, this represents a 1% change, aligning well with sound risk management principles.

In contrast, if you were to trade a mini lot on the same account, each pip would be worth about $1. A 100 pip move would then result in a $100 change - 10% of your account. This level of volatility could quickly deplete your trading capital if the market moves against you.

Understanding lot sizes allows you to precisely calculate your potential profit or loss before entering a trade. For instance, if you're planning to set a stop loss 50 pips away on a EUR/USD micro lot trade, you know your maximum loss would be 50 * $0.10 = $5. This level of precision is crucial for implementing effective trading strategies.

Great job on completing this lesson on lot sizes. You now understand how lot sizes work and their importance in risk management. In our next lesson, we'll explore how leverage interacts with lot sizes, adding another dimension to your trading decisions.

Lesson 2: Leverage and Margin Explained

Supercharge your trades with leverage:

Ready to amplify your trading power? Let's dive into leverage and margin - the turbochargers of forex trading.

Building on our understanding of lot sizes, we'll now explore how leverage and margin allow traders to control larger positions with a smaller amount of capital. These concepts are crucial for maximizing your trading potential.

Leverage is like borrowing money from your broker to increase your trading position size. It's expressed as a ratio, such as 50:1 or 100:1.

For example, with 100:1 leverage, you can control a $100,000 position with just $1,000 of your own capital.

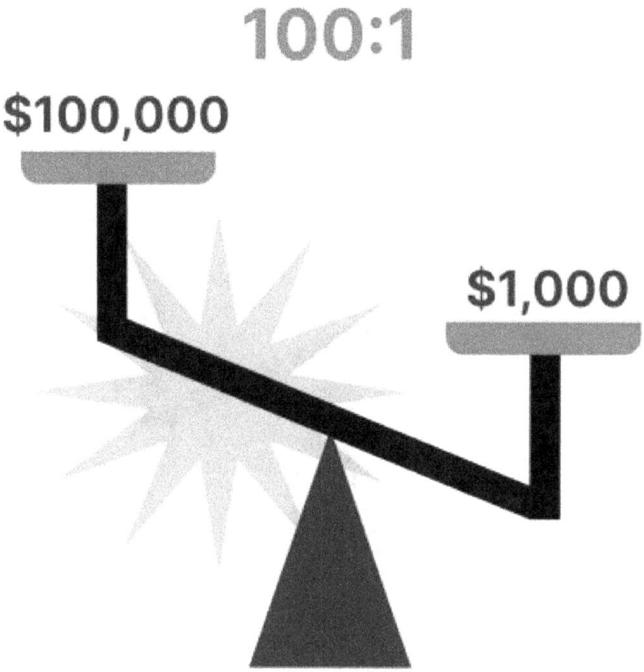

Margin, on the other hand, is the amount of money required in your account to open and maintain a leveraged position. It's typically expressed as a percentage of the full position size. For instance, a 1% margin would be required to open a position with 100:1 leverage.

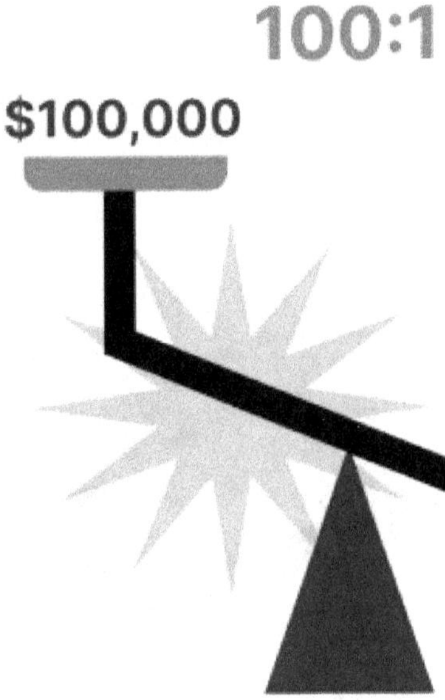

Let's look at an example. Suppose you want to trade 1 standard lot of EUR/USD (100,000 units), and your broker offers 100:1 leverage. The margin required would be: 100,000 / 100 = $1,000. This means you need $1,000 in your account to control a $100,000 position.

Leverage amplifies both potential profits and losses. While it can lead to significant gains, it can also result in substantial losses, potentially exceeding your initial investment.

It's crucial to understand that leverage doesn't change the pip value of a trade. Instead, it allows you to control larger positions with less capital. Remember our discussion on lot sizes? A 10-pip move on a standard lot of EUR/USD is still worth $100, regardless of the leverage used.

Brokers often offer different leverage ratios. Common ratios include:

- 50:1 (2% margin)
- 100:1 (1% margin)
- 200:1 (0.5% margin)

Higher leverage means you can control larger positions with less capital, but it also increases risk.

Test your leverage knowledge:

Let's apply what we've learned about leverage and margin. What's the margin for a mini lot at 50:1 leverage?

Answer: As we learned earlier, a mini lot is 10,000 units of currency. With 50:1 leverage, we divide 10,000 by 50, which equals 200. So, the margin required for a mini lot at 50:1 leverage is indeed $200. This is the amount you need in your account to open the position.

Margin call is an important concept related to leverage and margin. It occurs when your account equity falls below the required margin level. Your broker may close some or all of your open positions to prevent further losses. This is why proper risk management, which we'll explore in future lessons, is crucial when using leverage.

To calculate the margin level, use this formula:

Margin Level = (Equity / Used Margin) × 100%

For example, if your equity is $1000 and your used margin is $500, your margin level is: (1000 / 500) x 100% = 200%. Most brokers issue a margin call when this falls below 100%.

Remember, while leverage can amplify profits, it also increases risk. It's essential to use leverage responsibly and always consider your risk tolerance. Many successful traders use lower leverage to reduce risk and maintain longevity in the market.

You've now mastered the basics of leverage and margin, adding powerful tools to your trading arsenal. As we progress through this section, we'll explore how to use these concepts responsibly in your trading strategy. Up next: setting realistic trading goals that align with your newfound knowledge.

Chapter 2: Trading Challenges and Goal Setting

Lesson 1: Setting Realistic Trading Goals

Building on our understanding of lot sizes, leverage, and margin, we'll now focus on setting trading goals that align with market realities and your personal circumstances.

Effective trading goals follow the SMART criteria:

1. Specific

1. Measurable
2. Achievable
3. Relevant
4. Time-bound

Let's break these down in the context of forex trading.

•Specific: "Increase my win rate" is vague. "Achieve a 55% win rate on EUR/USD trades" is specific.

•Measurable: "Trade better" is not measurable. "Reduce average loss per trade by 10%" is quantifiable.

•Achievable: Consider your skills, resources, and market conditions.

•Relevant: Goals should align with your overall trading strategy and risk tolerance.

•Time-bound: Set a clear timeframe, e.g., "over the next 3 months".

Let's analyze a trader's goal: "Make $5000 per month trading forex."

Is it SMART? It's specific and measurable, but is it achievable and relevant without context? It lacks a time frame and doesn't consider the trader's account size or risk management.

A SMART version: "Increase account by 10% monthly over 6 months, risking no more than 2% per trade, with a $50,000 account."

Higher leverage can amplify profits, allowing for more ambitious goals. However, it also magnifies losses. Your goals should balance the potential of leverage with prudent risk management.

When setting profit goals, consider:

1. Account size: A 50% monthly return might be feasible on a $1000 account but unrealistic on $100,000.

1. Leverage used: Higher leverage enables larger positions but increases risk.

1. Trading style: Day trading might target more frequent, smaller gains compared to swing trading.
2. Market volatility: More volatile pairs might offer larger profit potential but with higher risk.

Example: With a $10,000 account, 100:1 leverage, and risking 1% per trade, a trader might set this goal:

"Achieve 5% monthly return over 6 months, with maximum drawdown of 10%, making 50-60 trades per month on EUR/USD and GBP/USD pairs."

This goal considers account size, uses specific pairs, sets a risk limit, and defines a trading frequency.

Align your goals with market reality:

Let's test your goal-setting skills with a practical scenario. Which goal is most realistic for a novice trader with a $5000 account and 50:1 leverage?

Answer: "2% monthly return, max 2% risk per trade, 20-30 trades/ month" is the most realistic goal for a novice trader with a $5000 account. It incorporates proper risk management (2% max risk per trade), sets a realistic return expectation (2% monthly), and defines a manageable trading frequency (20-30 trades/month). This goal allows room for learning and adjustment without excessive pressure.

Let's calculate the implications of this goal:

- 2% monthly return on $5000 = $100 target monthly profit

- 2% risk per trade on $5000 = $100 maximum loss per trade

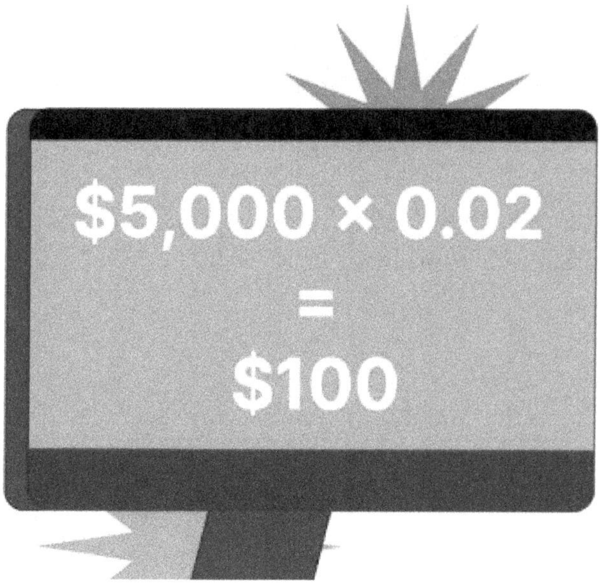

With 20-30 trades per month, the average profit per trade needed is:

- $100 / 20 = $5 per trade (if making 20 trades)

- $100 / 30 = $3.33 per trade (if making 30 trades)

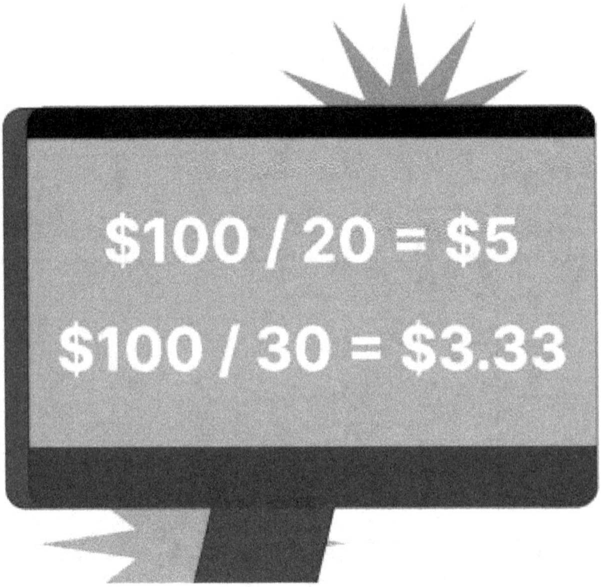

Now, let's consider how leverage affects this goal. With 50:1 leverage, the trader can control positions up to: $5000 x 50 = $250,000

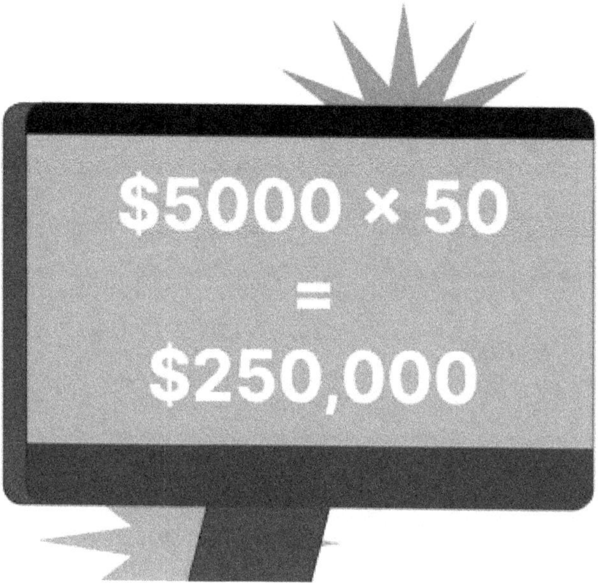

However, this full amount shouldn't be used. A more conservative approach might be using 10% of this, or $25,000 max position size. With EUR/USD at 1.1000, this allows for a maximum position of about 2.27 mini lots.

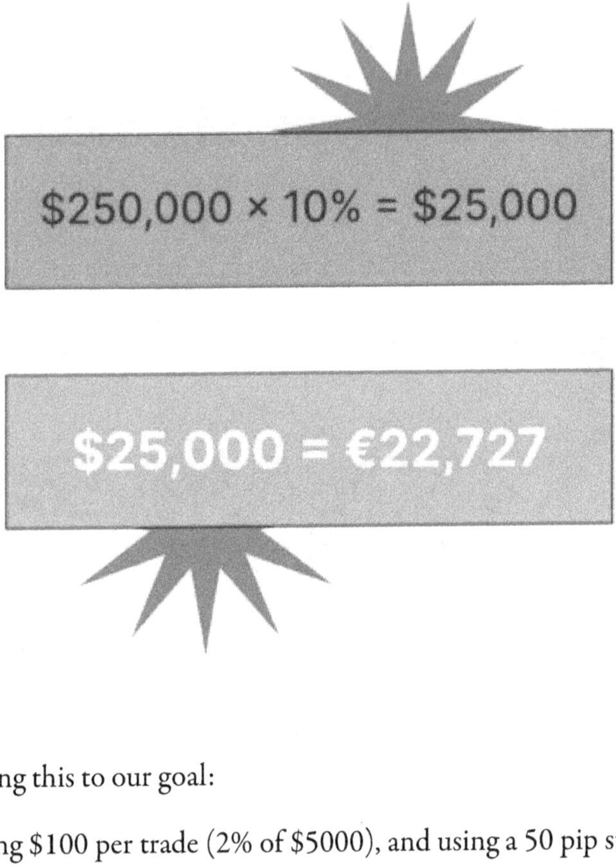

Applying this to our goal:

If risking $100 per trade (2% of $5000), and using a 50 pip stop loss on EUR/USD:

Position size = $100 / 150 x $1 per pip) = 2 mini lots. This aligns with our calculated max position size and demonstrates how the goal fits with prudent risk management.

You've now learned to set and analyze realistic trading goals, considering account size, leverage, and risk management. Next, we'll explore common challenges that might hinder achieving these goals, and strategies to overcome them.

Lesson 2: Overcoming Common Trading Challenges

Navigating trading pitfalls:

You've set your SMART goals. Now, let's tackle the obstacles that could derail them.

We'll focus on five common trading challenges:

1. Emotional trading

1. Overtrading
2. Lack of a trading plan
3. Poor risk management
4. Unrealistic expectations

Each challenge can significantly impact your ability to achieve your trading goals.

Emotional trading occurs when feelings override your trading plan. Let's examine a case:

A trader sets a stop loss at 50 pips for a EUR/USD trade. The price approaches the stop loss, but the trader, fearing a loss, moves the stop loss further away. The price continues to drop, resulting in a larger loss than initially planned.

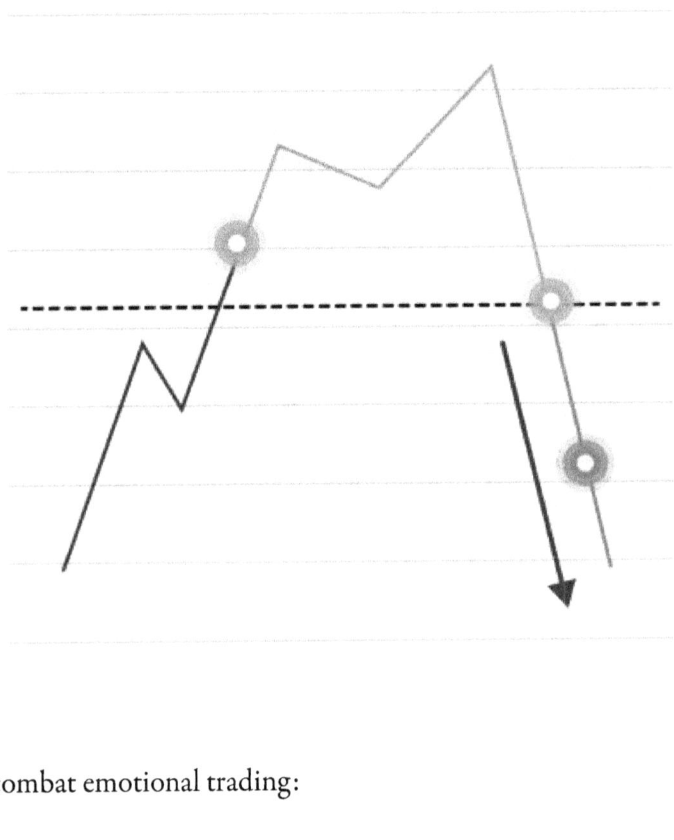

To combat emotional trading:

1. Use a trading journal to track your emotional states

1. Implement a rule-based system for entries and exits
2. Use automation for stop losses and take profits

Example: "If EUR/USD breaks below the 20-day moving average on the 4-hour chart, enter a short position with a stop loss 30 pips above the entry and a take profit at the next support level."

Overtrading often stems from a fear of missing out (FOMO) or trying to recover losses. Consider this scenario: A trader with a $10,000 account and a goal of 2% monthly return ($200) makes 100 trades in a month. Each trade incurs a $5 commission. Total commission cost: $500, exceeding the monthly profit goal.

Quality trumps quantity in trading. Excessive trading can lead to higher transaction costs and emotional fatigue, potentially resulting in poor decision-making. Focus on high-probability setups that align with your trading plan.

To address overtrading:

1. Set a maximum number of trades per day/week

1. Implement a minimum time between trades
2. Use a checklist to validate trade setups

Example: "Maximum 5 trades per day. Wait 30 minutes between trades. Each trade must meet at least 3 out of 5 criteria on my checklist."

Analyze this trading plan:

Let's evaluate a trader's plan for completeness: "Trade USD/JPY daily. Enter when RSI crosses above 30. Take profit at 50 pips. Trade 0.1 lots per $10,000 account balance." Which crucial element is missing from this plan?

Answer: The stop-loss strategy is the crucial missing element. Without a defined stop loss, the trader is exposed to potentially unlimited losses. A complete trading plan must include a clear strategy for exiting losing trades. This could be a fixed pip amount, a percentage of the entry price, or based on technical levels.

Poor risk management can quickly deplete your account. Let's analyze a risk management scenario: A trader with a $20,000 account risks 5% per trade. After a string of 7 losses, the account is down to $13,191.69. The trader needs a 51.6% return just to break even.

If the trader had risked 2% per trade instead, what would the account balance be after 7 losses? The answer is $17,236.52, requiring only a 16% return to break even.

Unrealistic expectations often lead to excessive risk-taking. Let's examine the probability of different return scenarios:

Assuming a 55% win rate and a 1:1 risk-reward ratio:

- 10 trades: 42% chance of profit
- 100 trades: 84% chance of profit
- 1000 trades: 99.9% chance of profit

This demonstrates the importance of a large sample size and the role of probability in trading outcomes.

You've now explored common trading challenges and strategies to overcome them. Remember, these challenges are interconnected - addressing one often helps with others.

In our next section of the book, we'll delve into the specific skills needed for advanced trading strategies.

SECTION 5: BROKERS, ORDERS, AND MARKET MECHANICS

Ever wondered what really goes on behind the scenes when you buy or sell stocks? This section pulls back the curtain on the stock market's inner workings. We'll break down how brokers do their thing, demystify those confusing order types, and show you how it all comes together to make stock prices bounce around. No fancy jargon here - just real, practical knowledge you can use to navigate the market with confidence.

Received skills:

MARKET ANALYSIS

ORDER EXECUTION

RISK MANAGEMENT

What will you learn:

- Broker Operations: Understand the role of brokers in facilitating trades and managing your investments.
- Order Mastery: Learn to use various order types effectively to implement your trading strategies.
- Price Dynamics: Grasp how different orders and market participants collectively influence stock prices.

Chapter 1: Introduction to Brokers

Lesson 1: Section Overview

If you've been following along with our Trading Basics and Technical Analysis sections, you're already building a solid foundation. Now, it's time to dive deeper into the nuts and bolts of how trades actually happen.

In this section, we're going to pull back the curtain and show you what really goes on behind the scenes when you click that "buy" or "sell" button. Trust me, it's not magic - it's market mechanics, and understanding this stuff can give you a serious edge.

We'll start by getting to know the unsung heroes of trading - brokers. These are the folks who turn your trading decisions into real market actions. We'll explore different types of brokers and how to choose the right one for your needs.

Next, we'll demystify order types. Market orders, limit orders, stop orders - by the end of this section of the book, you'll be slinging these terms around like a Wall Street pro. More importantly, you'll know exactly when and how to use each type to your advantage.

But we're not stopping there. We're going to show you how these orders actually drive stock prices. You'll see firsthand how the actions of traders like you shape the market in real-time. It's pretty mind-blowing stuff!

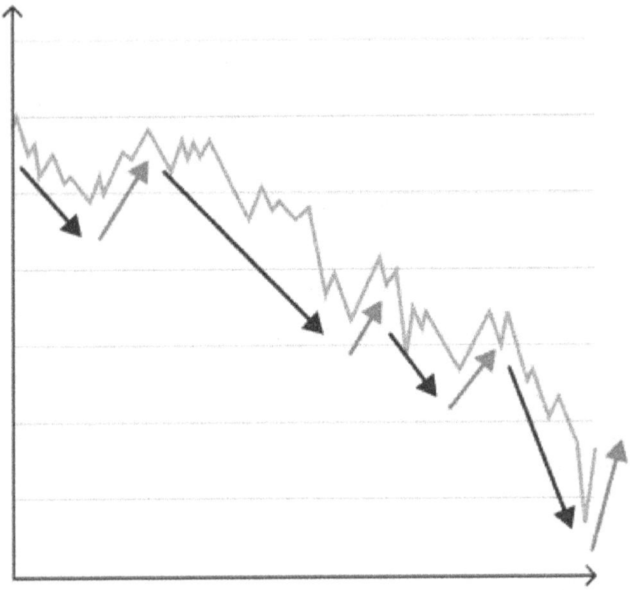

Now, I know some of this might sound a bit technical, but don't worry. We're going to break it all down step by step, with plenty of real-world examples. By the end of this section, you'll have a whole new perspective on how the market works.

So, are you ready to take your trading knowledge to the next level? Great! Let's dive in and start unraveling the mysteries of brokers, orders, and market mechanics. Trust me, once you understand this stuff, you'll never look at a stock chart the same way again. Let's get started!

Lesson 2: The Role of Brokers in Trading

Your gateway to stocks: Brokers

Let's say you've made a decision that you want to get into the stock market, that you want to actually buy some stocks.

But as you dig into it, you realize that you need an online broker. Now, you're thinking, "Why do I need an online broker? What do they actually do for me?" Those are great questions! Let's start unpacking that together.

Keep in mind that even if you're considering trading in markets other than the stock market, you'll still need a broker. This applies whether you're interested in currencies, options, futures, or any other market. However, we'll focus on stocks here, as it's a common starting point for beginners.

So you're going to buy stock, and the first step here is definitely finding an online broker, and you can't get around that!

Opt for a discount online broker rather than a small regional bank so you don't end up paying crazy fees. You can easily find reputable brokers with a simple search. We will learn how to do that in greater detail in later lessons.

So, what happens once you pick your online broker? It's pretty cool, actually. You become the boss!

You tell your broker what you want to buy, and they go off into the big, wild world of the stock market to make it happen.

Now, remember, being the boss means you've got to pay your broker for their work. This is where those fees and commissions come into play.

After your order they head into the busy market, filled with individuals and institutions like hedge funds and mutual funds. They actively engage with market participants to secure the best deal for you. Basically, they do all the negotiating and heavy-lifting for you - that's what brokers are all about!

Online brokers charge a commission for each transaction, similar to how online platforms may charge a delivery fee for each order. Brokers charge for each stock trade, similar to delivery fees, with fees being a few dollars or a small percentage of the trade, depending on the broker.

Once your broker finds a willing seller who matches your order requirements, the magic happens. They secure the stock for you and ensure it's transferred to your account. Now, voilà, you're officially a stockholder!

But remember, this isn't a face-to-face, handshaking kind of deal. Everything happens electronically, super quick. Imagine hitting a button, and just like that, your order is processed. Modern trading is fast and efficient, thanks to technology.

Direct stock purchasing:

Investors often wonder about buying stocks directly without involving a broker. However, this approach comes with significant challenges. Can you guess why it's usually not feasible for regular investors to buy stocks directly without a broker?

Answer: While it might seem simpler to buy stocks directly, the stock market's complexity makes this impractical for most individual investors. Brokers provide valuable services that justify their fees. Buying stocks directly without a broker is complex, time-consuming, and potentially more expensive. Brokers simplify the process, provide market access, and often offer more cost-effective solutions for individual investors.

Unless you plan to get your brokerage license from the National Association of Securities Dealers (NASD) and set up shop yourself (which is hard - and expensive - to do), you need to work with a broker to be able to buy and sell stocks.

That's why online brokers are invaluable. They act as your gateway to the stock market, handling all the intricate processes.

When the time comes to sell your stocks, the process is similar. You'll give your broker the sell order, and they'll jump back into the market, this time looking for buyers. Again, it's all done electronically and efficiently.

Unlike banks, which can guarantee interest on savings, brokers cannot guarantee profits from investments due to the inherent risks in the stock market.

To sum up, an online broker is your key to participating in the stock market. They handle buying and selling orders, negotiate on your behalf, and ensure transactions are smooth and quick. This makes trading accessible and manageable for everyone, regardless of experience level. Keep exploring, keep learning, and don't hesitate to ask questions. Happy trading!

Lesson 3: Brokers and Brokerage Services

Types of brokers and brokerage services:

Before you can pick the type of broker that best fulfills your needs, you need to understand the kinds of services that each kind of broker provides. So, let's dive into that in this lesson!

Not all brokers are the same. They differ in their costs, the types of services they provide, and their capabilities. It's important to choose one that aligns with your specific needs.

If you want someone to assist you with buying decisions and implementing those decisions, you need to check out the full-service brokers.

They provide research, trading ideas, and complete transactions for you, but at a higher commission. Usually, they contact you with trading ideas. All you need to do is say yes or no.

So, full-service brokers might look good at first, but there are a couple of big downsides to think about. First, as I said, all those extra services can mean you end up paying more.

Second, there's a chance of getting advice that's not in your best interest. Like, if your broker also sells insurance, they might try to get you to buy it just so they can make a commission, which might sway what you decide to do.

For more independence, consider discount brokers. They offer essential services at lower costs, suitable for traders comfortable with making their own decisions without much hand-holding.

Still, discount brokers come with their own drawbacks, such as limited guidance and lack of personalized attention. This means you'll need to take charge, doing your own research and learning to improve your chances.

No broker, including discount brokers, can guarantee high returns on investments due to the inherent risks in the stock market.

Once you've decided between a discount broker and a full-service broker, the next step is to pick one from the many available. But don't make your choice based solely on price. It's crucial to understand the services they offer to ensure they can support the kinds of trades you're looking to make.

The first easy step is to check the brokers' reputations on forums and online review platforms. This way, you can get a feel for their reliability and see if there are any common issues reported.

When choosing a broker, it's essential to consider the types of orders they support. By "order", we refer to the methods and conditions under which you can buy or sell securities. We'll talk more about this in the next chapter.

Next, the type of data you can access is really important. Most of them will give you basic stuff like up-to-date stock prices which are called stock quotes.

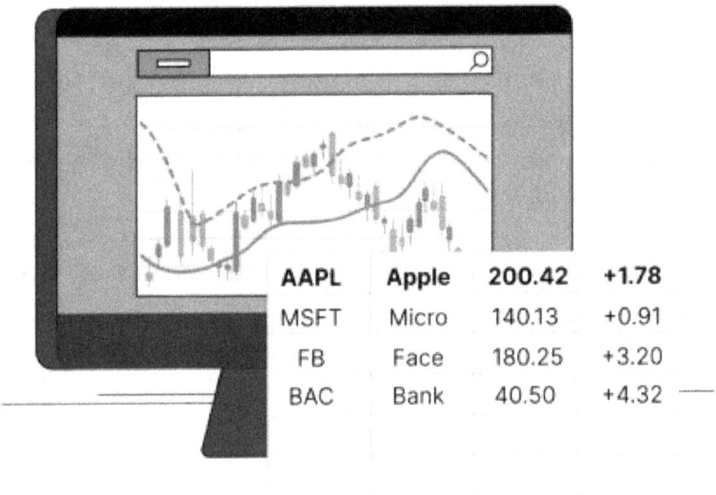

Some offer more detailed market data, which includes not just the latest sales info but also past sales data. If you need more detailed data, make sure the broker you choose can provide it, or think about getting it from somewhere else. Different brokers charge differently for these data services.

You should also think about how you'll get this data. Some brokers let you access it right from your home computer instead of their servers.

It might cost more, but you get the info faster. The speed of your internet also affects how quick and reliable this data is.

Then there's the software your broker provides to help you see and understand this data. This is really important for making good trading decisions. The software turns raw stock market data into charts.

Some brokers might charge for this software, but they might lower the cost or even make it free depending on how much you trade or how big your portfolio is. There are also free charting tools online.

Alright, that's a wrap on this lesson about picking the right broker! We've talked about the different kinds, from the full-service ones who do a lot but might cost more, to the budget-friendly discount brokers. Remember, it's all about what fits your style and needs. Next, we'll explore different brokerage accounts to find the best fit for your trading style. Stay tuned!

Lesson 4: Broker Basics Review

1. What is the primary role of an online broker in stock trading?

Answer: Execute trades on behalf of investors.

1. Why can't individual investors typically buy stocks directly without a broker?

Answer: It's complex, time-consuming, and potentially more expensive.

1. How do online brokers typically charge for their services?

Answer: Commission for each transaction.

1. What type of broker provides research and trading ideas?

Answer: Full-service brokers.

1. Which statement about brokers and investment returns is true?

Answer: Brokers cannot guarantee profits on investments.

1. What's a potential downside of using a full-service broker?

Answer: Higher commissions and potential conflicts of interest.

1. What's an advantage of using a discount broker?

Answer: Lower costs for essential trading services.

1. How do modern stock trades typically occur?

Answer: Electronically, without face-to-face interactions.

1. What should investors consider when choosing a broker?

Answer: Types of orders supported and data access.

1. What type of software do brokers often provide?

Answer: Charting tools for analyzing market data.

Chapter 2: Orders and Mechanics

Lesson 1: How Do Orders Work?

Intro to orders:

Now, we are going to be learning about orders and order types. It's important to understand the basics when you're buying or selling stocks.

We've already discussed the key figure you need to contact when you're ready to buy or sell in trading - your broker. But what are you going to tell them, and how do you tell them that?

It's very simple! You actually need to send them an order and tell them an order of what exactly you want them to do for you.

Back in the day, you had to write a letter or call your broker to place an order. But nowadays, you can just go online and send your broker your order of what you want electronically. Now, even though the orders and what we put on them haven't changed over time, the way we send them has changed, and we're going to cover that in later lessons.

But today, let's talk about what exactly you need to put on your order. Let's start with an obvious thing - you're going to let your broker know which stock you want to buy or sell.

So the first thing is the name of the company. You don't need to give your broker the full name. Instead you should give them something that's called the ticker.

What is a ticker? A ticker is simply an abbreviation for a company's name. For example, Apple Inc.'s ticker is AAPL. If you want to buy Apple shares, you tell your broker, "I want to buy AAPL." Similarly, the ticker for Samsung is SSNLF, so you would say, "I'd like to buy SSNLF." To trade shares of any company, it's important to know its ticker.

Test your trading intuition:

When placing an order with your broker, you need to specify several key details. One crucial element is the "side" of your order. Before giving you the answer, let's test your trading intuition! In trading terminology, what do you think the "side" of an order indicates?

Answer: The "side" of an order simply indicates whether you want to buy or sell. This is a fundamental aspect of any trade, as it determines whether you're entering a position (buying) or exiting one (selling).

Are you looking to purchase the stock, or are you planning to sell it? Clearly specifying this - as either a buy or sell order - is crucial.

So far, we've covered the basics. Now, let's delve into something more interesting: the type of order you need to tell your broker. There are many kinds, but we'll start with the two most basic ones in this lesson.

The first one, which is the market order, the simplest of all; and the second one, which is the limit order, which is the second simplest type of order.

So, what's the difference between a market and a limit order? A market order basically tells your broker that you want to buy or sell that stock immediately, no matter what price it's at.

On the other hand, a limit order tells your broker, "I want to buy or sell that stock at a limit price or better. I do not want to get a worse price than the price I'm telling you to get it at."

So, when would you choose a limit order, and when would you choose a market order? It's quite simple: You choose a market order when it's time-sensitive but not price-sensitive.

If you really want to get the stock right away and you don't care what price it is, send a MARKET order to get it. On the other hand, if you care about the price but you don't mind waiting for the stock to reach that price, then you send a LIMIT order.

Test your limit order knowledge:

Let's explore how limit orders work in the stock market. Imagine you're interested in buying shares of XYZ Corp, but you don't want to pay more than $10 per share. You decide to place a limit order. If you set a limit order to buy XYZ

Corp stock at $10 per share, but the current market price is $11, what will happen?

Answer: When you place a limit order to buy at $10, but the current price is $11, your order will remain unfilled until the stock price drops to $10 or lower. This is the key feature of limit orders - they allow you to specify the maximum price you're willing to pay, ensuring you never pay more than you're comfortable with. It's important to understand that a limit order sets a maximum (when buying) or minimum (when selling) price at which you're willing to trade. The order won't be executed above (for buy orders) or below (for sell orders) this price.

Each type of order has its own drawbacks to consider. The issue with a limit order is that if the stock never reaches your specified price and continues to rise, the order won't be executed. This means you could miss out on a potentially profitable opportunity.

The drawback of a market order is that while you may get the stock immediately, you might end up with a less favorable price. Had you been more patient, you might have secured a better deal.

So, you always have to know when to use which one, and we're going to cover that in future guides. But these are the two most basic orders.

Now, if you give a market order, you don't need to give your broker a price, but if you use a limit order, in this case only, you're going to have to give a price to your order, and you can say $10 or whatever price it is that you want to sell it at or buy at, depending if it's a buy or sell order.

Market orders do not require you to specify a price, as they are executed at the next available market price. However, limit orders do require specifying the price at which you wish to buy or sell.

The final key detail to specify when placing an order is the quantity - the number of shares you want to buy or sell. This is crucial because the quantity determines the size of your investment. For example, if you decide to buy 200 shares of a stock, you're instructing your broker to purchase that specific amount on your behalf. Whether you choose 100, 200, or 300 shares, always consider how the quantity aligns with your investment goals and risk tolerance.

To sum up, an order is an instruction you give to your broker about how you want to buy or sell stocks. In an order, you need to include the ticker symbol of the stock, whether you're buying or selling, the type of order (such as market or limit), the number of shares, and the price if it's a limit order. Nowadays, it's very simple. You log in online, enter all of these details, click send, and your broker receives your orders right away.

Lesson 2: Orders Driving Prices

Orders driving prices:

In this lesson, we'll explore the driving forces behind price movements. Essentially, every price shift is dictated by the orders that traders place. Let's illustrate this concept with an example.

Imagine starting your own car company and listing it on the NYSE with the ticker MYCAR. Your company would have "shares outstanding," which are the total number of shares your company has issued.

For example, let's say MYCAR has 100,000 shares outstanding. Not all shares may be available for trading, which is where the "float" comes in. The float is the number of shares available for trading, such as MYCAR's 75,000 shares. The remaining 25,000 shares might be held by the company or private investors, not available for trading. Thus, others looking to buy all available shares would aim to purchase 75,000 shares.

Imagine a world with only 9 people who trade in the market. Participant 1 (P1) owns 40,000 shares in a company, and Participant 2 (P2) holds 10,000 shares.

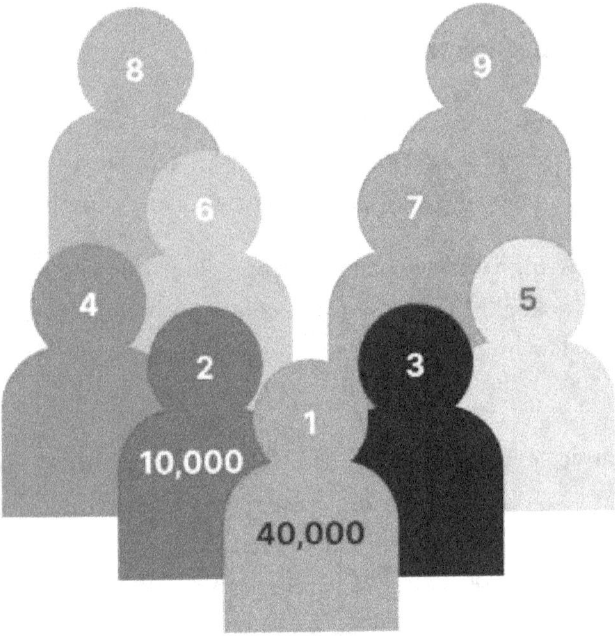

Similarly, P3 has 2,000 shares, P5 holds 2,000, P6 owns 5,000, P7 possesses 1,000, P9 has 10,000. P4 and P8 have zero shares.

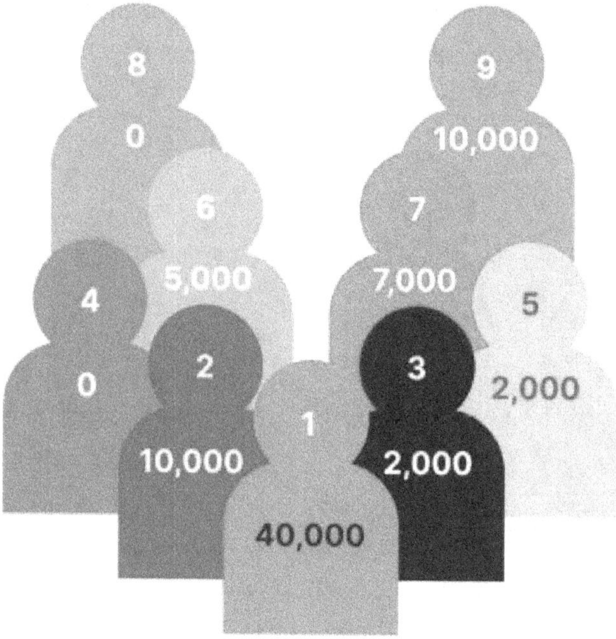

Although these 9 individuals own shares, they haven't traded them yet. Without trades, there's no market price for the stock. We're assuming that these participants acquired their shares through your company's IPO, which was discussed earlier. To trade, they need to place orders in the market!

P1 wants to buy 3,000 shares at a limit price of $41. He sends an order to his broker, specifying it's a buy, the stock's ticker, and that it's a limit order. Then, the broker informs his order to the exchange. At the exchange, a computer system equipped with a matching algorithm, pairs buyers and sellers for trade executions. The buyers' orders are listed in one column and the sellers' in another.

Now, P2 wants to buy 5,000 shares at $39. His order, once sent, goes to the exchange. Where does it appear in the matching system's book? Below Pl's order! The system prioritizes prices for buyers.

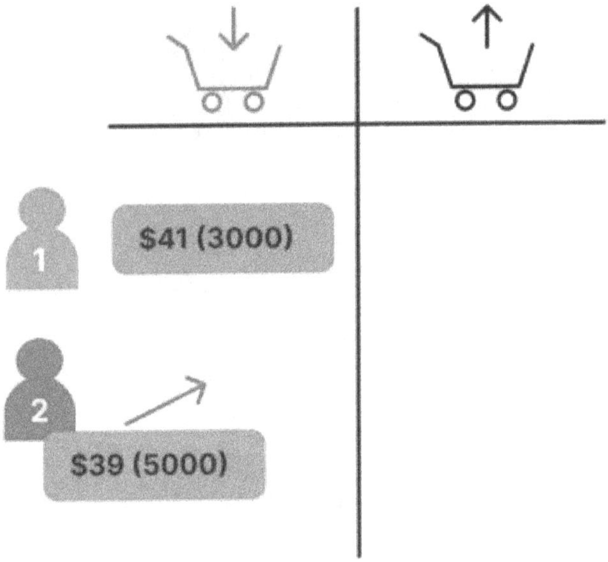

In the stock market, higher buy bids get priority. So if you're willing to pay more, you're placed higher on the list for execution. Conversely, for sellers, lower selling prices receive higher priority. The exchange's algorithm prioritizes price first, then time - higher bids or lower asks top the list, and among equal prices, earlier orders get precedence.

P2, already having placed a buy order, now seeks to sell 5,000 shares at $55. Owning 10,000 shares, he aims to buy at $39 and sell at $55. His order is added to the seller's side on the exchange.

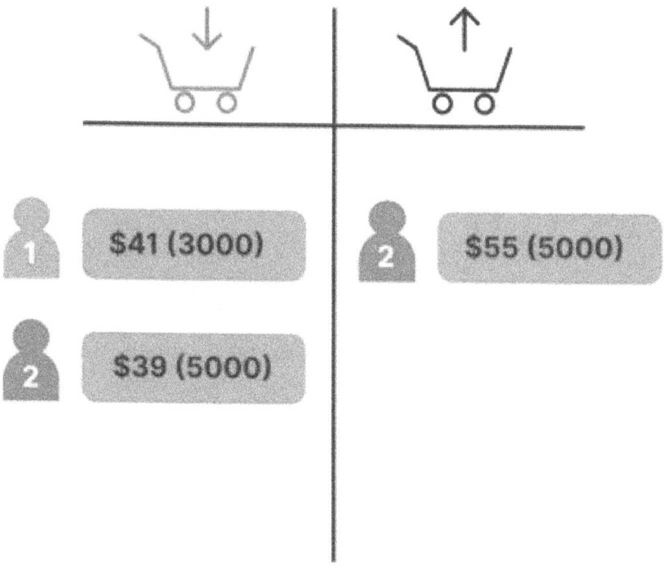

This is known as Level 2, or the order book, which includes all buyers and sellers in the market. From this, we derive Level 1, which represents the best available bid and offer prices in the market.

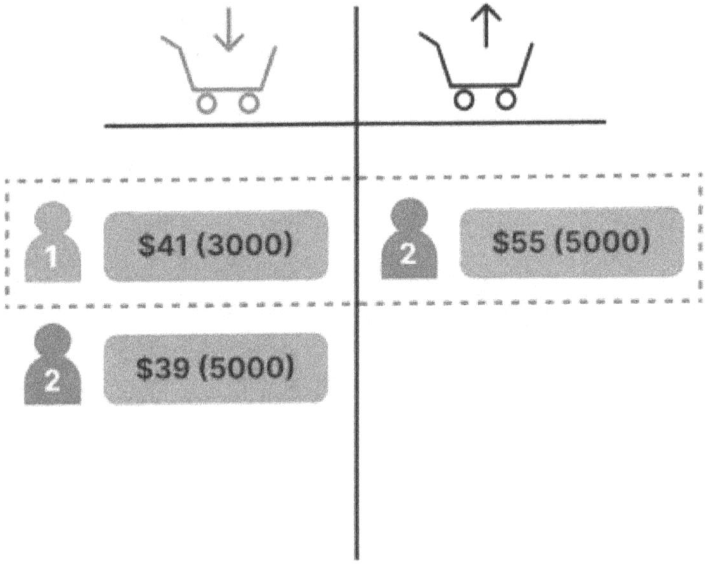

In other words, it is the highest price someone is willing to pay to buy and the lowest price someone is willing to sell at. For instance, $41 for 3,000 shares to buy and $55 for 5,000 shares to sell. When someone asks for Level 1 prices, they're asked about these immediate buying and selling prices. Level 1, showing the bid and ask, is derived from Level 2, the order book, and updates with each new order affecting the top bid or offer.

Then, P2 submits a second sell order for 5,000 shares at $59. It is placed below his $55 order, as higher-priced sell orders like this are less favorable and rank lower in the order book.

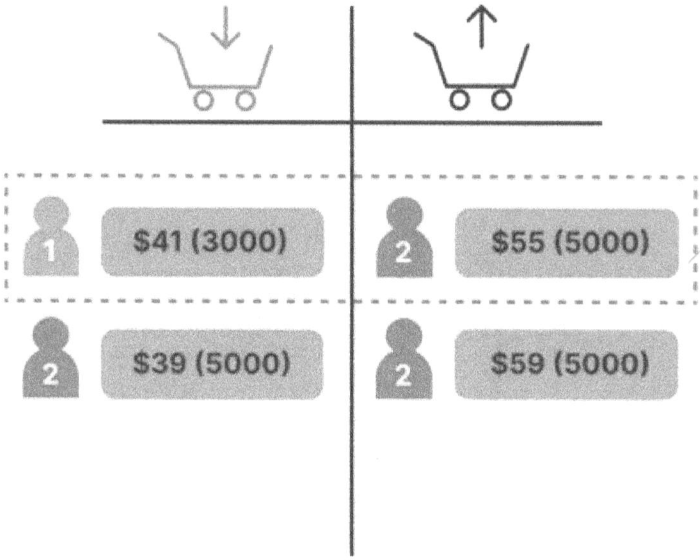

No trades have occurred yet as no matching orders have been placed. On a chart, you'd only see an ask price with no last traded price. At this time, P3 offers to sell 2,000 shares at $52. This order, placed on the sell side, gets priority over higher-priced orders and tops them in the book, as buyers prefer lower prices. While, P4 remains inactive, which is common; not everyone places orders.

P5 wants to buy 1,000 shares at $50. This order, offering a better price for sellers, tops the buy side in the order book, pushing previous orders down. With this change, Level 1 also updates - buyers can now buy at $52 instead of $55. As the highest bid shifts to $50, Level 1 updates again, reflecting this new top bid of $50 for 1,000 shares.

When a significant new order alters the book, it can affect Level 1. These updates show how incoming orders continuously impact stock prices.

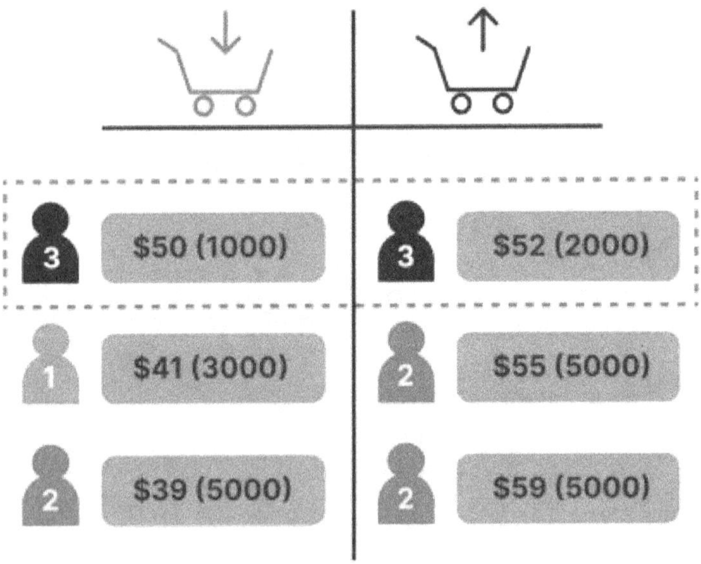

P6 offers to buy 2,000 shares at $48, slotting between the $50 and $41 offers. P7 aims to sell 1,000 shares at $51, a better price than $52, so it tops that order. With these changes, Level 1 updates to reflect the best buy and sell prices, but no trades have occurred yet.

Now P8 enters, wanting to buy 5,000 shares at $46, updating the book. However, Level 1 doesn't change as this order doesn't affect the best bid or ask prices.

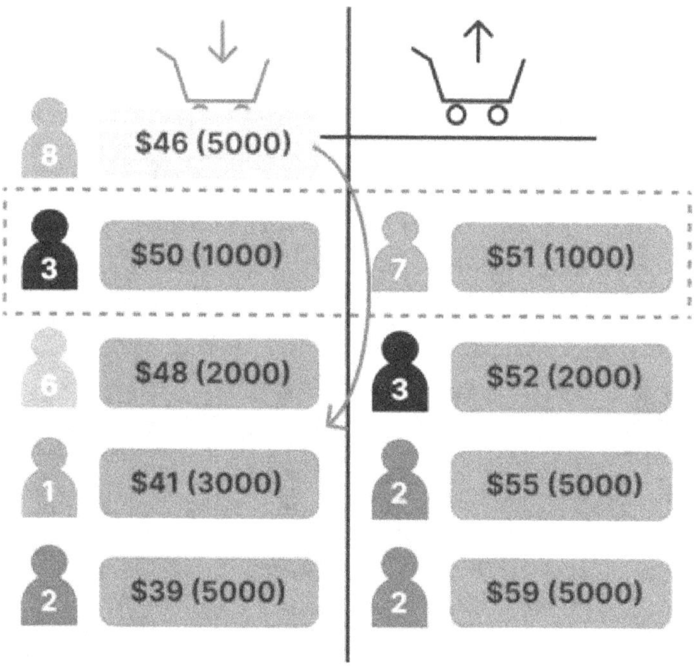

P9 decides to sell 5,000 shares at market price, without specifying a price. Since he's selling, his order heads to the buyers' side for execution, matching with someone willing to buy, like the order for 1,000 shares at $50. This sale is logged in the Time & Sales record, detailing the transaction's time (e.g., 5:00 pm), price ($50), and quantity (1,000 shares). Time & Sales is a key tool in trading, working alongside Level 1 and 2.

After selling 1,000 shares at $50, P9 still has 4,000 shares left to sell from his initial 5,000. His order continues down the line, next matching with a buyer at $48 for 2,000 shares.

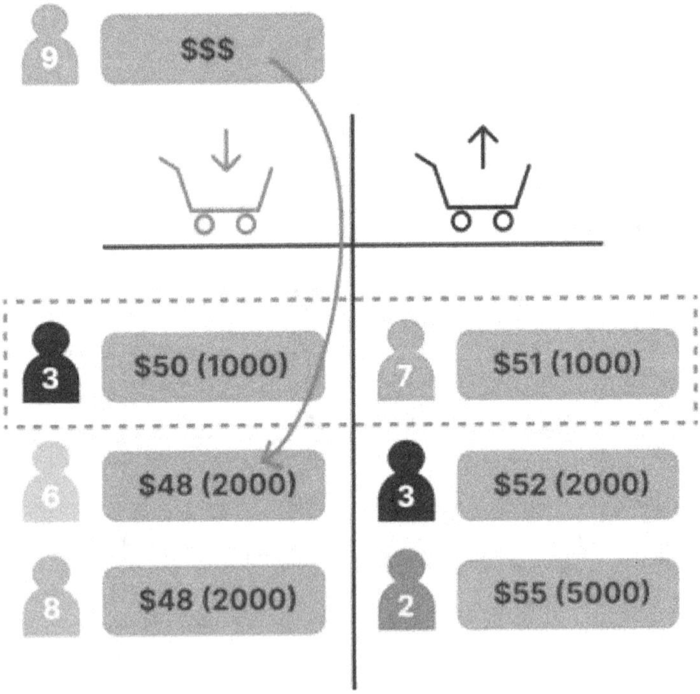

Next he matches with P6 to to sell 2,000 shares at $48, and it recorded instantly in the Time & Sales log. With 2,000 shares left, P9 finds another buyer at $46 wanting 5,000 shares. P9 sells his last 2,000 shares, leaving the buyer still seeking 3,000 more. These transactions, happening at 1pm and almost simultaneously, are all recorded in the Time & Sales log.

So, P9 has successfully filled his orders. Notably, the seller's action led to the first execution. Suddenly, a trade occurred and was recorded in the Time & Sales log.

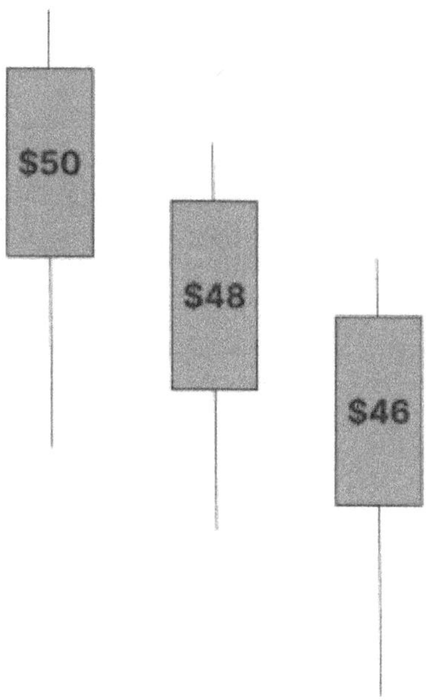

Now, if you check this stock in our fictional world, you'll see it's trading at $46, which is the most recent price the stock was traded at.

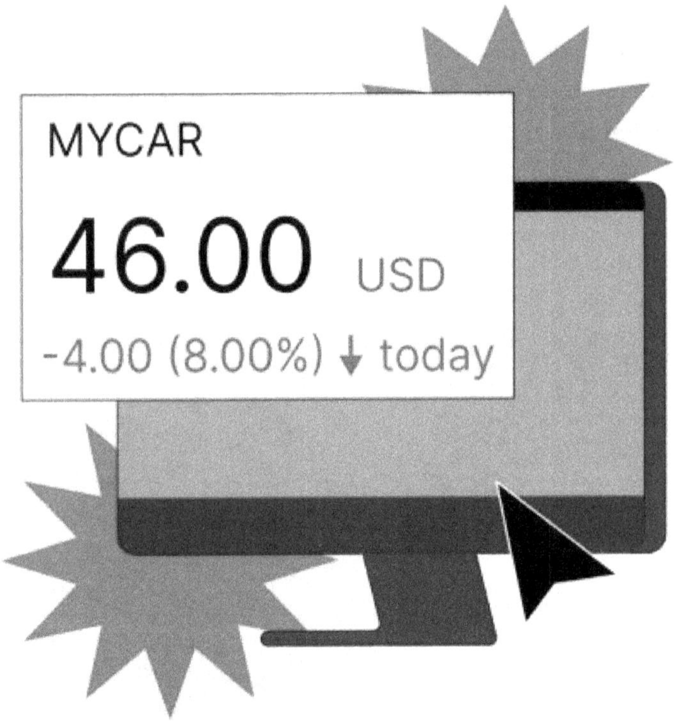

Alright, so wrapping it up, we've seen how prices in the stock market are like a dance of supply and demand. It's all about the orders people place, right? This lesson really shows how each participant, with their buying or selling orders, plays a part in nudging those prices up or down. It's like everyone's moves in this big market dance floor affects the rhythm of the prices!

Lesson 3: Order Types and Market Mechanics Review

1. What is a ticker in stock trading?

Answer: An abbreviation for a company's name.

1. What does the "side" of an order indicate?

Answer: Whether the order is to buy or sell.

1. Which order type is executed immediately at the current market price?

Answer: Market order.

1. What is the main advantage of using a limit order?

Answer: It sets a maximum/minimum price for the trade.

1. What is the "float" in stock trading?

Answer: Number of shares available for trading.

1. What is Level 2 in stock trading?

Answer: The complete order book of buyers and sellers.

1. How are buy orders prioritized in the order book?

Answer: Higher prices get priority.

1. What information is typically recorded in the Time & Sales log?

Answer: Time, price, and quantity of executed trades.

1. What determines the current trading price of a stock?

Answer: The most recent executed trade price.

1. How does a market order to sell interact with the order book?

Answer: It matches with the highest available buy orders.

Chapter 3: Deep Dive into Order Types

Lesson 1: Buy or Sell?

Diving deeper into order types:

In this lesson, we'll cover various order types used in trading. Knowing how to use these orders effectively is key to implementing your trading strategies.

We'll focus on five main order types: buy limit, sell limit, buy stop, sell stop, and market orders. Each serves a specific purpose in trading. Let's explore each one in detail.

Let's start with buy limit orders. A buy limit order tells your broker to buy a stock at or below a specific price. It's useful when you have a maximum price you're willing to pay for a stock.

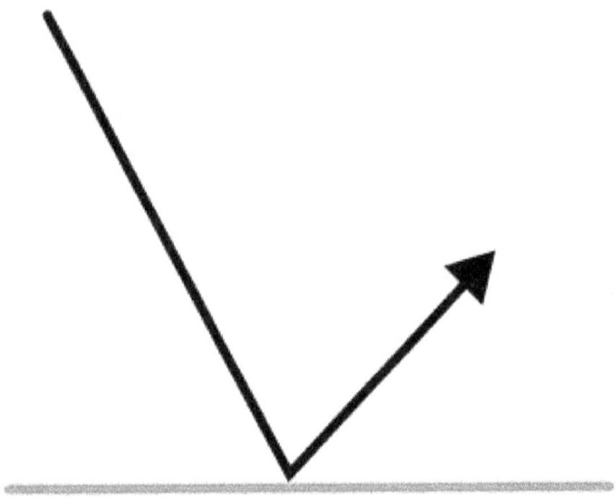

Buy limit orders:

Let's dive deeper into how buy limit orders work in the stock market. Imagine you're interested in purchasing shares of ABC Corp, but you believe the current price is a bit high and you want to wait for a better deal. If ABC Corp stock is currently trading at $50 per share and you set a buy limit order at $48, under what condition will your order be executed?

Answer: When you set a buy limit order at $48 while the stock is trading at $50, your order will only execute if the price drops to $48 or lower. This is the key advantage of buy limit orders - they allow you to specify the maximum price you're willing to pay, ensuring you don't overpay if the stock price declines to your desired entry point.

Now, let's look at sell limit orders. Conversely, a sell limit order instructs your broker to sell a stock at or above a certain price. Use this when you have a minimum price you want to receive for selling your

shares.

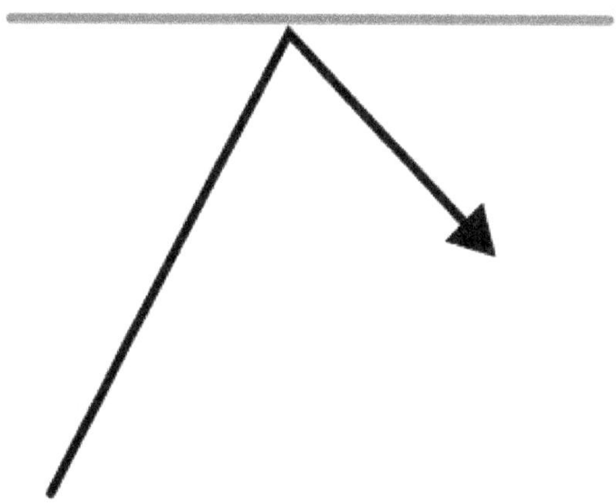

Sell limit orders:

Now let's explore how sell limit orders work in the stock market. Imagine you own shares of XYZ Corp and you're looking to sell them, but only if you can get a price higher than the current market price. If XYZ Corp stock is currently trading at $60 per share and you set a sell limit order at $62, under what condition will your order be executed?

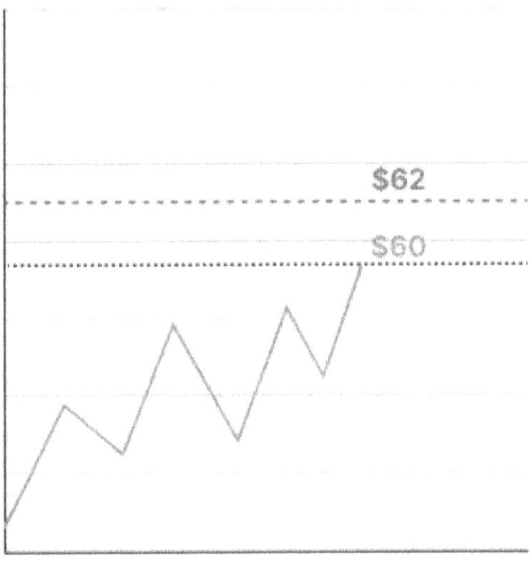

Answer: When you set a sell limit order at $62 while the stock is trading at $60, your order will only execute if the price rises to $62 or higher. This is the key advantage of sell limit orders - they allow you to specify the minimum price you're willing to accept, ensuring you don't sell for less than your desired exit point if the stock price increases.

Moving on to stop orders, let's first look at buy stop orders. A buy stop order is placed above the current market price. It becomes a market order when the stock reaches your specified price. Traders often use this when they think a stock will continue rising after breaking a certain level.

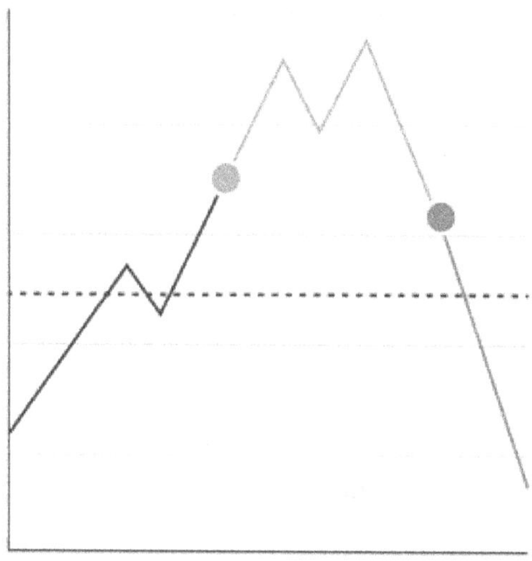

Decoding buy stop orders:

Let's explore this different type of order: the buy stop order. This order type is often used when traders anticipate a stock's price will continue to rise once it reaches a certain point. If ABC Corp stock is currently trading at $50 per share and you place a buy stop order at $52, what will happen when the stock price reaches $52?

Answer: When you set a buy stop order at $52 while the stock is trading at $50, your order becomes a market order to buy as soon as the price hits $52. This type of order is often used when traders believe a stock will continue to rise once it breaks through a certain price level. It helps you enter a position in an upward-trending market. It's important to understand that a buy stop order is different from a limit order. With a buy stop order, you're looking to buy when the price moves up to a certain level, not when it drops below a certain price.

Now, let's examine sell stop orders. A sell stop order works the opposite way. It's placed below the current market price and turns into a market order if the stock falls to that price. It's commonly used to limit potential losses.

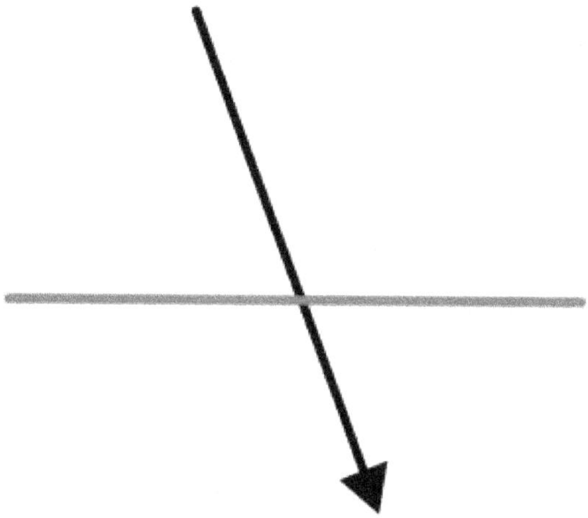

Unraveling sell stop orders:

Let's take a closer look at this important order type: the sell stop order. This order is often used by traders to limit potential losses or protect profits on a stock they own. If XYZ Corp stock is currently trading at $60 per share and you place a sell stop order at $58, what will happen when the stock price reaches $58?

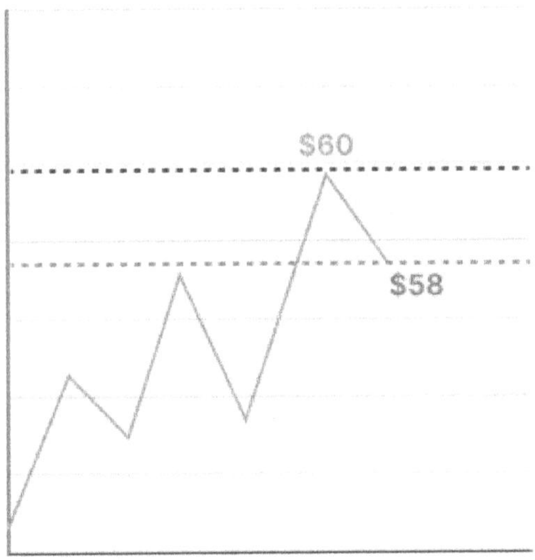

Answer: When you set a sell stop order at $58 while the stock is trading at $60, your order becomes a market order to sell as soon as the price hits $58. This type of order is often used to limit potential losses or protect profits on a stock you own. It helps you exit a position in a downward-trending market or if the stock price falls below a level you're comfortable with.

Lastly, let's briefly revisit market orders. As we discussed in previous lessons, market orders are straightforward - they execute immediately at the best available price. They're quick, but you have less control over the execution price.

Understanding market orders:

Let's compare market orders with the limit and stop orders we've discussed. Market orders are different because they prioritize immediate execution over price. If XYZ Corp stock is currently trading at $60 per share and you place a market order to buy 100 shares, which of the following is most likely to occur?

Answer: When you place a market order, it's executed as quickly as possible at the best available price. In this case, you'd likely buy 100 shares at or very close to $60 each. While this ensures quick execution, it doesn't guarantee a specific price, especially in fast-moving markets. This is different from limit orders, which give you price control but may not execute, and stop orders, which trigger at a certain price but then execute as market orders.

That covers the main order types, including market orders. Each has its place in different market conditions and trading strategies. It's worth practicing with these in a demo account before using them in real trading. Remember, these orders are instructions to your broker. How they're executed depends on market conditions and your specified parameters.

Lesson 2: Order Placement

Order types in action:

In this lesson, we'll explore how the order types we've learned can be used for three key purposes in trading: entry orders, stop loss orders, and target (profit) orders.

Understanding this flexibility is crucial for effective trading

strategies.

Remember, every order is just an order. Your entry could be someone else's stop loss, your target could be another trader's entry, and so on. It's important to put equal effort into planning all aspects of your trade: entry, stop loss, and target.

Let's start with entry orders. Any order type can be used to enter a trade, depending on your strategy. For example, you might use a buy limit order to enter a long position at a lower price, or a buy stop order to enter once the price breaks above a certain level.

Stop loss orders are crucial for risk management. Depending on whether you're in a long or short position, you might use a sell stop (for long positions) or a buy stop (for short positions) as your stop loss.

Target or profit orders are how you plan to exit a profitable trade. For a long position, this might be a sell limit order. For a short position, it could be a buy limit order.

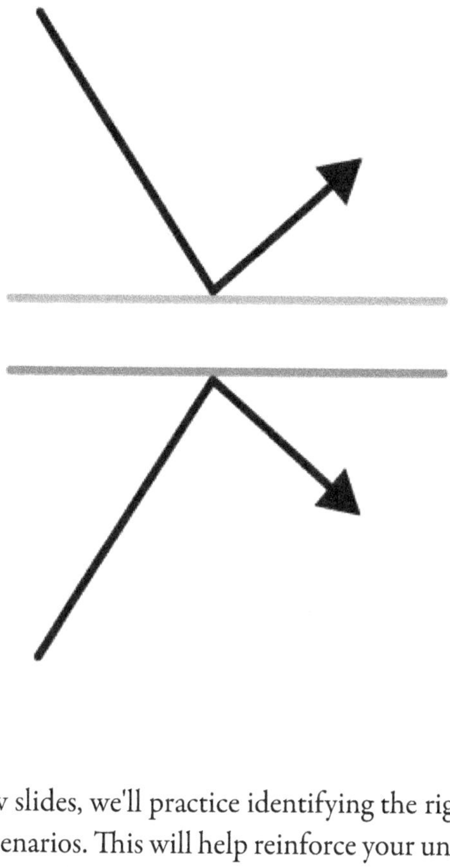

In the next few slides, we'll practice identifying the right order types for different scenarios. This will help reinforce your understanding of how to use these orders effectively in your trading.

Entry order scenario:

Let's practice with an entry order scenario. Imagine you're watching ABC stock, currently trading at $50. You believe it's overvalued and want to enter a short position if it reaches $52. Which order type would be most appropriate for this entry?

Answer: A Sell Stop Order is perfect for this scenario. It to your broker to sell 6t(enter a short position) when the price rises to your specified level of $52. This allows you to automatically enter your short position if the stock reaches the price you believe represents an overvalued state.

Stop loss:

Now that we've entered our short position at $52, let's consider our stop loss. We want to limit our potential loss if the stock continues to rise against our position. If you want to set your stop loss at $54, which order type would you use?

Answer: A Buy Stop Order is the correct choice for a stop loss on a short position. If the stock price rises to $54, this order will trigger, buying back the shares and closing your position to limit your loss.

Target:

Finally, let's set a target for our trade. We believe the stock might fall to $48, where we'd like to take our profit. Which order type would you use to automatically close your short position at $48?

Answer: A Buy Limit Order is perfect for this situation. It instructs your broker to buy back the shares (closing your short position) when the price falls to your target of $48, allowing you to secure your profit automatically.

Let's review the complete trade setup:

1. Entry: Sell Stop Order at $52 (to enter the short position);

1. Stop Loss: Buy Stop Order at $54 (to limit potential losses)
2. Target: Buy Limit Order at $48 (to take profit).

From this example we can see how different order types work together in a single trade strategy.

Remember, the same order types can be used differently for long positions. For instance, a Buy Stop Order could be an entry for a long position, while a Sell Stop Order could be its stop loss.

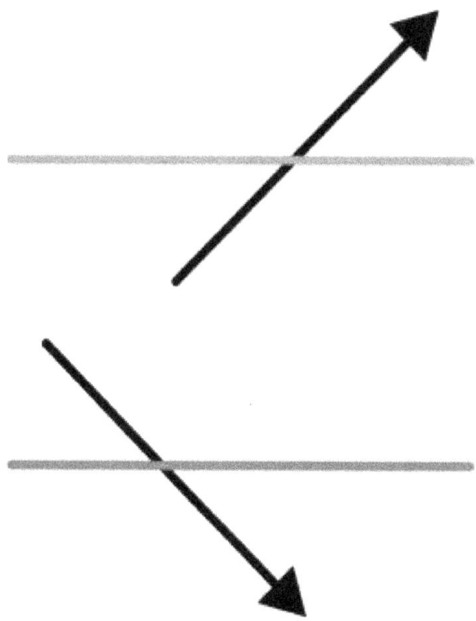

Practice creating trade setups with different scenarios. Consider both long and short positions, and think about which order types make the most sense for entries, stop losses, and targets in each case.

In conclusion, understanding how to use different order types for entries, stop losses, and targets gives you flexibility in executing your trading strategies. Always consider the current price, your prediction for price movement, and whether you're entering a long or short position when choosing your order types.

Lesson 3: Advanced Order Types and Trading Strategies Review

1. What does a buy limit order instruct your broker to do?

Answer: Buy a stock at or below a specific price.

1. When does a buy stop order become a market order?

Answer: When the stock reaches the specified price.

1. What is the primary purpose of a sell stop order?

Answer: To limit potential losses or protect profits.

1. Which order type prioritizes immediate execution over price?

Answer: Market order.

1. In a short trade, what type of order is typically used as a stop loss?

Answer: Buy stop order.

1. What type of order would you use to enter a short position when a stock rises to a certain price?

Answer: Sell stop order.

1. For a long position, which order type is commonly used as a profit target?

Answer: Sell limit order.

1. What is true about the relationship between different traders' orders?

Answer: One trader's entry could be another's stop loss.

1. Which aspect of trading should receive equal planning effort?

Answer: Entry, stop loss, and target orders.

1. What factor should NOT be considered when choosing order types for a trade?

Answer: The opinions of other traders.

SECTION 6: BASICS OF RISK MANAGEMENT

Ready to take your trading skills to the next level? Dive into the world of risk management and discover the secret sauce that separates amateur traders from the pros. In this section, you'll learn how to protect your capital, maximize your profits, and trade with confidence. Whether you're just starting out or looking to refine your strategy, this section of the book will equip you with the tools you need to succeed in the fast-paced world of trading.

Received skills:

RISK ASSESSMENT

POSITION SIZING

STRATEGY DEVEL

What will you learn from this section:

- Risk Management: Master the fundamentals of risk assessment and learn to protect your capital effectively.

- Position Sizing: Calculate optimal position sizes to balance potential profits against acceptable losses.

- Strategy Development: Create and backtest your own trading strategies using historical market data.

Chapter 1: Intro to Risk Management

Lesson 1: Intro to Risk Management

Remember when we first talked about candlesticks, and you were trying to wrap your head around all those order types? Well, look at you now! Now you're ready to make some trades! But guess what? We're about to take it to the next level.

In this section of the book, we're diving into the stuff that separates the amateurs from the pros: risk management and strategy development.

Now, I know what you're thinking - "Risk management? Sounds boring." But trust me, this is the secret sauce that'll keep you in the game when others are blowing up their accounts.

We're going to get our hands dirty with some real-world examples. I'm talking about calculating position sizes that won't give you a heart attack every time the market twitches. We'll look at how to spot the perfect moment to enter a trade, and more importantly, when to get out - both when you're right and when you're wrong.

But here's the really cool part - we're going to develop our own trading strategy. Yeah, you heard that right. By the end of this section, you'll have your very own approach to the markets. We'll look at different market conditions, how to spot them, and how to adapt your strategy to whatever the market throws at you.

And you know what else? We're going to test the heck out of that strategy. I'm going to show you how to use a simple spreadsheet to track your trades. It might not sound exciting, but let me tell you, there's nothing quite like seeing your strategy come to life in cold, hard numbers.

Before we dive deeper, let's test your intuition:

Carl is a new trader who has been enjoying a winning streak. He's won 9 out of his last 10 trades, each winning trade earning him $100. However, he hasn't implemented any risk management strategies yet. Is Carl guaranteed to be profitable in the long run if he maintains his 90% win rate, even without implementing risk management strategies? Take a moment to think about this. What's your gut feeling?

Answer: A high win rate doesn't guarantee profit without proper risk management. If Carl loses $1000 on one trade, even after winning 9 out of 10, he ends up with a net loss of $100. This highlights the importance of risk management for long-term success.

Now, I'm not going to lie to you - this part of the book is going to be challenging. We're dealing with advanced concepts here. But I promise you, if you stick with it, you'll come out the other side with skills that can genuinely change your trading game.

So, what do you say? Are you ready to take your trading to the next level? Great! Let's get started on this journey together. Trust me, by the time we're done, you'll be looking at the markets in a whole new way.

Lesson 2: Order Placement and Risk Management

Understanding risk and position sizing:

In this lesson, we'll walk through a simple example to illustrate how position sizing and risk management work in practice. Let's break down order placement and risk management at the most basic level with an example!

Let's set the scene. Imagine we're in a trending market, and we've identified a potential entry point.

We're going to focus on a buy order for this example. Don't worry too much about the profit target for now - we'll get to that later. Our main goal here is to understand the fundamentals of risk and position sizing.

For our example, let's say we want to enter the market at a price of 0.8550. We could use a limit order, a market order, or a buy stop - the specific order type isn't crucial for this example. What's important is that we're predicting the market will go up from our entry point.

Now, here's where risk management comes in. We need to decide where to place our stop loss. This is the point where we'll exit the trade if the market moves against us, minimizing our potential loss. Let's set our stop loss at 0.8500, 50 pips below our entry.

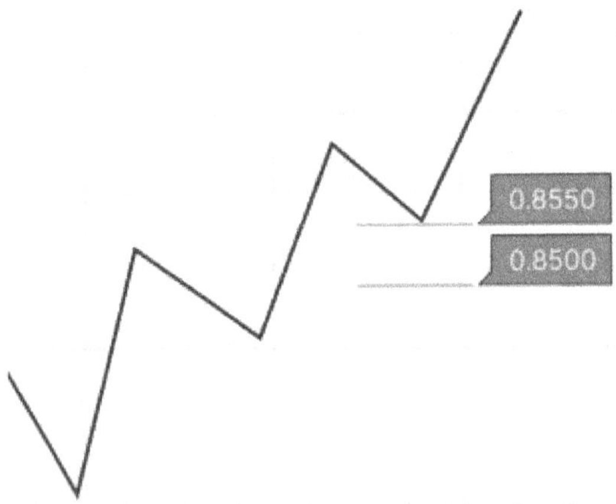

Hold up, what's a pip anyway? It's like the smallest step a currency pair can take. For most pairs, we're talking about the fourth decimal place. So if EUR/USD moves from 1.2000 to 1.2001, that's a one pip move. It's tiny, but in forex, these little guys add up fast!

The yen pairs are an exception - for those, we look at the second decimal point. For example, in USD/ JPY at 131.20, the '1'is one unit and the '2' is ten units.

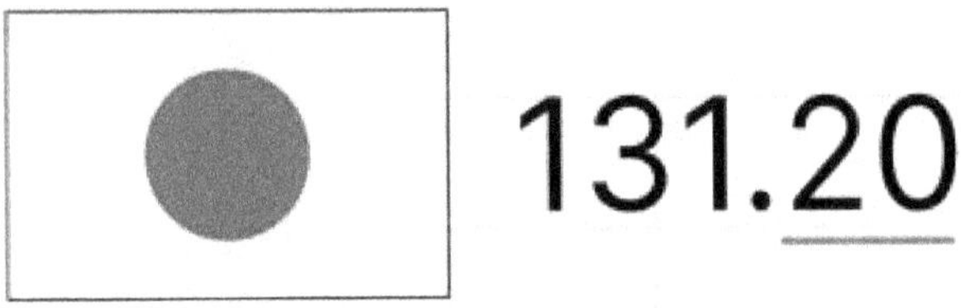

Back to our example. We've established a 50-pip risk between our entry and stop loss. Now, let's talk about our trading account. Let's say we have a $10,000 account. This is just an example - your actual account might be larger or smaller.

Here's a key principle of risk management: never risk more than a small percentage of your account on any single trade. For our example, we'll use 1% as our maximum risk. So, what's 1% of $10,000?

Calculating 1% risk:

Let's calculate 1% of a $10,000 account to limit our risk per trade. So, what's 1% of $10,000?

Answer: The correct answer is $100. To calculate 1% of $10,000, we multiply 10,000 by 0.01, which equals 100. This means we should risk no more than $100 on any single trade to adhere to the 1% risk management rule. This approach helps protect our capital while still allowing for potential profits.

So, $100 is the maximum amount we're willing to risk on this trade. Now, how do we use this information to size our position correctly?

Let's calculate:

Remember, we have a 50-pip stop, and we're willing to risk $100. To find out how much we should risk per pip, we divide $100 by 50 pips. How much should we risk per pip?

Answer: It gives us $2 per pip. We calculated this by dividing our total risk ($100) by the number of pips to our stop loss (50). This means for every pip the market moves in our favor, we gain $2, and for every pip it moves against us, we lose $2.

So this means that for every pip, if the market moves in our favor, we gain $2. For every pip it moves against us, we lose $2. If we hit our stop loss at 50 pips, we'll lose our maximum risk of $100.

Now, let's think about our potential profit. If we're aiming for a 2:1 reward-to-risk ratio, where would our take profit level be? If we're risking 50 pips, we'd be looking to gain 100 pips.

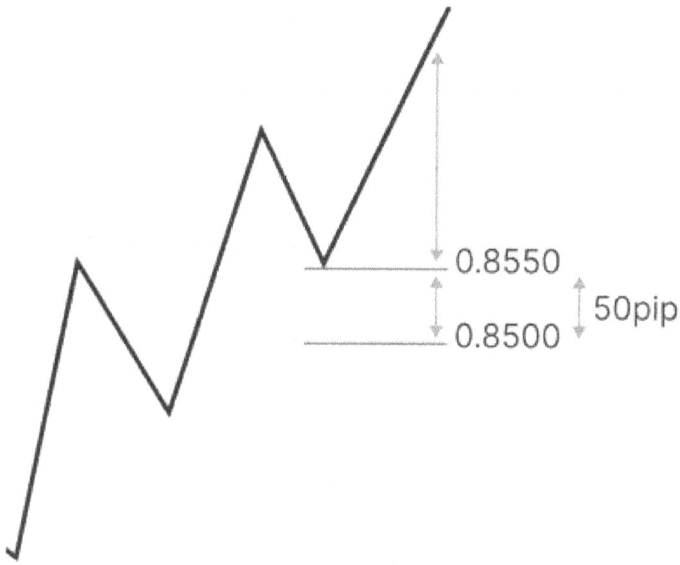

At $2 per pip, a 100-pip move in our favor would result in a $200 profit. So we're risking $100 to potentially gain $200. This is what we mean by a 2:1 risk-reward ratio.

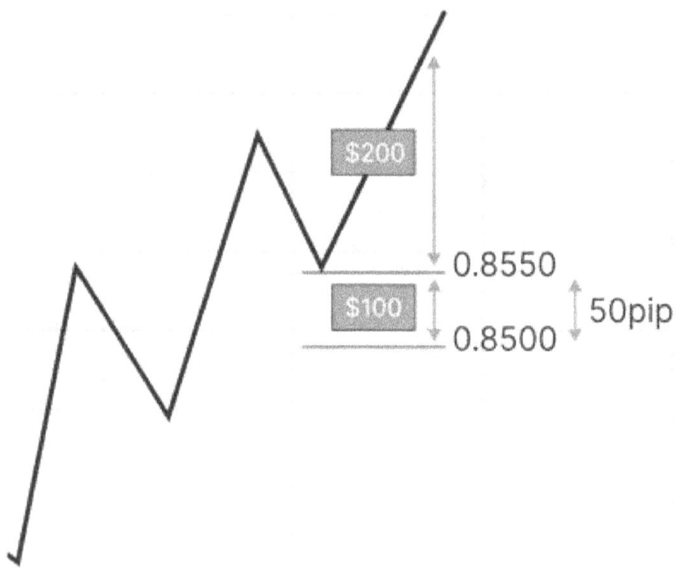

Great job! The key takeaway is this process: Determine your account risk (1%), calculate your stop loss in pips, divide your dollar risk by pip risk to find the value per pip, and use it to calculate position size and

potential profit. This method is essential for managing risk and ensuring no single trade can wipe out your account while allowing for solid profits when your analysis is correct.

Lesson 3: Practical Strategy Development

Putting theory into practice:

Now that we've covered the basics of risk management and order placement, it's time to take everything we've learned and develop our first trading strategy.

This is where the rubber meets the road!

During this lesson, we will bring together six essential elements of a trading setup: market conditions, phases, price action patterns, indicators, support and resistance levels, and candlestick patterns. We'll use these components to develop a basic trading strategy.

A trading strategy is essentially a series of events or patterns that occur frequently in the market. By identifying these patterns and building rules around them, we can create a consistent approach to trading.

Remember, the concepts we've covered can be applied to various trading styles - whether you're looking for trends, reversals, or ranging markets. Your strategy will depend on your preferred approach and market conditions.

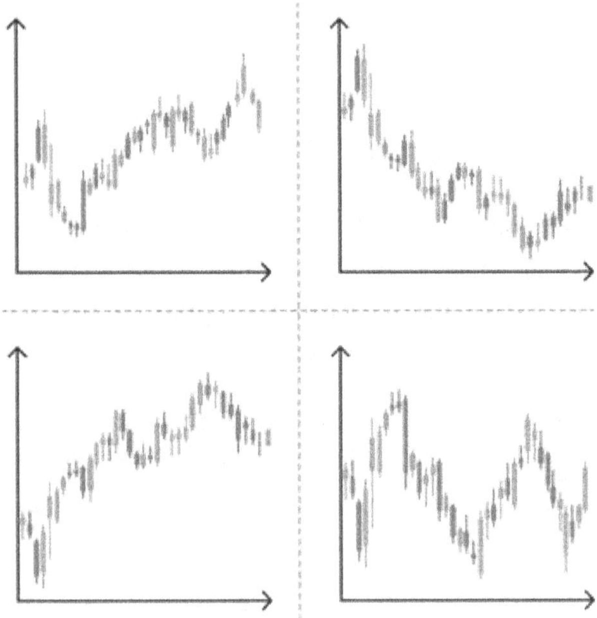

Now let's focus on our practical exercise. Using the horizontal line tool on your charting platform, practice identifying support and resistance levels. This exercise will train your eye to spot key price levels quickly.

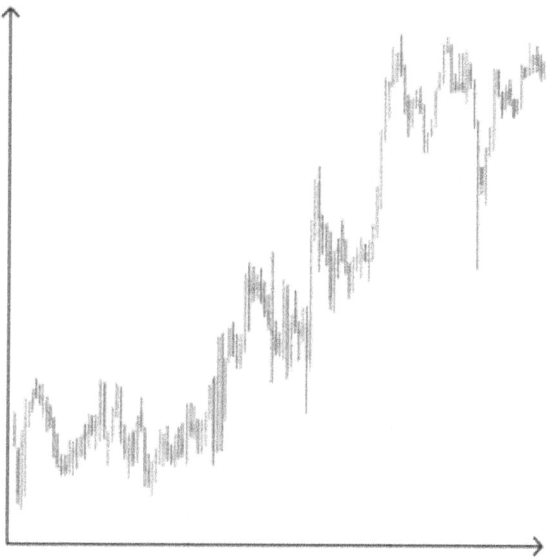

Practice time!

We've covered and practiced support and resistance lines in previous lessons. Let's reinforce those skills to build your confidence. On the following chart, how many support and resistance lines can be drawn?

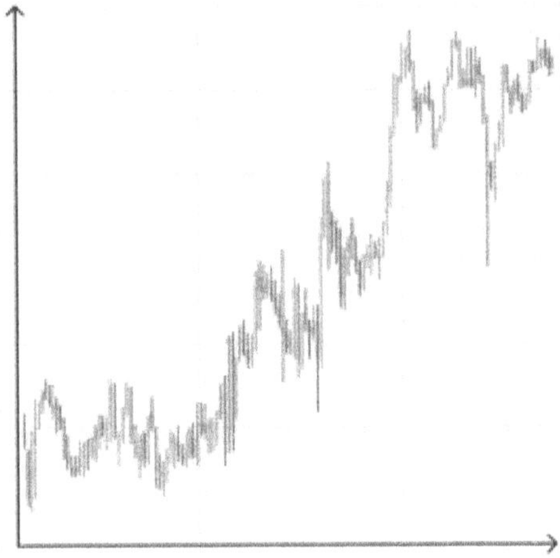

Answer: There are 5 levels of support and resistance lines. Support and resistance lines often appear at key price points where buying or selling pressure has previously halted price movements. Remember, identifying these levels becomes easier with practice and experience.

As you practice, you'll notice something interesting: previous resistance often becomes support, and vice versa. This behavior doesn't always occur, but it's frequent enough to be a valuable part of your analysis, especially in trending markets.

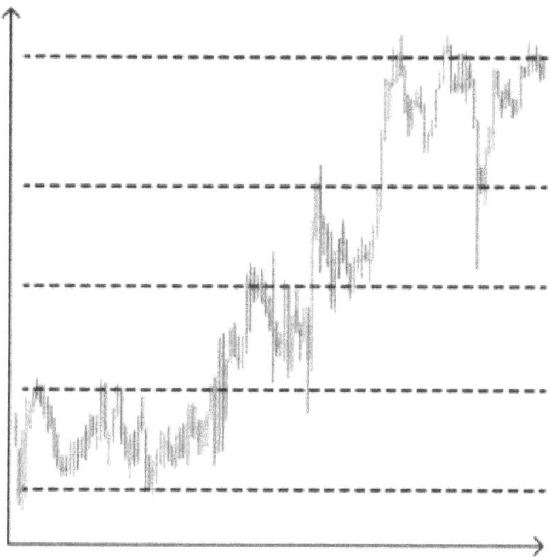

This exercise will help you in two ways: it will train your eye to identify market structure, and it will demonstrate how powerful these support and resistance levels can be in your trading decisions.

Now that we've practiced identifying key levels, let's develop a simple strategy based on what we've learned. We'll create a set of rules to identify potential trade setups.

Here's our basic strategy:

1. Identify an uptrend (market condition)

1. Wait for a pullback (market phase)
2. Look for a support level (support and resistance)

3. Watch for a bullish candlestick pattern at the support level
4. Enter a long position if all conditions are met

Remember, this is just an example. You can adapt this strategy based on your preferred trading style, whether you're looking for trends, reversals, or range-bound markets.

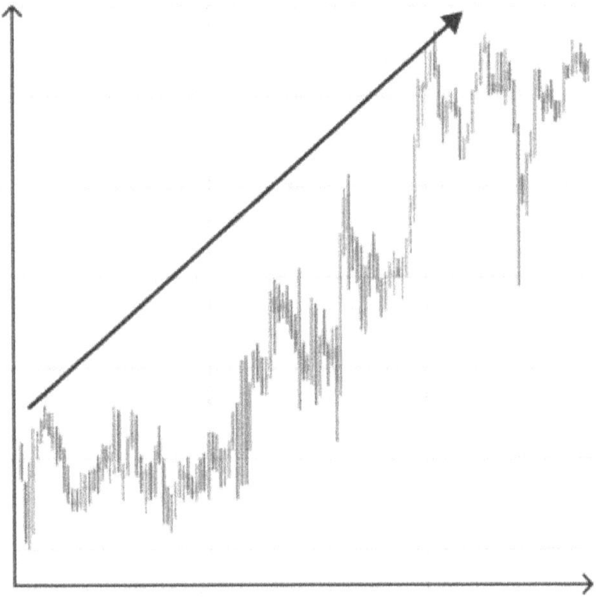

Great work completing this chapter! You now understand the basics of risk management, position sizing, and strategy development. In our next chapter, we'll dive deeper into identifying specific trade setups. Keep up the fantastic work!

Chapter 2: Identifying High-Probability Trades

Lesson 1: Choosing The Right Time Frame

Your trading window:

Let's talk about time frames - they're like choosing the right lens for your trading camera. Pick the wrong one, and you might miss the big picture or get lost in the details.

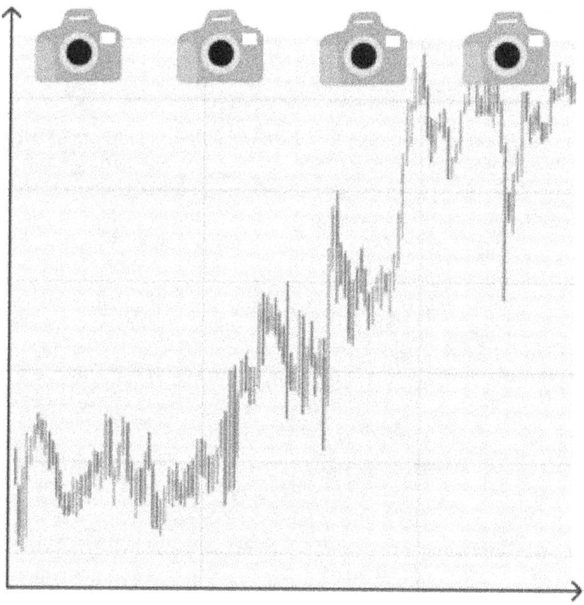

Now, you might be wondering, "What's the best time frame?" Well, here's the kicker - there isn't a one-size-fits-all answer. It depends on you, your schedule, and your trading style.

Here's the deal: consistency is king in trading. You need to pick a time frame that fits your life like a glove. Ask yourself: When can you reliably sit down and focus on the markets without interruptions?

Think about your daily routine. Are you juggling a 9-to-5 job? Got kids to pick up from school? These aren't just life details - they're crucial factors in your trading decisions.

If you can only check the markets once a day, the daily chart is your go-to. It's like the Goldilocks of time frames - not too short, not too long, just right for getting a solid market overview.

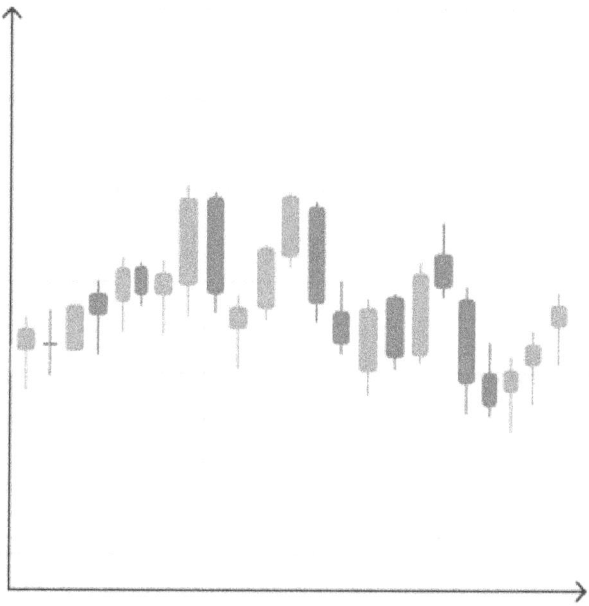

Each candle on a daily chart represents a full day of trading. It's less noisy than shorter time frames, which means less false signals and less stress for you. Perfect for beginners or those with busy schedules.

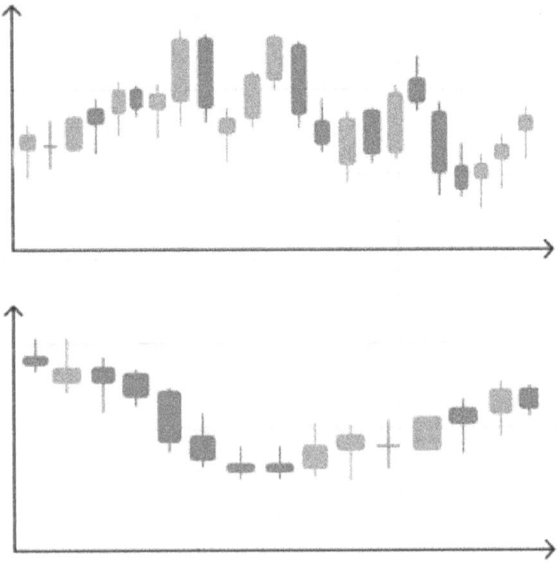

Got time to check the markets 2-3 times a day? The 4-hour chart might be your sweet spot. It offers more opportunities than daily charts but requires more attention.

But here's the catch - those check times need to be consistent. There's no point in randomly popping in and out of the markets. Trading is a discipline, not a hobby you do when you're bored.

The 1-hour chart is like the fast lane of trading. More opportunities, but also more noise and potential for overtrading. It's not for the faint-hearted or the easily distracted.

If you're considering the 1-hour chart, ask yourself: Can I realistically check the markets more than 3 times a day, every day? Be honest with yourself - this isn't about what you want to do, but what you can consistently do.

Remember, as a beginner, less is often more. You don't need to be glued to your charts 24/7 to be successful. In fact, that's a recipe for burnout and poor decisions.

Here's a pro tip: start with the daily chart. Get comfortable with that, understand how the market moves in that time frame. You can always switch to shorter time frames later if needed.

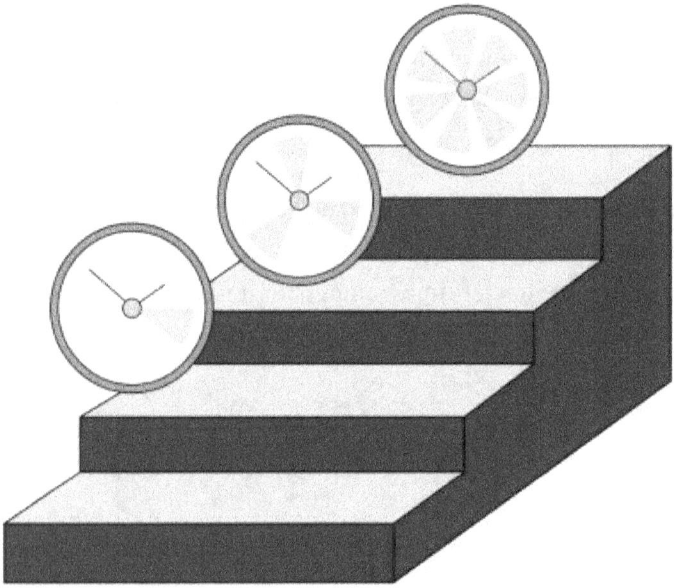

Switching between time frames or missing trading sessions isn't just inconvenient - it can be costly. In trading, your edge is often small. Missing a single good setup can wipe out weeks of gains.

Time frame quiz:

You're working a full-time job and can only dedicate one hour each evening to trading. Which time frame would likely be most suitable for your situation?

Answer: The daily chart is perfect for you. It allows for thorough analysis once a day, fits your available time, and strikes a good balance between capturing meaningful market moves and filtering out unnecessary noise.

Choosing your time frame is a personal decision, but it's one that can make or break your trading. In our next lesson, we'll dive into how to actually use these time frames to spot high-probability trades. Stay tuned, and remember - consistency is key!

Lesson 2: Developing A Bearish Trend Trading Strategy

Bearish trend trading strategy:

Now that we've nailed down our time frame, let's dive into a specific strategy. We're going to focus on trading bearish trends using the daily chart.

First things first - what's a bearish trend? It's when the market is moving from the top left of your chart to the bottom right. You'll see a series of lower highs and lower lows. Think of it as the market going downhill.

In this downtrend, we're looking for continuation setups. That means we want to sell when the market pulls back, aiming to profit as it resumes its downward movement.

The key to this strategy is identifying the pullback phase. This is when the market takes a breather, moving temporarily against the main trend. It's like a sprinter catching their breath before the next sprint.

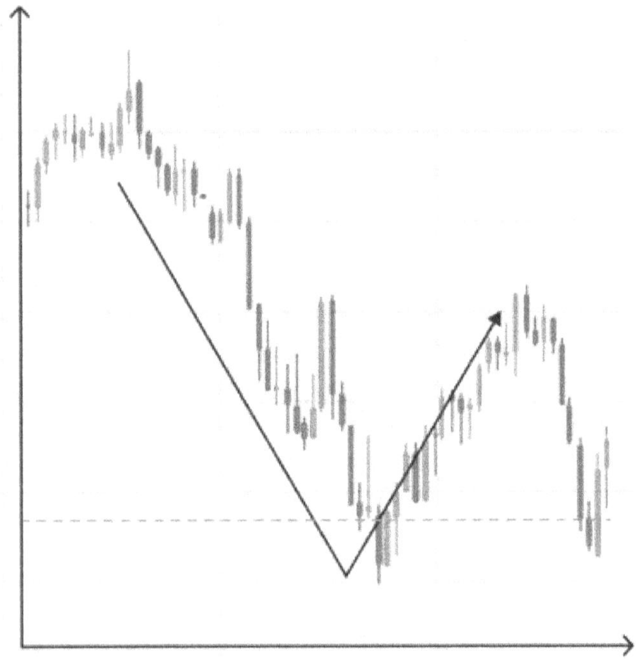

During the pullback, price often returns to a previous support level. But here's the twist - in a downtrend, that old support might now act as resistance. This is a key area to watch for potential entries.

Now, let's talk about our entry trigger. We're looking for what I call a "lower low, lower close" candle. It's exactly what it sounds like - a candle that makes a lower low than the previous candle and also closes lower.

In other words, we're waiting for a day where the market not only dips below yesterday's low but also ends the day lower than it started. This signals that the bears are back in control.

Once we spot this candle, here's what we do: place a sell stop order 2 pips below the low of our "lower low, lower close" candle. This ensures we only enter if the market continues to move in our favor.

Now, let's talk about protecting ourselves. We'll put our stop loss 2 pips above the highest high of the recent pullback. This gives the market some wiggle room while still protecting our downside.

For our profit target, we're aiming for the lowest close of the previous bearish run. This level often acts as support and can provide a nice risk-reward ratio.

Speaking of risk-reward, this strategy often gives us setups with 2:1 or even 3:1 reward-to-risk ratios. That means we're risking 1 to potentially gain 2 or 3. Not too shabby, right?

Now, a word of caution. This all looks neat and tidy on a historical chart. But in real-time, it's messier. You'll need patience and discipline to wait for the right setup and to hold through the trade.

Remember, no strategy works 100% of the time. You'll have losing trades. The key is to stick to your rules, manage your risk, and think in probabilities, not certainties.

Bearish strategy quiz:

In a bearish trend, you see a pullback followed by a candle that closes at 1.2010, with a low of 1.2005. The previous candle had a low of 1.2015. Where would you place your sell stop order?

Answer: Our entry rule for this strategy is to always place our entry in relation to the low of the "lower low, lower close" candle, not at the low itself or at the close. Thus, we place our sell stop order 2 pips below the low of the "lower low, lower close" candle. In this case, that's 2 pips below 1.2005, which gives us 1.2003. So, the correct entry would be at 1.2003.

Great job! You've now got the basics of a bearish trend trading strategy. In our next lesson, we'll walk through some real-chart examples and discuss how to fine-tune this approach. Keep practicing identifying these setups - it gets easier with time!

Lesson 3: Bearish Trend Strategy in Practice

Meet Andy - your trading buddy!

Let's follow Andy, a part-time trader who works full-time as a nail technician. He's been studying our bearish trend strategy and is ready to put it into practice. We'll see how he identifies, analyzes, and executes his first trade.

Choosing the right time frame:

It's Monday evening, and Andy has just finished his dinner. He sits down at his trading desk for his daily market review. He's chosen to trade the dally chart because it fits perfectly with his work schedule. Why is the daily chart suitable for Andy's situation?

Answer: The daily chart is perfect for Andy because it aligns with his schedule, allowing him to conduct thorough analysis once per day after work without interfering with his full-time job.

Identifying the trend:

Andy opens his EUR/USD chart and starts his analysis. He notices the market has been making lower highs and lower lows for the past three weeks. The most recent low was at 1.0850. What type of trend is Andy identifying?

Answer: Andy is correctly identifying a bearish trend, shown by the consistent pattern of lower highs and lower lows on his chart. This is the first requirement for our bearish trend strategy.

Analyzing the pullback:

The market has been pulling back for the past four days. Andy marks the previous support level at 1.0920, which could now act as resistance. He sees today's candle made a high of 1.0915. What should Andy look for next?

Answer: Andy should wait for a "lower low, lower close" candle - this is our strategy's specific entry trigger that shows bearish momentum is returning after the pullback.

Entry signal analysis:

Wednesday arrives, and Andy sees a new candle: Low at 1.0890 (lower than Tuesday's 1.0895) and close at 1.0888 (lower than its open). Is this a valid entry signal?

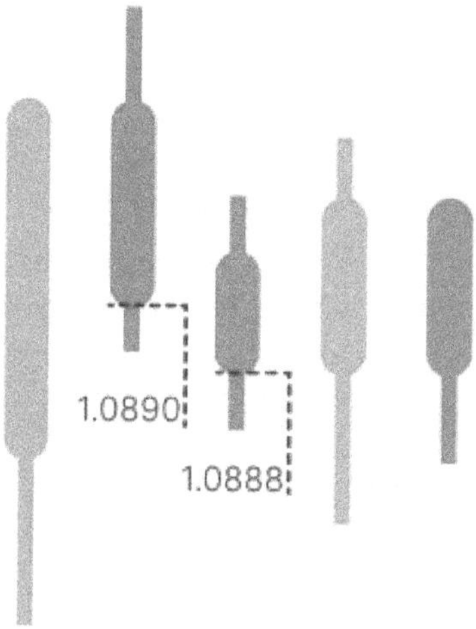

Answer: Yes, this is a valid entry signal. The candle made both a lower low than the previous day AND closed lower than its open - meeting our "lower low, lower close" criteria.

Setting up the trade:

Andy needs to determine his entry price based on our strategy rules. Where should Andy place his sell stop order?

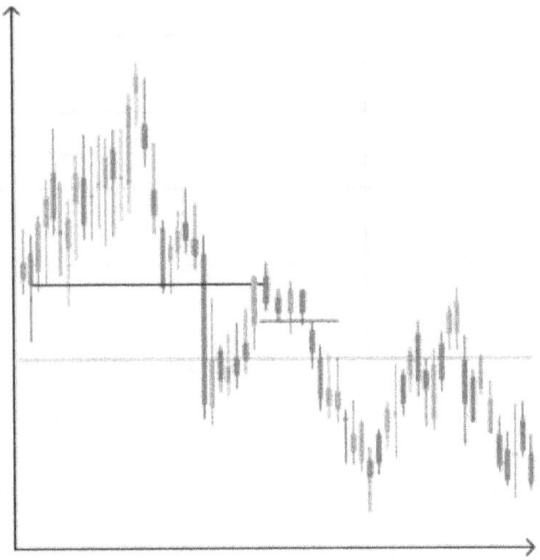

Answer: The correct entry is 2 pips below the signal candle's low (1.0890), which gives us 1.0888. This ensures we only enter if bearish momentum continues.

Risk management:

For his stop loss, Andy looks at the highest point of the pullback: 1.0915. Following our rules, where should he place his stop loss? What is the correct stop loss placement?

Answer: The correct stop loss is 1.0917, placed 2 pips above the pullback high of 1.0915. This gives the trade enough room while maintaining clear invalidation.

Calculating risk-reward:

Andy identifies his target at the previous low of 1.0850 and calculates. Should Andy take this trade?

Answer: Andy should skip this trade. While the setup looks good, the reward-to-risk ratio is only 1.3:1 (38/29 = 1.3), which is below our minimum requirement of 2:1.

Finding a better setup:

The next day, Andy spots another setup with better measurements:

Entry: 1.0868 Stop Loss: 1.0887 (19 pips risk) Target: 1.0850 (38 pips reward). Is this trade worth taking?

Answer: This is a valid trade! The reward-to-risk ratio is 2:1 (38/19 = 2.0), meeting our minimum requirement. All other criteria are also met.

Managing the trade:

Andy's order gets triggered and the market moves in his favor. He's tempted to move his stop loss to breakeven. What should Andy do?

Answer: Andy should stick to his original plan. Changing trade management rules mid-trade based on emotions often leads to suboptimal results.

Reviewing success:

The market reaches Andy's target of 1.0850, and his trade closes automatically with a 2:1 reward-to-risk ratio. What was the key to Andy's success?

Answer: Andy's success came from strictly following ALL the strategy rules, including skipping a tempting but subpar setup and waiting for one that met ALL criteria, including the minimum reward-to-risk ratio.

Wrapping up, Andy's journey shows us that trading success comes from discipline, not prediction. By patiently waiting for valid setups and following his rules without exception, he turned our strategy into profitable trades. Remember - the best trades are often the ones

you choose to skip.

Chapter 3: Backtesting

Lesson 1: The Important of Backtesting

Why backtest?

Welcome to our lesson on backtesting! We're about to explore a crucial aspect of trading that separates successful traders from the rest. Let's dive into why backtesting is so important and how it can transform your trading journey.

Backtesting is all about using historical data to test our trading strategies. It's like a simulator that lets us see how our strategies would have performed in the past. This process is essential for any trader looking to build confidence in their system before risking real money.

Remember, there's no certainty in the markets. Anyone claiming they can guarantee a set amount of pips or money per week is mistaken.

Our focus is on long-term profitability, and backtesting helps us understand the probabilities of what might happen next.

Backtesting provides valuable insights:

1. What's likely to happen based on historical patterns

1. Your longest drawdown periods
2. Maximum losses and biggest gains
3. Seasonal patterns in your strategy's performance

This information is crucial for maintaining emotional control. For example, if you've had three losses in a row, you can look back at your backtest results and see that this is normal for your strategy, helping you stay calm and stick to your plan.

It's important to view trading as a business. Just like any other business, you have overheads (broker fees, platform costs, losses) and profits (winning trades). Backtesting helps you understand your "business model" and create a plan for long-term profitability.

Backtesting creates a framework - a policy for making profits. It gives you something to refer back to when times get tough, reminding you what "normal" looks like for your strategy.

Quiz time!

Let's test your understanding of the importance of backtesting in trading strategy development. A fellow trader tells you, "Backtesting isn't necessary if you have a good intuition for the markets." Based on what you've learned, how should you respond?

Answer: You should to challenge their assumption and ask for evidence. As we've learned, backtesting is a crucial step in developing a robust trading strategy. It provides concrete data on how your strategy would have performed historically, which is far more reliable than intuition alone. Always be prepared to question claims that dismiss the importance of data-driven approaches in trading.

Now that we understand why backtesting is so important, let's dive into the process. In our next lesson, we'll walk through a practical example of how to backtest a strategy. Get ready to take your trading to the next level!

Lesson 2: Setting Up Backtesting Spreadsheet

Creating backtesting spreadsheet:

Welcome to our lesson on setting up a backtesting spreadsheet! We'll use Google Sheets for this example, which you can access on your mobile device or computer. Let's dive in and create a simple yet effective tool for tracking your strategy's performance.

Our spreadsheet will include these key elements:

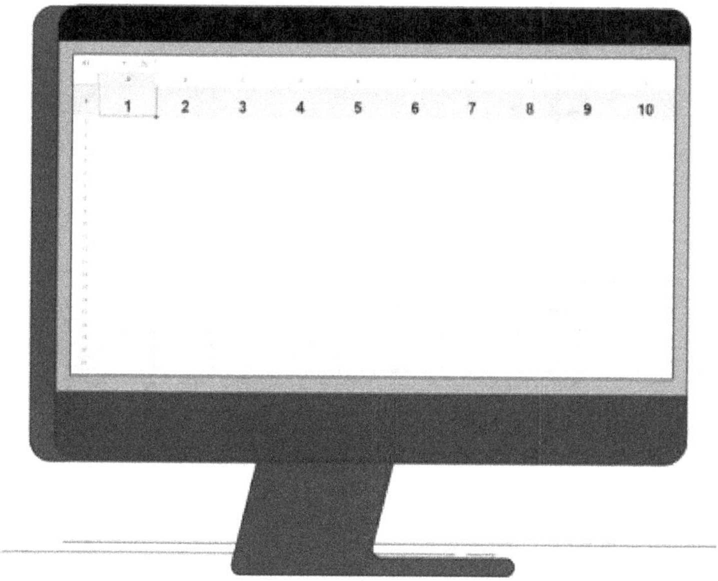

For the first column, "Entry Date and Time," record when you entered the trade. This allows you to easily reference past trades and spot patterns. On daily charts, the time will typically be consistent (e.g., 5 PM EST), while shorter time frames will have varying entry times.

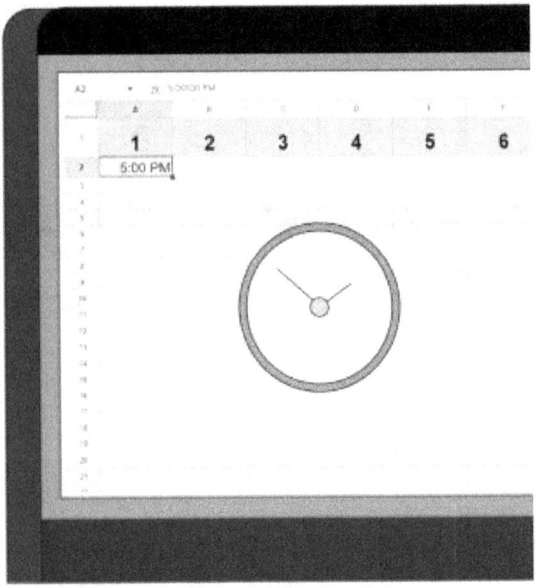

For the "Currency Pair" and "Time Frame" columns, record the market you're trading and the chart's time frame (e.g., daily, 4-hour, 1-hour). Tip: It's best to focus on mastering one currency pair before expanding to others.

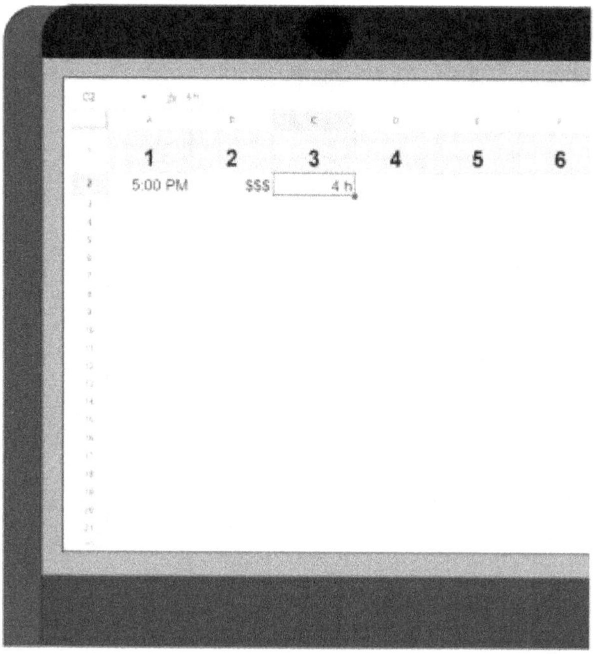

For the "Strategy Type" and "Entry Details," specify your strategy (e.g., trend, counter-trend, reversal, ranging) and entry type (e.g., lower low, lower close candle). This helps you track which strategies work best in different market conditions.

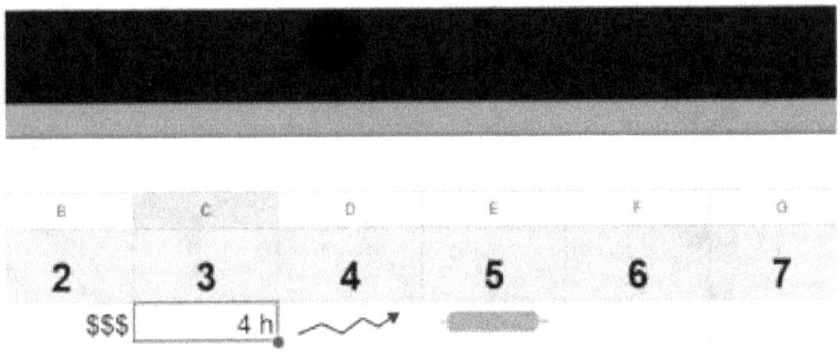

Let's explore "Setup Conditions." Create a scoring system to quantify trade strength: 1 point per price touch on support/resistance, 2 points for angled levels, and 1 point if it aligns with the market phase. For example, 3 touches (3 points), angular support (2 points), and market alignment (1 point) would score 6 points total. Higher scores often indicate better trade setups.

In the "Indicators" column, note any technical indicators you used, such as Fibonacci retracement levels (e.g., 38.2%, 61.8%), moving average crossovers, or RSI readings. For "Price Action," record specific patterns like Doji candles, hammer or Shooting Star formations, or engulfing patterns. This data can reveal which indicator levels or patterns are most reliable for your strategy.

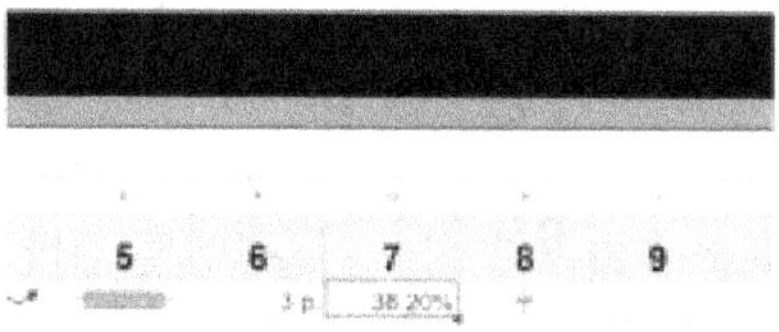

Record your entry price, stop-loss level, and profit targets. For example:

Entry: 2 pips below the lower low, Stop-loss: 2 pips above the highest high,

Target: At the lowest close.

You might also include additional target levels if you're testing multiple take-profit strategies.

Note when and how you exited the trade (stop-loss or target hit) and calculate your profit or loss. Include the exit date and time, exit price, and reason for exit (stop-loss hit, target reached, or manual close). This gives you a clear picture of your strategy's performance over time.

Quiz time!

In the Setup Conditions scoring system we discussed, how many points would you assign to a trade setup with 2 touches on a horizontal support level, aligned with the current market phase?

Answer: 3 points. Here's the breakdown: 2 points for the two touches on the support level (1 point each), and 1 point for aligning with the current market phase. The support is horizontal, so we don't add the 2 points for angular support. This gives us a total of 3 points for this setup. Remember, this scoring system helps us quantify the potential strength of a trade setup, allowing for more objective decision-making in our trading strategy.

Great job setting up your

spreadsheet! Remember, the power of backtesting lies in the patterns you'll discover. As you collect more data, you'll gain insights that can significantly improve your trading strategy. Look for correlations between your setup scores, indicator signals, and successful trades. Use this analysis to refine your strategy and improve your trading performance.

Lesson 3: Practical Application of Backtesting

Backtesting on practice:

Welcome to our practical lesson on backtesting! Now that we've set up our spreadsheet, it's time to put it to use. We'll walk through a real example of how to populate your backtesting data.

Let's start with a specific trade example. We'll use a daily chart of the AUD/USD pair. Remember, it's best to focus on one pair at a time when you're starting out.

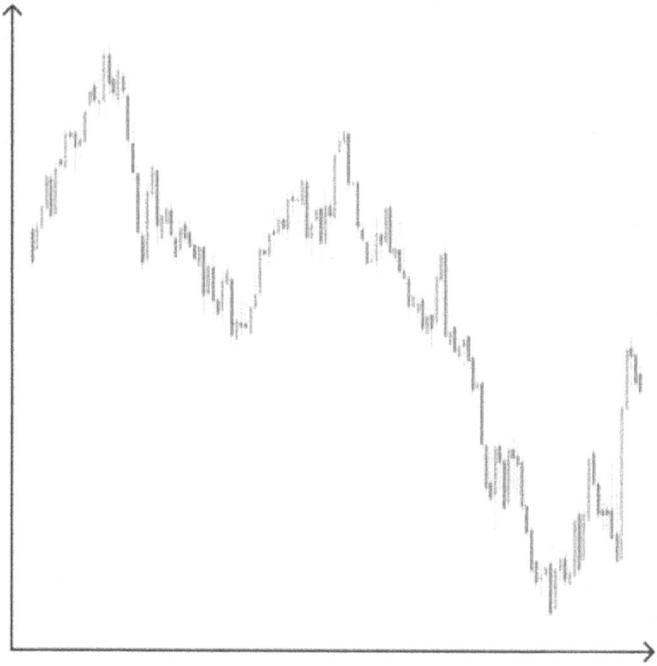

First, identify the market condition. In our example, we're in a bearish downtrend with a pullback phase. Note this in your "Strategy Type" and "Setup Conditions" columns.

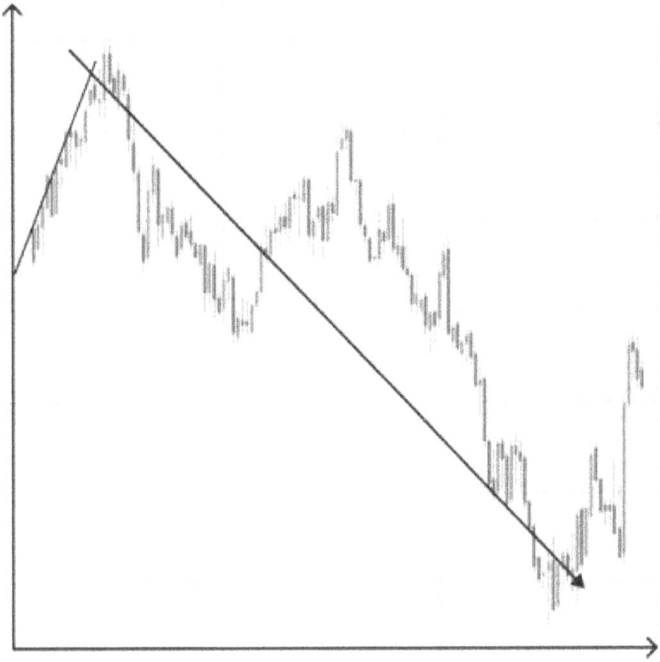

Now, let's score our setup. Count the touches on support/resistance levels. Use the horizontal line tool on your charting platform to mark these levels and count the touches. Let's say we have 5 touches in our example.

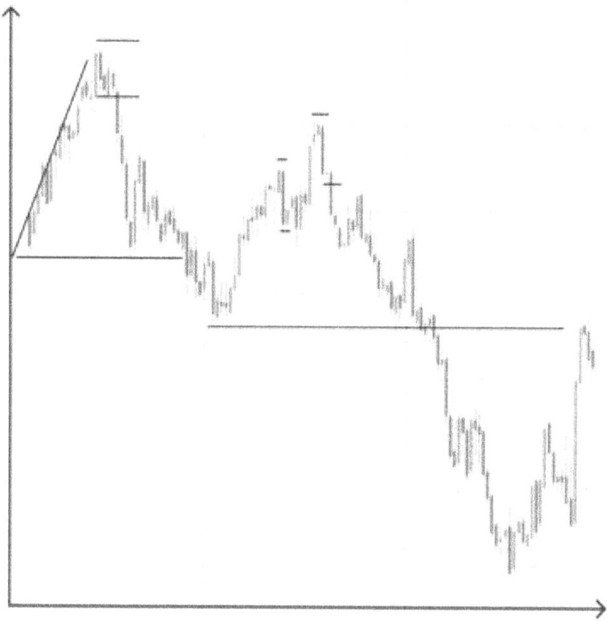

For indicators, we'll use Fibonacci retracement. Draw it from the recent low to the high. In our example, price has retraced to the 61.8% level. Note this in your "Indicators" column as "61.8% Fib retracement".

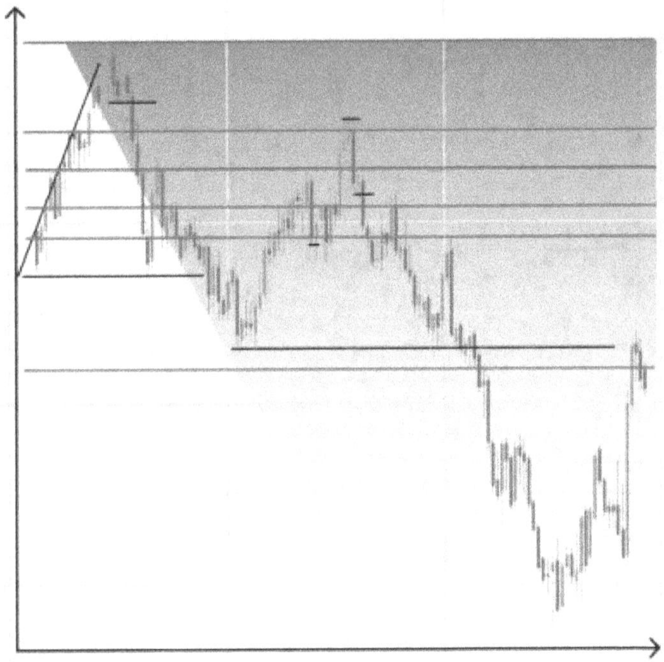

Our entry strategy is a lower low, lower close candle. We'll place our entry order 2 pips below the low of this candle. If the low is at 0.7011, our entry would be at 0.7009.

For the stop loss, we'll place it 2 pips above the highest high of the pullback. If the high is at 0.7135, our stop loss would be at 0.7137.

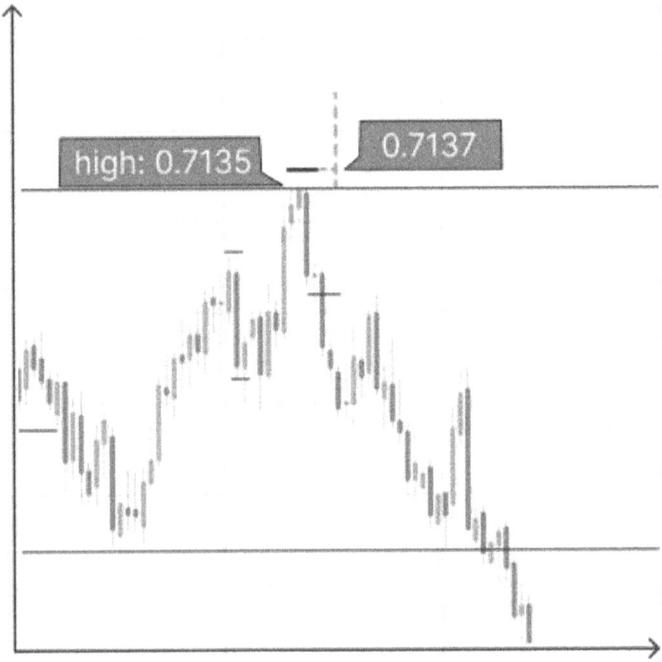

Our target will be at the lowest close of the previous downward move, plus 2 pips to account for potential front-running. If the lowest close was at 0.6735, our target would be at 0.6739.

Now, let's fill in our entry details. Date: August 16, 2022. Time: 22:00 (10 PM UK time for daily charts). Entry Price: 0.7009. Stop Loss: 0.7137. Target: 0.6739.

	08/16/2022
	10 PM
	0.7009
	0.7137
	0.6739

To complete our backtesting, we need to find when our target was hit. In this case, it was on September 6, 2022. Fill in your exit details: Exit Date: September 6, 2022. Exit Time: 22:00. Exit Price: 0.6739.

08/16/2022
10 PM
0.7009
0.7137
0.6739
09/06/2022
10PM
0.6739

Quiz time!

Let's recap what you've learned so far. How long was this trade active?

Answer: The trade was active for 3 weeks. We entered on August 16 and exited on September 6, which is about 21 days or 3 weeks. This is a good reminder that some trades can take several weeks to play out, especially on daily charts. It's important to have patience and trust in your strategy during these longer-term trades. Remember, in trading, we count all calendar days, not just trading days.

Well done on completing the backtesting exercise! You've learned to identify market conditions, score setups, use indicators, set entry and exit points, and record it all. Remember, good record-keeping is crucial for successful backtesting.

Look how far you've come! You now understand risk management, can develop strategies, use backtesting spreadsheets, and analyze your performance objectively. You're on your way to becoming a trading professional.

SECTION 7: BLUEPRINT FOR EFFECTIVE TRADING STRATEGIES

Master a battle-tested daily timeframe trading strategy that combines precision entry points with clear execution rules. This comprehensive section of the book transforms technical analysis concepts into actionable trading decisions, teaching you a specific strategy that's been proven profitable in real market conditions. Whether you trade forex, indices, or stocks, you'll learn how to identify high-probability setups using a systematic approach that requires just minutes per day to implement.

Received skills:

MARKET ANALYSIS

TRADE EXECUTION

RISK MANAGEMENT

What will you learn from this section:

- Phase Identification: Master the art of recognizing optimal market conditions for trade entry.

- Moving Averages: Leverage a powerful three-EMA system to predict market direction.

- Entry Precision: Develop expertise in identifying exact entry points using the 30% rule.

Chapter 1: Getting Started

Lesson 1: Section Overview

In this course we're taking everything you've learned and turning it into actionable trading results. I'll be showing you a proven strategy that's been consistently profitable in real market conditions.

You've already learned how to build strategies in our previous courses. But here's the thing - sometimes the best way to master something is to start with a proven framework. Think of it like learning to cook: before creating your own recipes, you master the classics first.

I'm going to share with you a specific daily time frame strategy that I personally use to generate consistent income. It's simple, effective, and most importantly - it works in real market conditions.

Let me walk you through what we'll cover in this section. We've organized everything into four focused parts to turn you into a confident strategy trader.

Part 1 is all about getting started right. Here we'll talk about market phase identification. I'll show you exactly how to spot the perfect conditions for our strategy!

In Part 2, you will learn how to get started right. Here we'll talk about market phase identification. I'll show you exactly how to spot the perfect conditions for our strategy!

Part 3 focuses on decision-making and execution. You'll learn when to pull the trigger and, more importantly, when to stay out. This is where the rubber meets the road - turning analysis into action.

Finally, Part 4 is all about practice and application. We'll look at real trades, real results, and how to adapt this strategy to your personal trading style. Because remember - no one ever became successful by just copying someone else's approach exactly.

One question before you go:

Before we continue, take a moment to consider this: Why do you think it's important to master proven trading strategies before creating your own?

Answer: By mastering proven strategies first, you learn the fundamental principles that make trading strategies successful. This knowledge becomes the foundation for understanding market behavior and eventually developing your own effective approaches.

Lesson 2: Market Phase Identification

Setting up for success:

Now that you understand what makes this course special, let's dive into the first crucial skill - identifying the right market conditions for our strategy. Think of it as checking the weather before planning a trip - you need to know what you're working with!

Remember how we talked about market cycles in previous courses? Well, now we're going to put that knowledge to practical use. Our strategy works best in specific market conditions, and I'll show you exactly how to spot them.

We'll be working with the daily timeframe - it's clean, it's clear, and it gives us the big picture view we need. Markets move in cycles between Phase 1 and Phase 2, and our strategy specifically targets one part of this cycle.

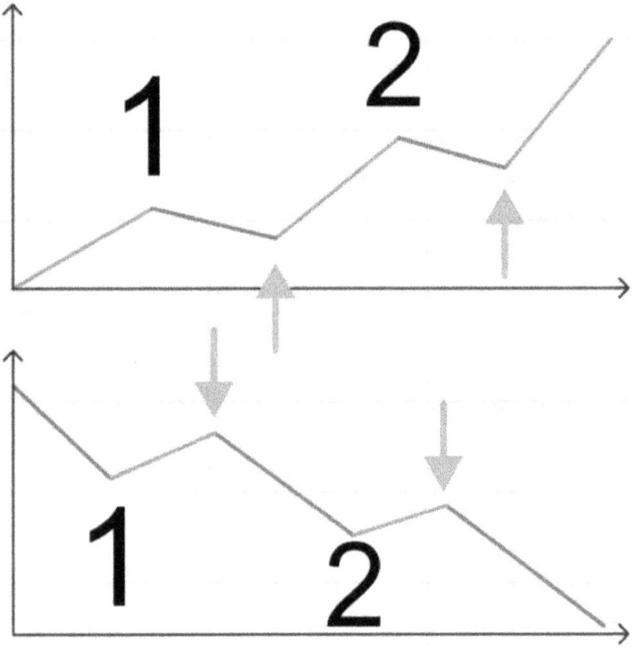

Here's what we're looking for: Phase 2 trends. In an uptrend, we get runs up followed by pullbacks. In a downtrend, we get runs down followed by pullbacks. These pullbacks are our bread and butter.

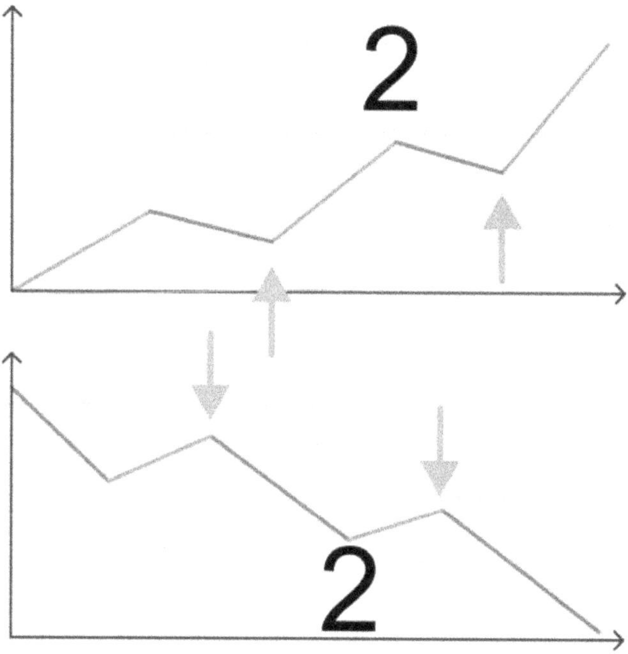

Think of it like an "if-then" scenario. IF we're in Phase 2, and IF we see a pullback, THEN we start looking for our setup. Simple as that.

What about Phase 1?

What do you think we should do when we identify Phase 1? When you identify Phase 1 market conditions, what should you do?

Answer: We stay out completely during Phase 1. Our strategy is specifically designed for Phase 2 pullbacks - trying to force it in Phase 1 is a recipe for poor results. Patience is key in trading; sometimes the best trade is no trade at all.

In bullish setups, we're watching for pullbacks down. In bearish setups, we're watching for pullbacks up. That's it - no complicated formulas, just clean, simple price action.

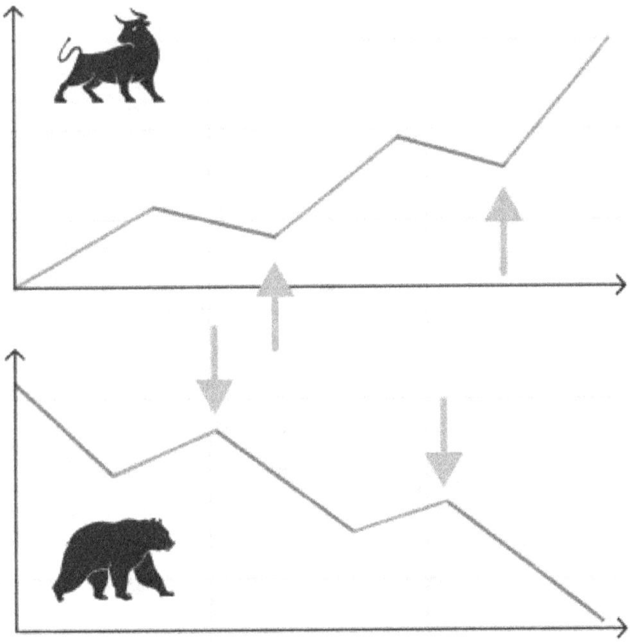

Another filter to consider is whether the price is interacting with previous support or resistance levels. Pay close attention to how these levels behave: when former support turns into resistance or previous resistance becomes support, it strengthens the probability of our setups being successful.

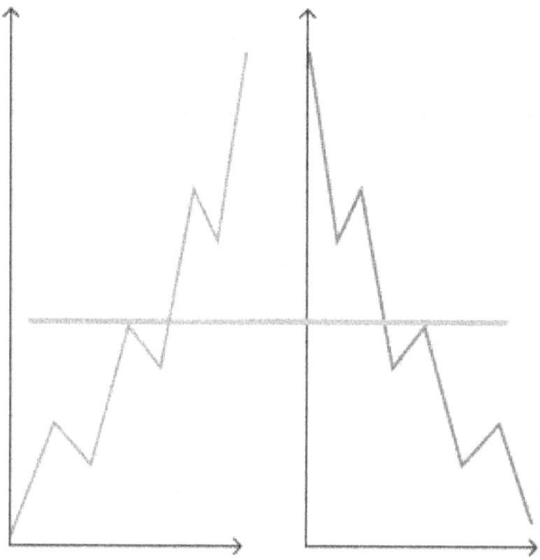

The beauty of this strategy is its versatility. While I'll show you how I trade it on my preferred markets, you can test it on any major market - forex, indices, stocks - it works across the board.

The first step in our strategy is to identify the market phase we're targeting. In this case, we're focusing on spotting a pullback within a bullish or bearish market to position ourselves for the next continuation and capture the following move.

Great job! That wasn't too hard, right? But this is just the beginning - the exciting part is yet to come! Before we move forward, keep in mind that the foundation of our strategy lies in identifying the market phase. We focus on spotting pullbacks within bullish or bearish markets to set ourselves up for the next continuation and capture upcoming moves. Let's build on this as we dive deeper into the strategy!

Chapter 2: Predicting Market Phase

Lesson 1: Moving Averages

The second step:

So the next thing we want to do is predict where the market is likely to go. Right now, a great tool that gives you a high-probability prediction that the market is likely to continue in the direction of the prevailing trend is moving averages.

What exactly are moving averages? A moving average is a tool that shows the average closing prices over a specific time period, smoothing out fluctuations to give a clearer picture of overall price trends.

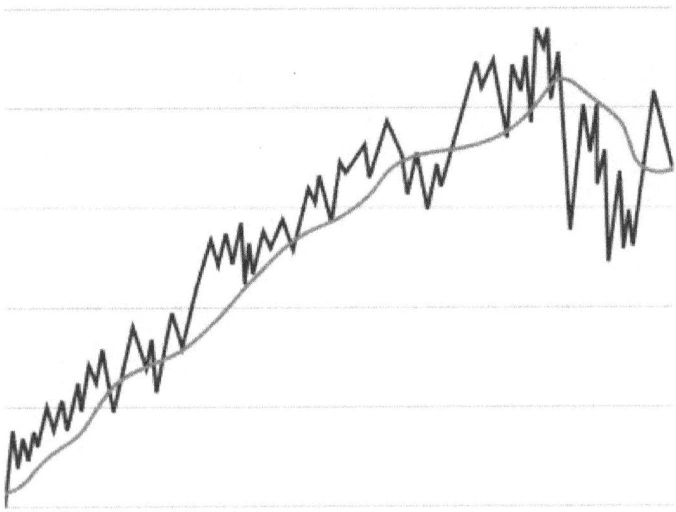

Imagine a price chart where each point represents a closing price. Now, if we average these prices over a certain period, we get a new point. A line of these averaged points forms the moving average.

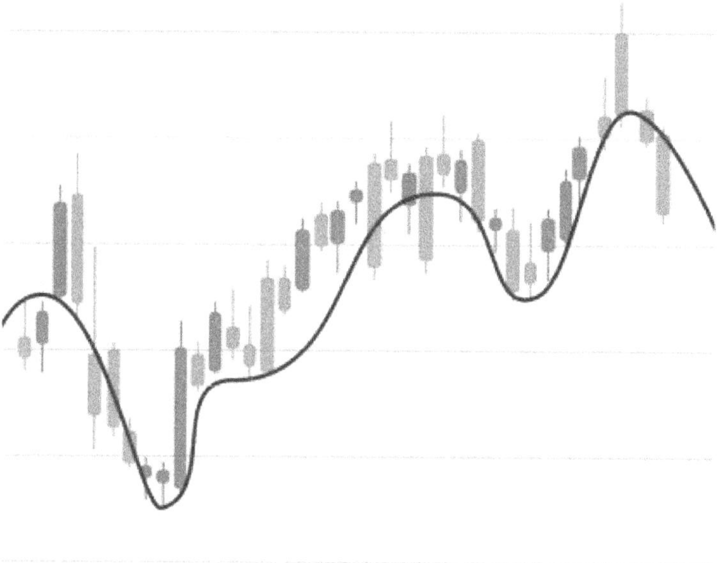

Understanding moving averages:

Moving averages are a fundamental tool in technical analysis, helping smooth out price data to identify trends. What does each point on a 20-day moving average represent?

Answer: Each point on a 20-day moving average represents the average closing price of the last 20 days. This is why the moving average line is smoother than the actual price chart.

Moving averages help traders monitor trends. If the price rises, the moving average will rise too, but more slowly and smoothly.

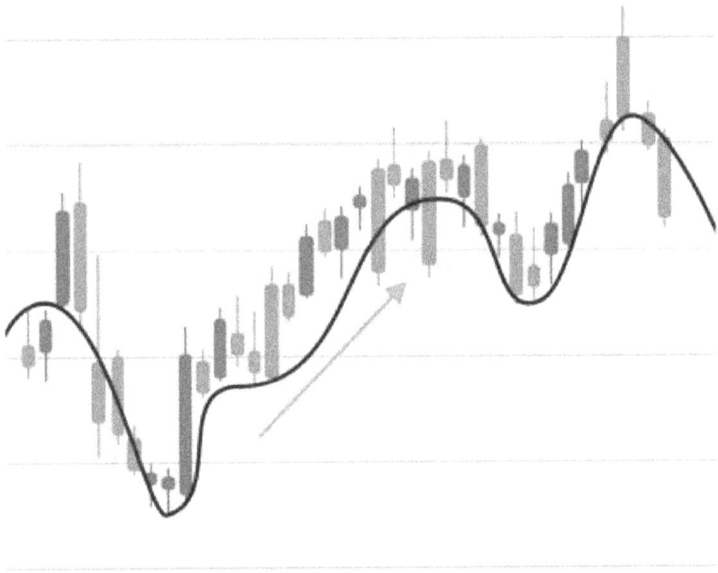

The most commonly used periods for moving averages (MAs) are 15, 20, 30, 50, and 200 days. Most traders prefer the 20- and 50-day MAs, while long-term investors often use the 180- or 200-day MAs.

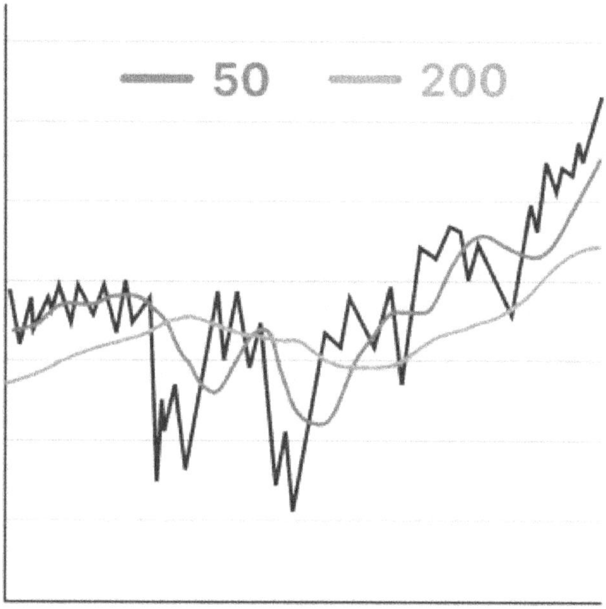

The moving average often acts as a support or resistance line. When the price crosses the MA, it can signal a potential trend change.

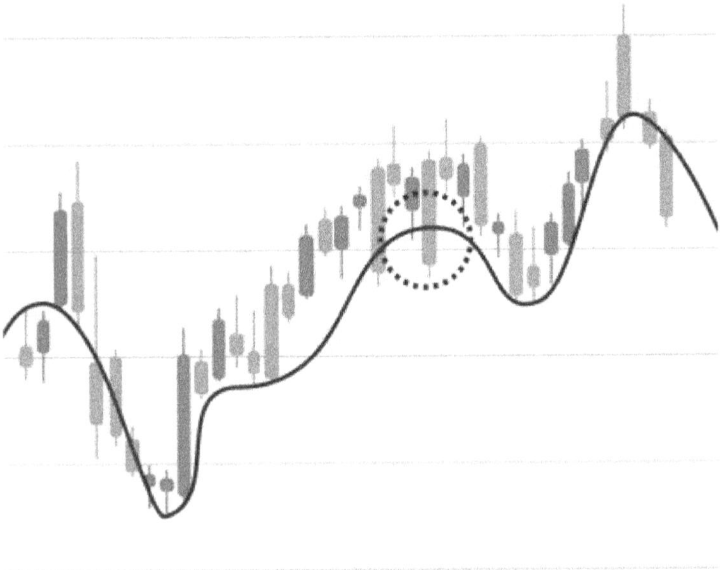

However, it's important to note that moving averages work best in trending markets. In sideways markets, they can generate false signals.

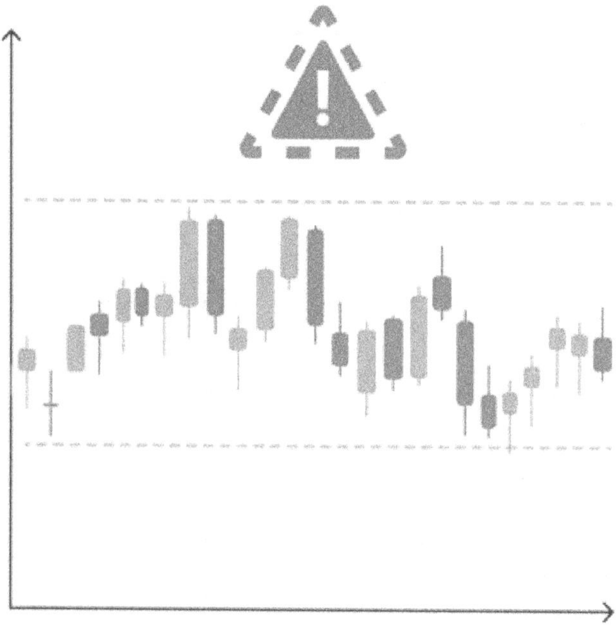

Quiz time!

Moving averages are used with different periods depending on the trading strategy. Which MA period is typically used in long-term investing?

Answer: The 200-day MA is often used in long-term investing. It provides a broad view of the trend, smoothing out short-term fluctuations that might not be significant for long-term investors. Long-term investors typically use longer periods to filter out short-term noise. Shorter periods like 5, 13, or 20 are more suitable for short-term trading.

Let's look at an example of how traders might use moving averages.

Using moving averages in trading decisions:

A trader believes the market is overheated and wants to profit from a fall. Is selling S&P 500 futures when it crosses below the 50-day moving average a good strategy?

Answer: Relying solely on moving average crossovers can lead to frequent false signals, especially in non-trending markets. If an investor sold futures at every moving average intersection, they would lose a lot of money. It's important to use moving averages in conjunction with other indicators and analysis.

There are different types of moving averages. Besides the simple moving average (SMA) that we just discussed, there's the exponential moving average (EMA). Each is calculated differently to emphasize various aspects of price data.

Exponential moving average gives more weight to recent prices, making it more responsive to new information. For now, there's no need to delve deeper into the specific formulas.

Here's a comparison of simple moving average and exponential moving average on the same chart. Notice how they respond differently to price changes.

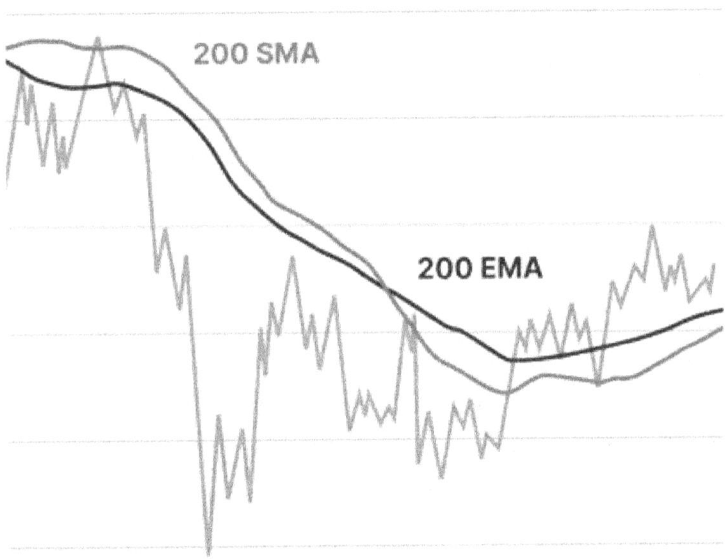

For our strategy, we'll be using exponential moving averages (EMAs). Why? Because exponential moving averages give more weight to recent prices, making them more responsive to current market conditions - exactly what we need for our trend-following strategy.

While all indicators lag behind price, exponential moving averages react faster to market changes than standard moving averages. This faster feedback is crucial when we're looking to catch trend continuations after pullbacks. Think of it like driving - you want to see what's happening now, not just what happened a mile back.

Now that you understand why we're using exponential moving averages, we're ready to take it to the next level. In our next lesson, we'll explore how to use three specific exponential moving averages in combination. When these three align, they create a powerful filter for high-probability trades. Get ready to add this tool to your trading arsenal!

Lesson 2: The Power of Three Exponential Moving Averages

The power of three:

Now that you understand moving averages, let's explore how we use three specific ones in our strategy. We're looking for a special "Fanning" effect that signals strong trending conditions.

As mentioned earlier, our strategy relies on three key exponential moving averages: the 8 EMA, 20 EMA, and 50 EMA. Picture them as three dancers moving in perfect harmony.

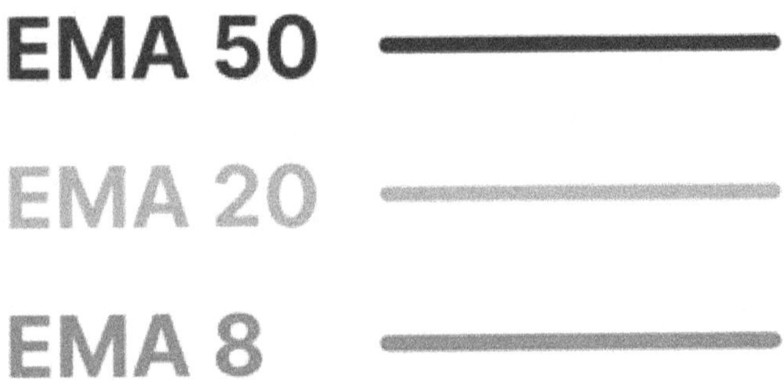

In a bullish trend, we want to see a specific order: the 8 EMA has to be above the 20 EMA, and the 20 EMA has to be above the 50 EMA. This creates a beautiful fanning effect.

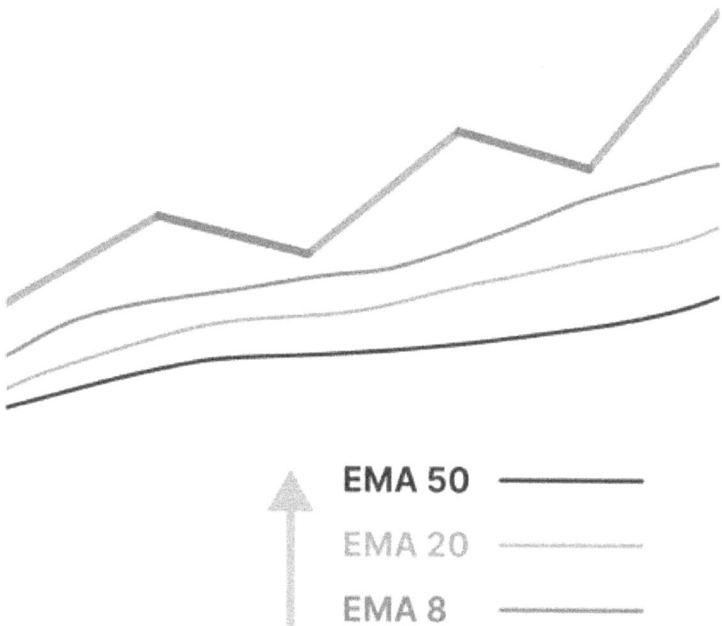

In a bearish trend, we're looking for the opposite arrangement: the 8 EMA needs to be below the 20 EMA, and the 20 EMA needs to be below the 50 EMA.

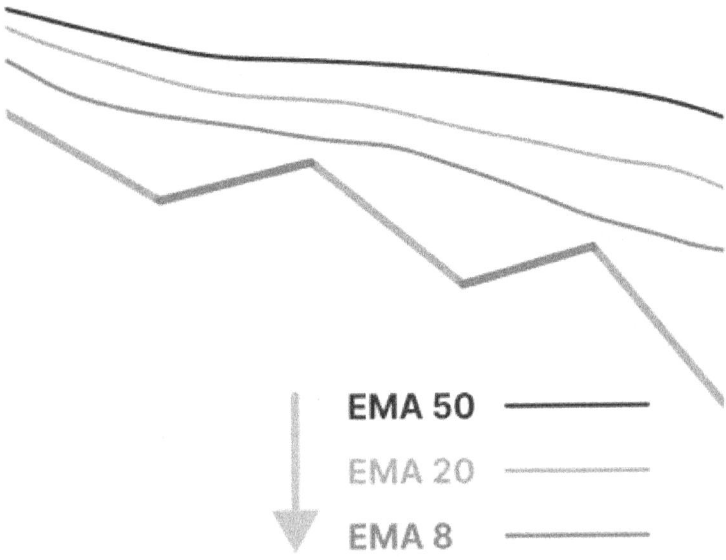

Here's the key point: regardless of trend direction, the 8 EMA should always be nearest to price, the 20 EMA second closest, and the 50 EMA furthest away.

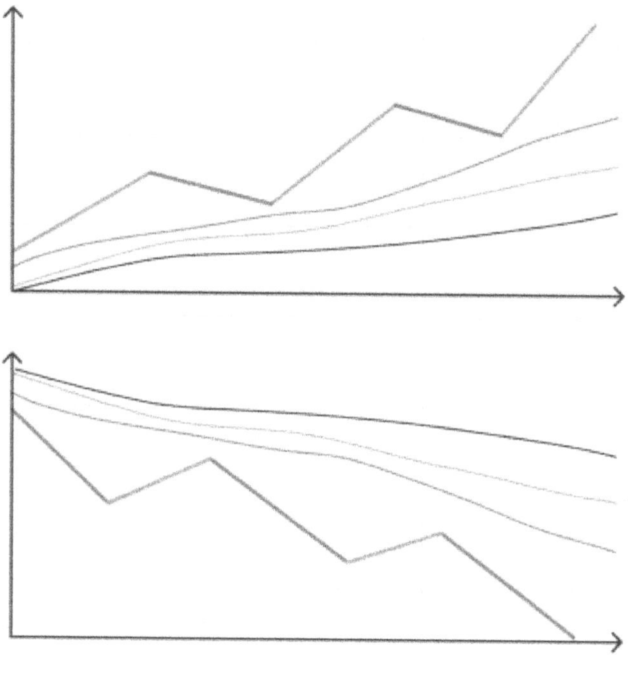

The more these exponential moving averages fan out from each other, the stronger our signal becomes. It's like a consensus - when all three

EMAs agree and spread out nicely, they're telling us the trend is strong.

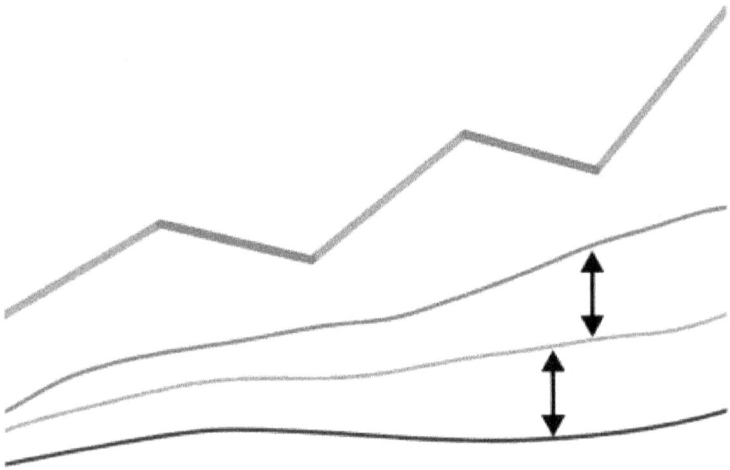

Now, let's talk about what we don't want to see. When these EMAs start crossing over each other during a pullback, that's our warning sign.

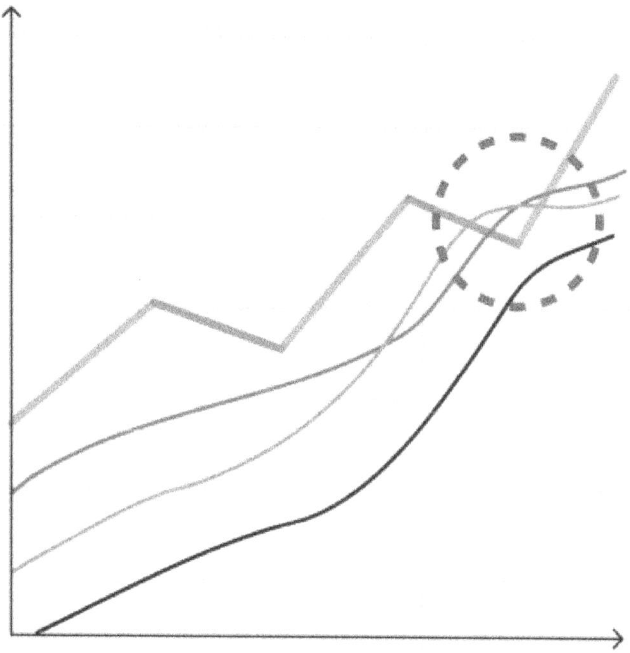

Why do we avoid crossovers? Because they signal one of two things: either a potential trend reversal or upcoming consolidation. Neither scenario is ideal for our strategy.

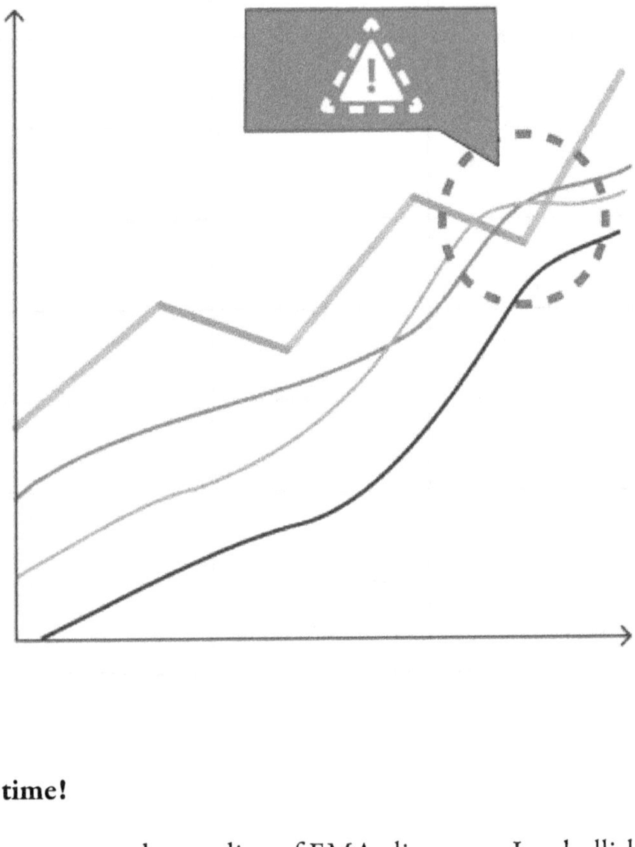

Quiz time!

Let's test your understanding of EMA alignment. In a bullish trend, which EMA should be closest to price?

Answer: Remember, the 8 EMA is our most responsive indicator, which is why it needs to be closest to price in any trend. The 8 EMA should always be closest to price because it responds most quickly to price changes. This helps us confirm trend strength and direction.

Think of these EMAs like three race cars. The 8 EMA is the fastest and stays closest to the action (price), the 20 EMA follows behind, and the 50 EMA takes the longest route.

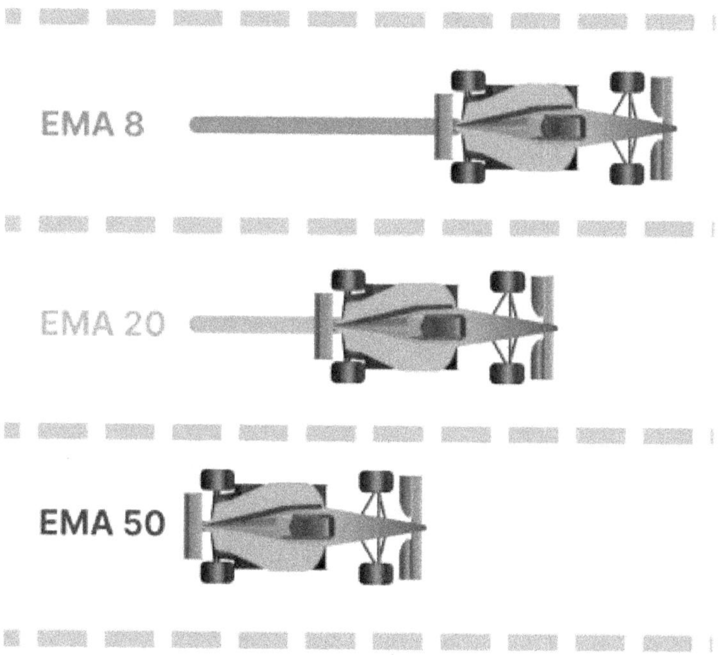

When our EMAs are properly aligned, they create a powerful filter that helps us avoid weak trends and false signals. This alignment must be present before we even consider looking for our entry patterns.

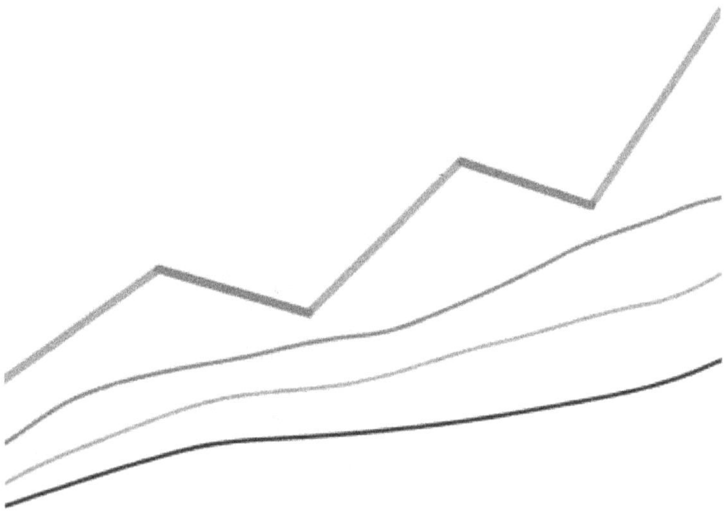

Great work! You now understand how to use three EMAs to confirm trend strength. In our next lesson, we'll learn how to make trading decisions based on this information.

Chapter 3: Decision Making and Execution

Lesson 1: Making Trading Decisions

Time to make decisions!

Now that we understand how to identify market phases and use exponential moving averages to predict market direction, let's focus on the crucial step - deciding when to enter a trade. This is where we turn our analysis into action!

The decision to enter a trade isn't random. It comes down to specific price action patterns that we'll identify together. These patterns are like fingerprints - unique signals that tell us when the probability is in our favor. But before we dive into the specific patterns, remember that we're looking for these signals during pullbacks. We never try to catch the absolute bottom or top -

instead, we want to enter when the trend is likely to continue.

Let's start with bearish setups. In a bearish market, we're watching for pullbacks to the upside. This is when price temporarily moves against the overall downward trend.

In these bearish setups, we're looking for a very specific type of candle. The magic happens when both the open and close of the candle occur in the lower 30% of the entire candle body.

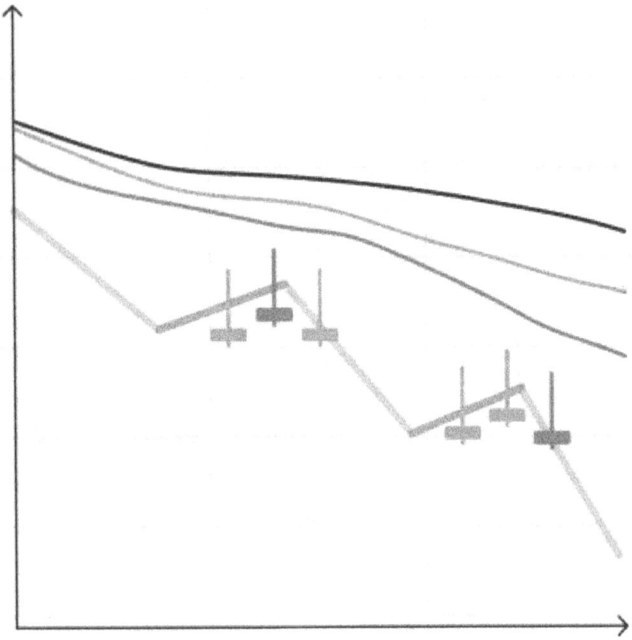

This lower 30% placement is crucial. It shows us that while buyers tried to push the price higher during the candle's formation, sellers ultimately won the battle, forcing the close into that lower portion.

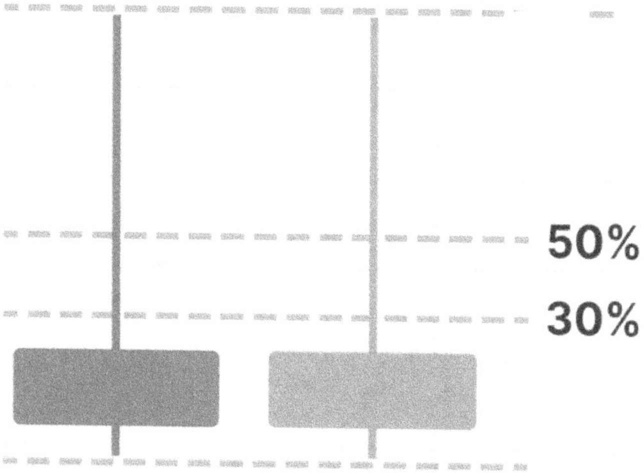

For bullish setups, we're looking at the mirror image. When the market is in an uptrend, we watch for pullbacks to the downside. These are temporary moves against the upward trend.

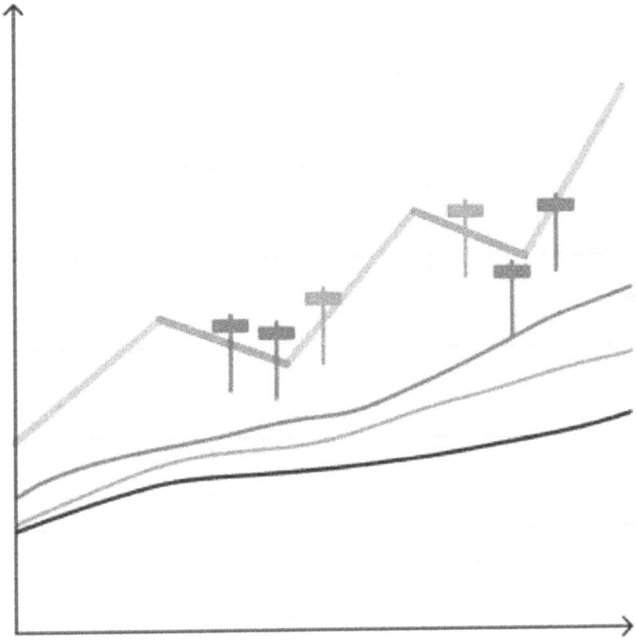

In bullish setups, we want to see the open and close in the upper 30% of the entire candle body. This tells us that although sellers tried to push the price down, buyers maintained control.

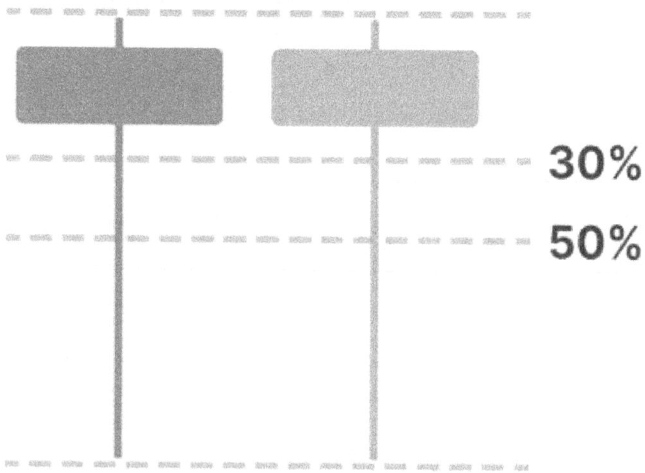

The upper 30% placement in bullish setups is like a battle scar - it shows us where sellers tried and failed to take control of the market. This failure becomes our opportunity.

To help you identify the 30% threshold consistently, you can use Fibonacci tools. When setting up your Fibonacci tool, you can add a 30% level. Some traders prefer 33.3% - one third of the candle. I personally like to see the open and close below the 30% mark in bearish setups.

In bullish setups, the same principle applies - but remember, we're looking for the open and close above the 70% mark when measuring from the bottom.

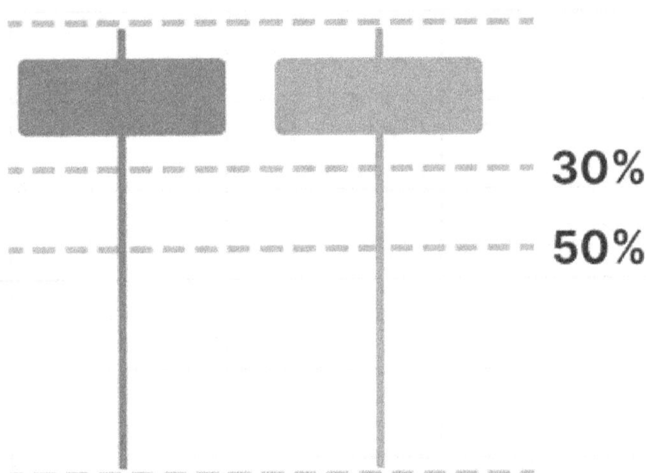

Now, let's talk about where these candles should appear. In a bearish setup, our signal candle must either touch or be above the 8 exponential moving average.

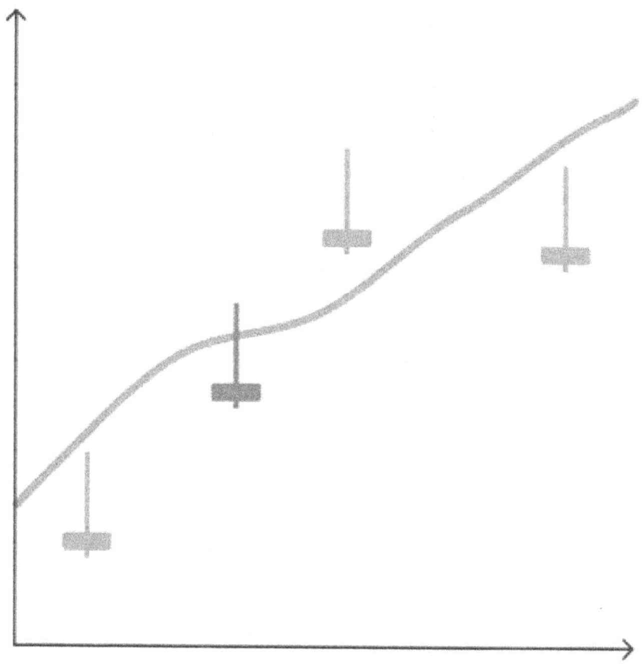

For bullish setups, it's the opposite. Our signal candle needs to either touch or be below the 8 exponential moving average.

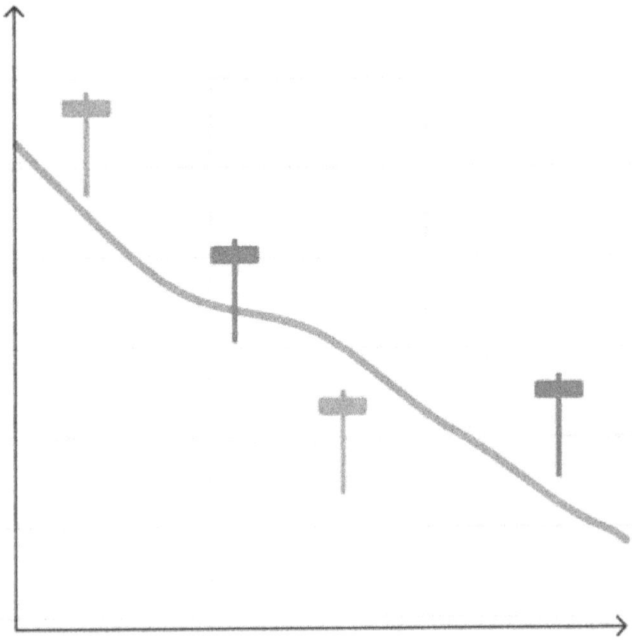

The relationship with the 8 exponential moving average is critical. Think of it as a magnet - price tends to interact with it during pullbacks before continuing in the trend direction.

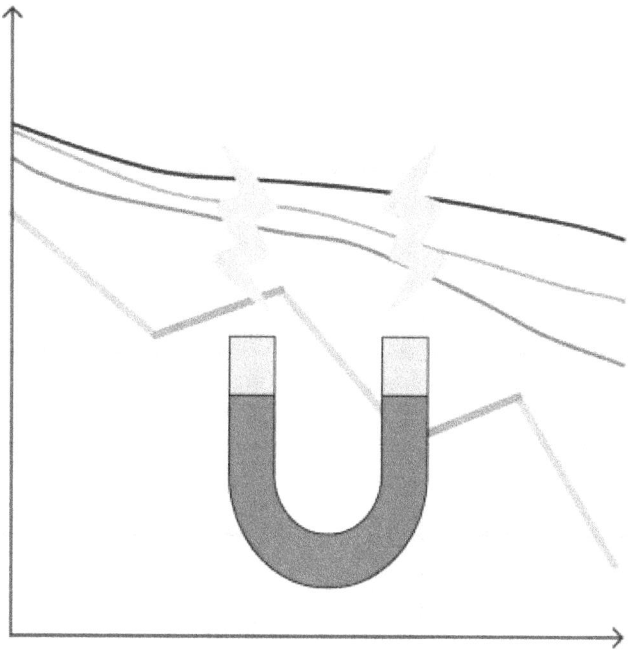

Quiz time!

Let's test your understanding of entry signals. In a bearish setup, where should the open and close of your entry candle be?

Answer: Remember, in a bearish setup, we want to see evidence that buyers failed to maintain control. When the open and close are in the lower 30% of the candle body in a bearish setup, it shows that sellers dominated the price action, pushing prices.

Sometimes you'll see a perfect looking candle, but if it's not touching or on the correct side of the 8 exponential moving average, we must pass on the trade. Patience is crucial.

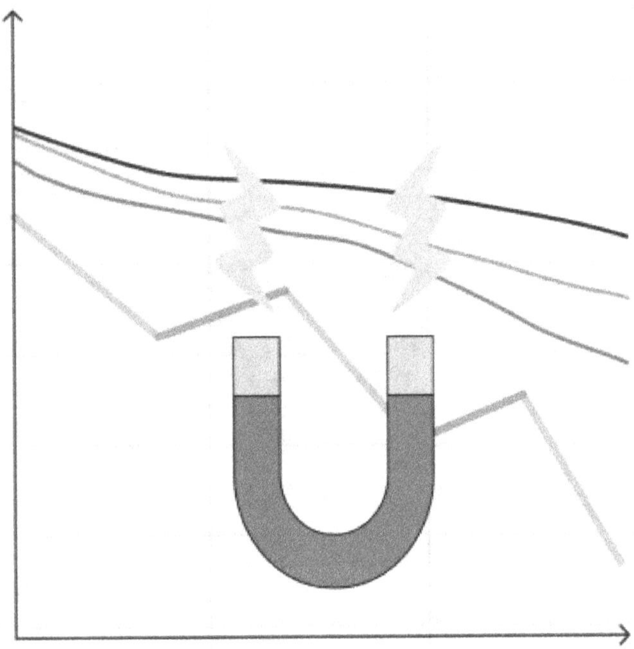

Here's what an invalid candle looks like in a bearish setup. Even though the open and close are in the lower portion, it never touched the 8 EMA, making it invalid for our strategy.

Valid vs Invalid bullish setups:

Let's test your understanding with bullish setups. Look at the four candlesticks marked on this chart and identify which one represents an invalid bullish entry signal. Which candlestick provides an invalid bullish setup signal?

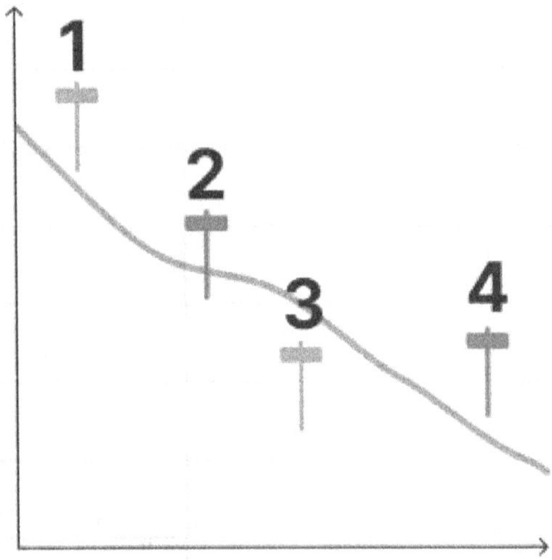

Answer: The correct answer is Candlestick 4. In a bullish setup, a valid entry requires the candlestick to touch or be below the 8 EMA. Candlestick 4 does not meet this requirement, making it an invalid entry signal. Candlestick 4 is indeed the invalid setup, as it does not touch or fall below the 8 EMA, which is essential for a valid bullish signal.

Trading is about probabilities, not certainties. Every setup that meets our criteria won't work, but by following these rules consistently, we put the odds in our favor.

Great work! You now understand exactly how to decide when to enter a trade. Remember, this strategy works because it puts probability on our side. We're not trying to predict the future - we're identifying situations where the odds favor a particular outcome.

Lesson 2: Trade Execution

Executing your trade:

Now that we've identified the trend, spotted the pullback, confirmed our prediction with exponential moving averages, and found our price action pattern, it's time for the exciting part - executing the trade!

Let me show you some real examples. Looking at this chart, you can see multiple setup candles. Each one represents a potential trading opportunity that meets our criteria.

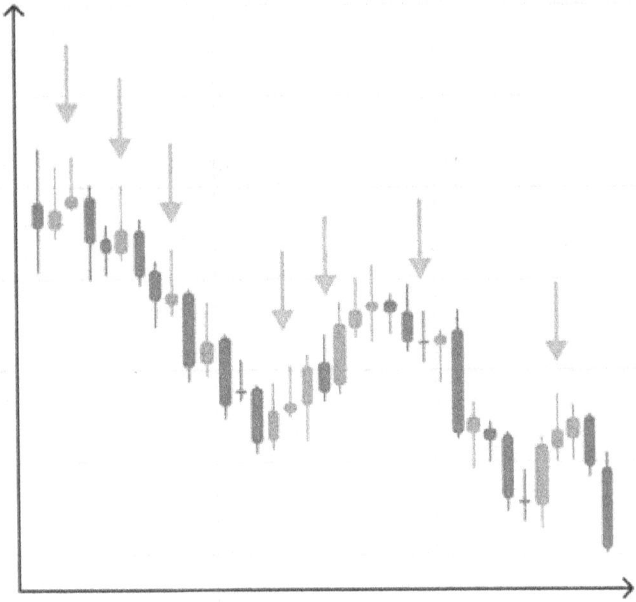

You might notice some candles that look like setups but weren't valid trades. Either they didn't close in the required 30% zone, or we didn't get triggered into the trade on the next candle.

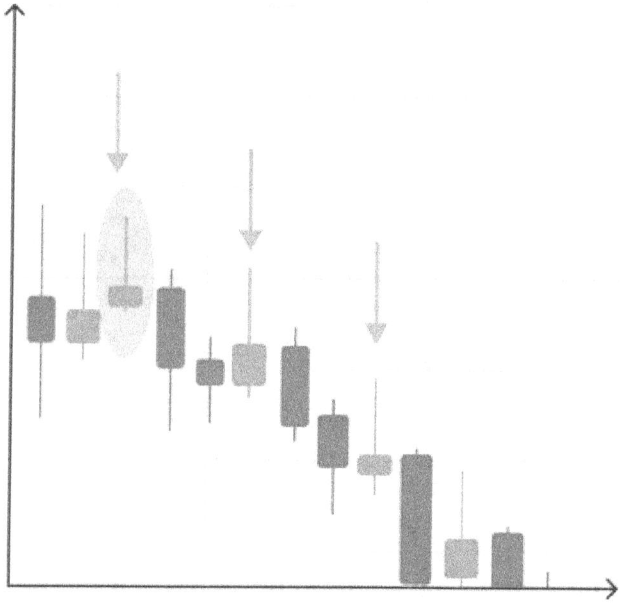

Let's focus on timing. A crucial rule: we must wait for our signal candle to close before taking any action. Why? Because a candle that looks perfect midday might not close in the lower 30 percent.

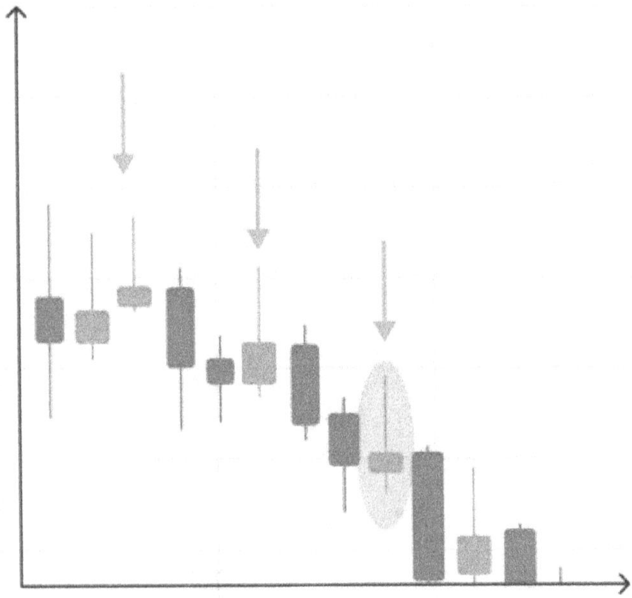

If you're trading on the daily timeframe, the day's candle (or bar) closes at 5:00 PM Eastern Time (ET) in New York and at 10:00 PM GMT

(Greenwich Mean Time) in London. This means a new daily candle starts right after these times in each time zone.

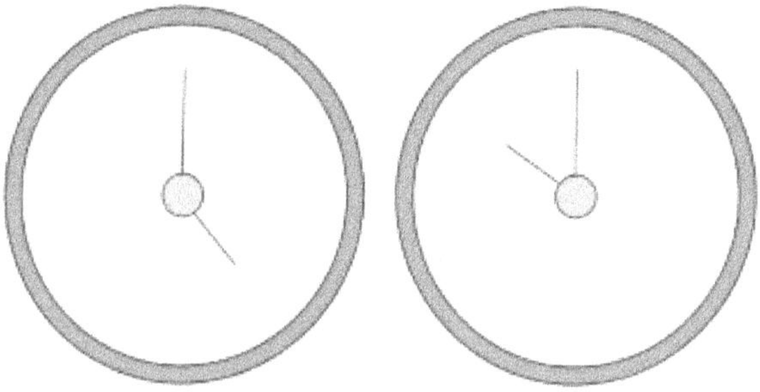

If you're in a different time zone, simply Google "what is 5 PM Eastern Standard Time in my country?" This will give you your local candle closing time.

Now, let's talk about order types. For bearish setups, we use a sell stop order. This is an instruction to your broker to enter a short position when price moves below a specific level.

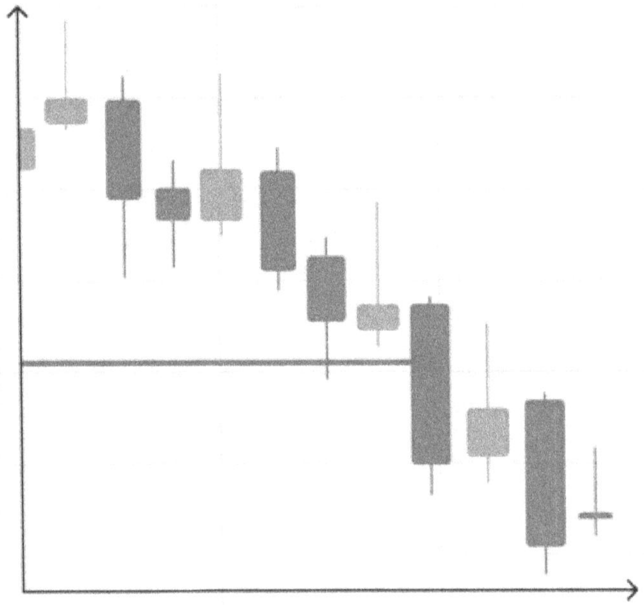

Place your sell stop order exactly two pips below the low of your signal candle. Not the close - the low. This is crucial for proper execution.

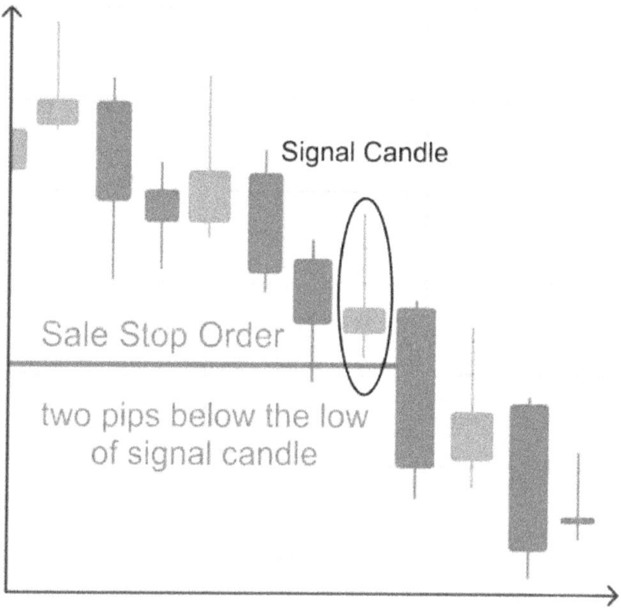

Once you're triggered into the trade, you need to protect yourself with a stop loss. We use a buy stop order for this in our bearish setups.

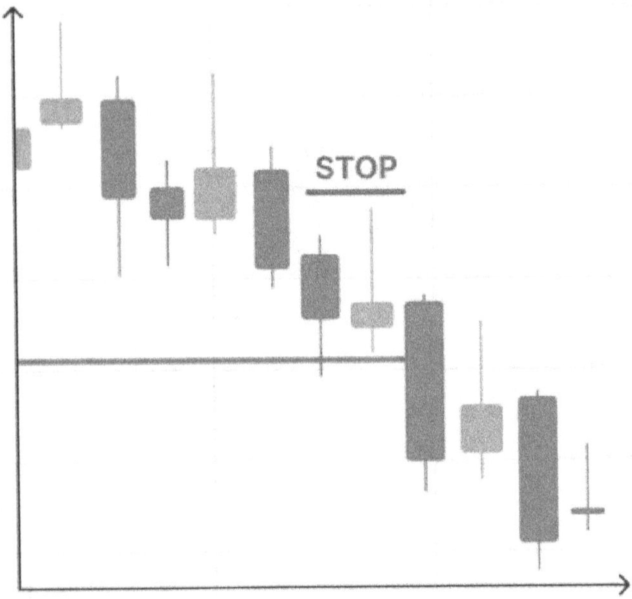

Your protective buy stop order goes exactly two pips above the high of your signal candle. This creates a clear invalidation point for your trade.

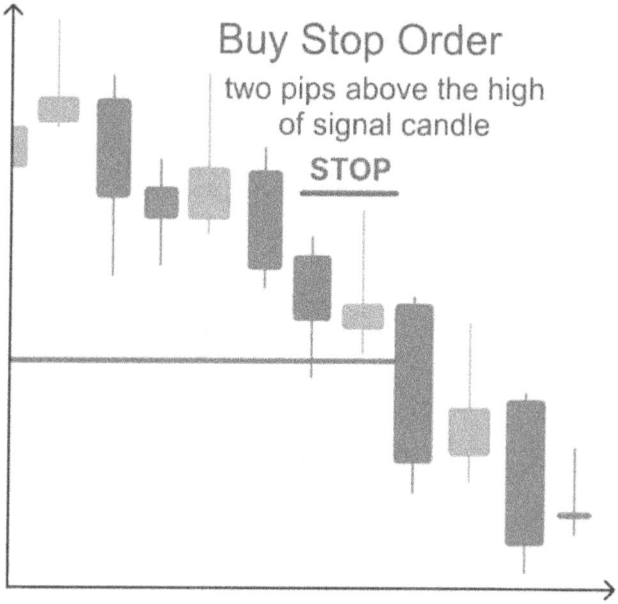

Now for the profit target. While you can experiment with larger targets later, let's start with a simple one-to-one risk-to-reward ratio.

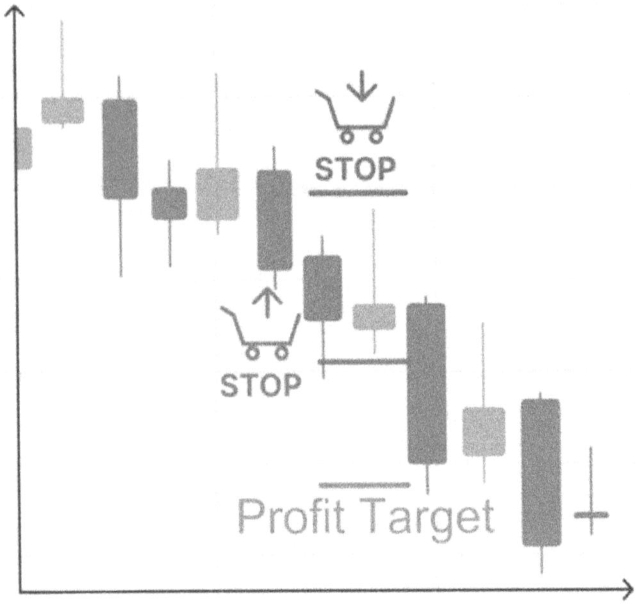

For taking profits in a short trade, we use a buy limit order. This tells your broker to close your position by buying back at a specific price.

To calculate your target, measure the distance in pips between your entry and stop loss. Then project that same distance down from your entry for your target.

Why start with one-to-one? Because even with this conservative target, this strategy can be very profitable due to its high strike rate, especially when using the 30% rule and exponential moving averages.

Remember, these are daily timeframe trades. While we're using a one-to-one ratio, these trades might take several days to complete. One advantage of the daily timeframe is fewer rollover costs compared to longer-term trades. You're typically in and out within a few days.

Let's review our three orders for a bearish setup:

1) Sell Stop for entry: 2 pips below signal candle low (only after the candle has closed at 5PM EST/10 PM GMT)

2) Buy Stop for protection: 2 pips above signal candle high

3) Buy Limit for target: Equal distance from entry as your stop

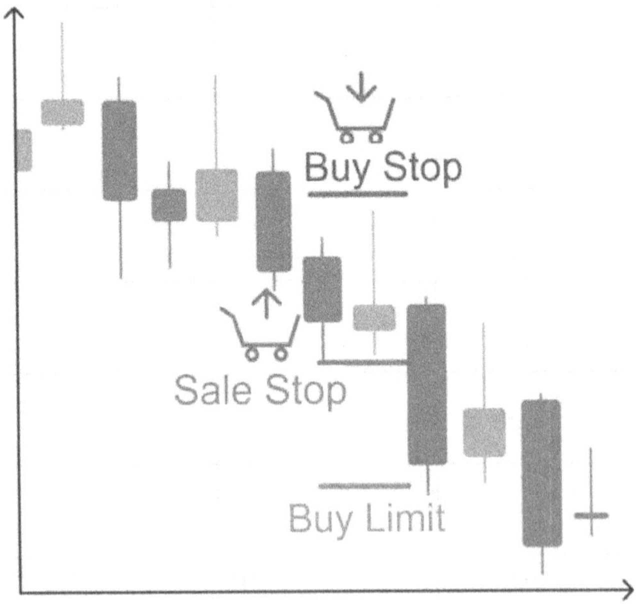

Order execution:

Now that we've covered all the order types and their placement, let's make sure you understand the crucial timing aspect of trade execution. When you spot a potential setup forming during the trading day, you might be tempted to place orders immediately. When should you place your entry order?

Answer: Patience is crucial in trading. We must wait for the signal candle to close to confirm it meets our criteria, especially the 30% rule, before placing any orders.

For bullish setups, we use the mirror image of these orders: Buy stop for entry, sell stop for protection, and sell limit for target.

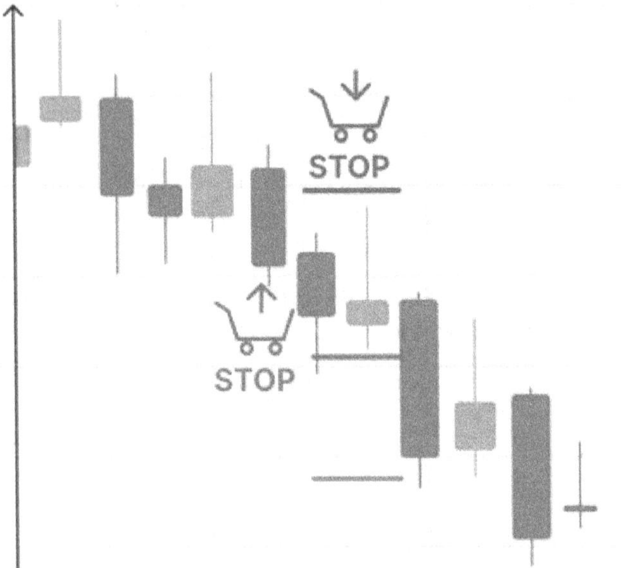

Let's review our three orders for a bullish setup:

1) Buy Stop for entry: 2 pips above signal candle high (only after the candle has closed at 5PM EST/10 PM GMT)

2) Sell Stop for protection: 2 pips below signal candle low

3) Sell Limit for target: Equal distance from entry as your stop

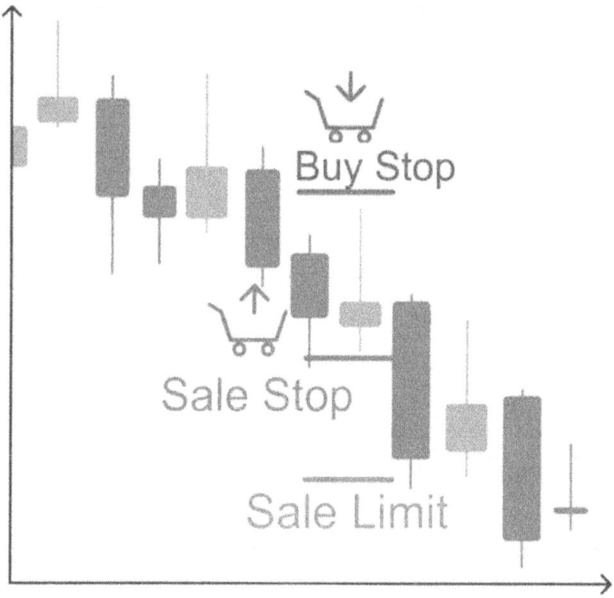

Great work! You now understand exactly how to execute your trades. Next, we'll look at position sizing and risk management to protect your capital. Remember, you can modify these targets as you gain experience, but start with these conservative settings to build your confidence in the strategy.

Chapter 4: Putting It All Together

Lesson 1: The Complete Strategy

Putting it all together:

Congratulations on making it this far! Let's review everything we've learned and see how all the pieces fit together. This is your complete trading blueprint.

Remember, successful trading isn't about catching every move. We're not trying to buy the exact bottom or sell the exact top. Instead, we're looking for high-probability setups in established trends.

For bearish setups, we're looking to enter somewhere in the middle of the move - either as price is moving down or during the pullback up. The same applies to bullish setups in reverse.

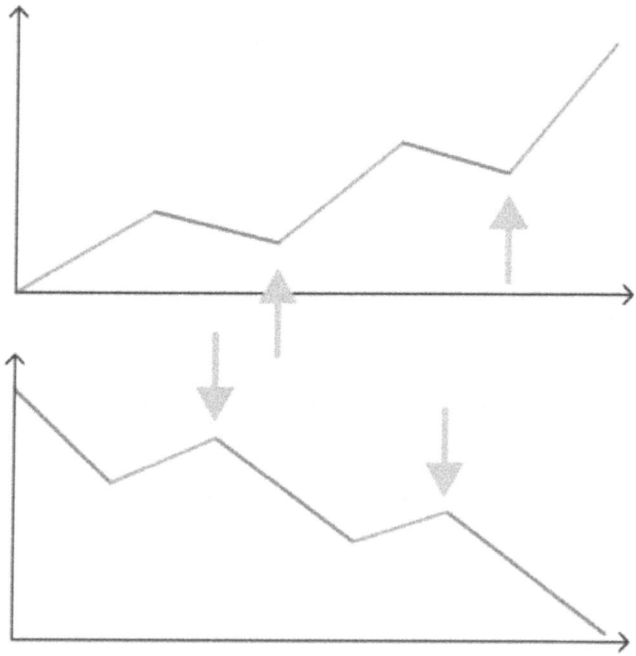

Let's start with a complete checklist for bearish trades. First, you must identify a bearish market - this is your Phase 2 downtrend.

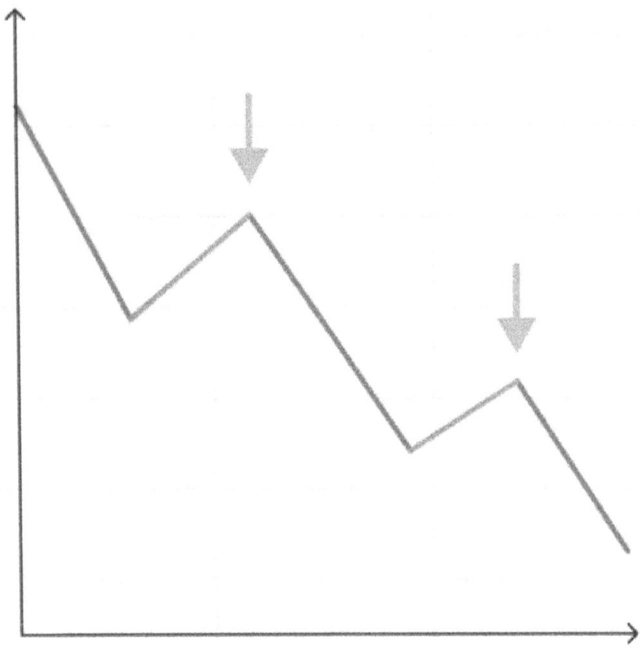

Your exponential moving averages must be perfectly aligned: The 8 EMA closest to price, below the 20 EMA, which must be below the 50 EMA. This "fanning" effect confirms trend strength.

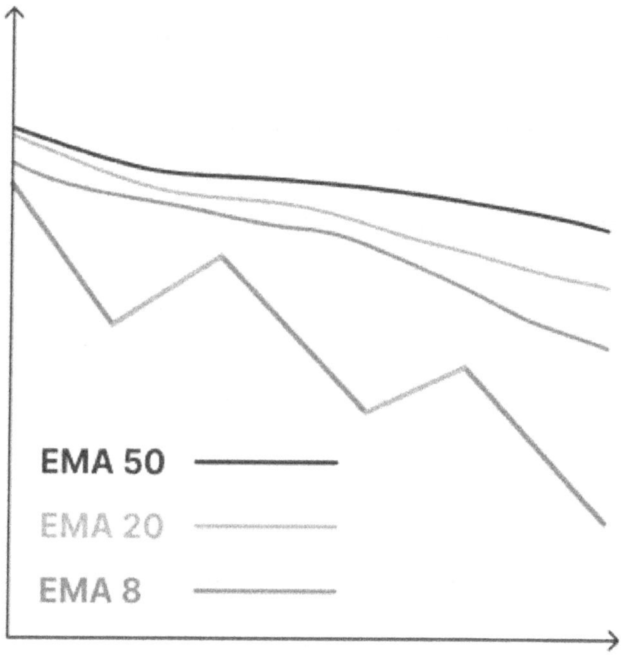

Look for your signal candle - remember, the open and close must be in the lower 30% of the candle body. This candle must either touch or be above the 8 EMA.

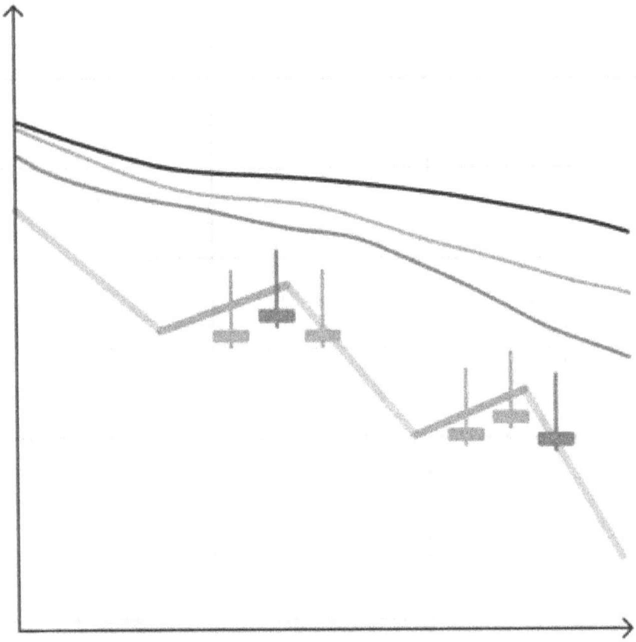

Once you have your signal candle, place your sell stop order 2 pips below the candle's low - but only after the candle has closed at 5 PM EST/10 PM GMT.

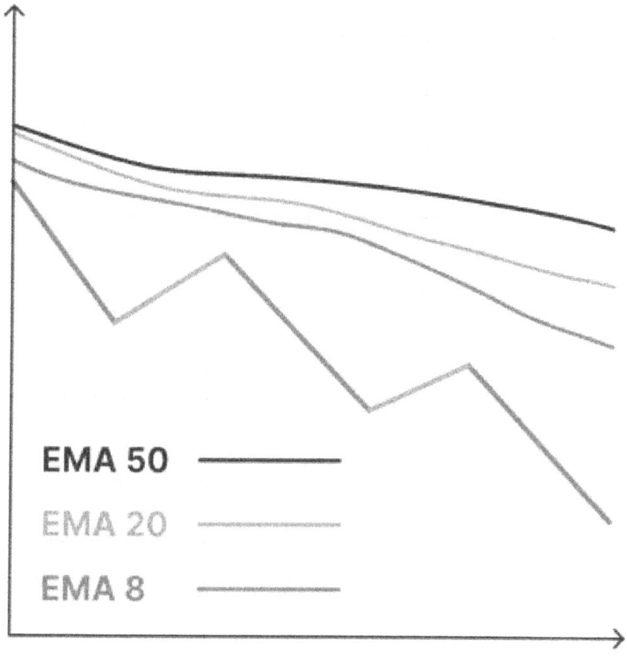

Your protective buy stop (stop loss) goes 2 pips above the signal candle's high. Your buy limit (target) is placed at an equal distance - creating a 1:1 risk-to-reward ratio.

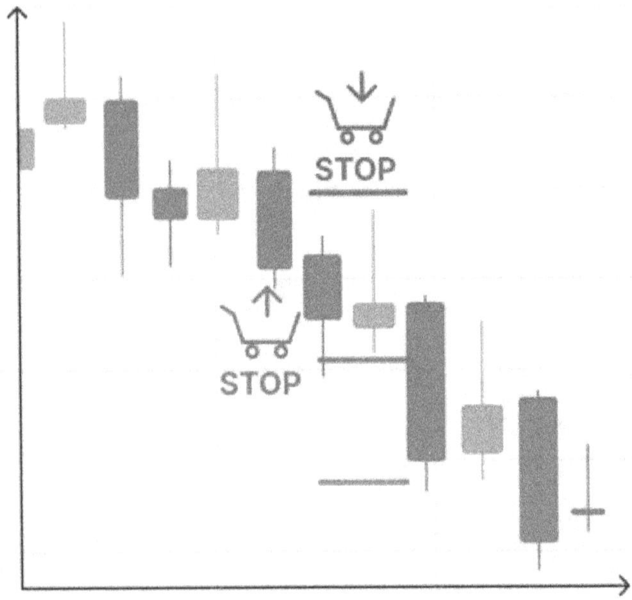

For bullish trades, we're looking for the mirror image. First, identify a bullish market in Phase 2.

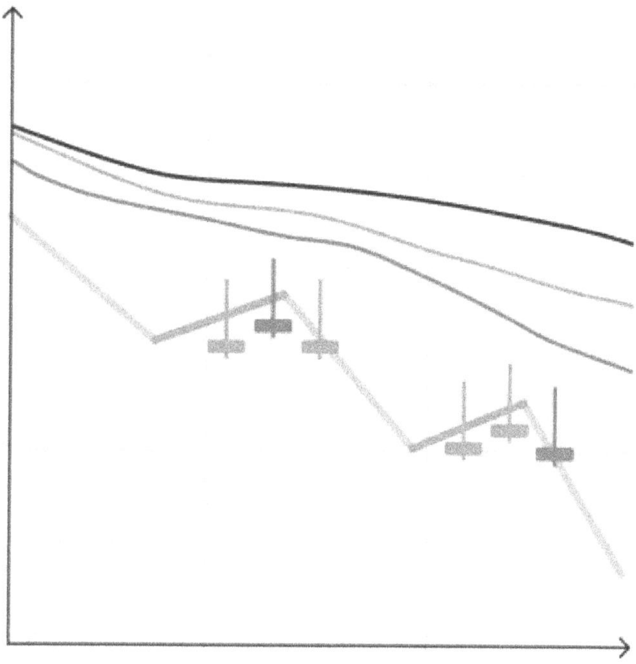

Your EMAs must fan upward: 8 EMA nearest to price, above the 20 EMA, which must be above the 50 EMA. This confirms upward trend strength.

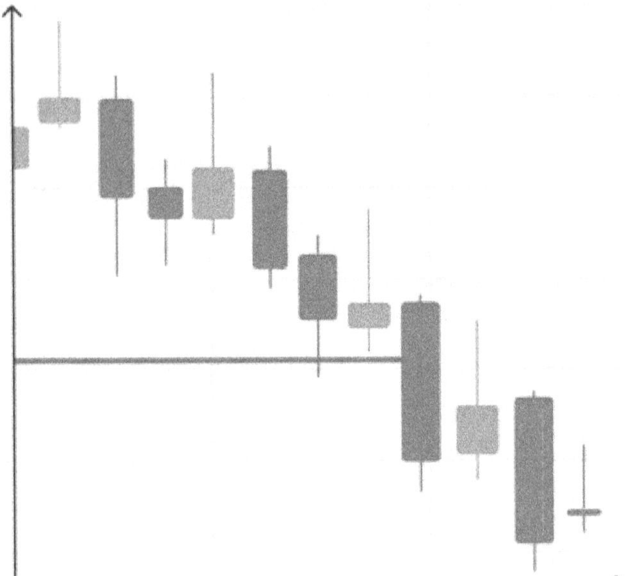

Your signal candle must have its open and close in the upper 30% of the candle body. The candle must either touch or be below the 8 EMA.

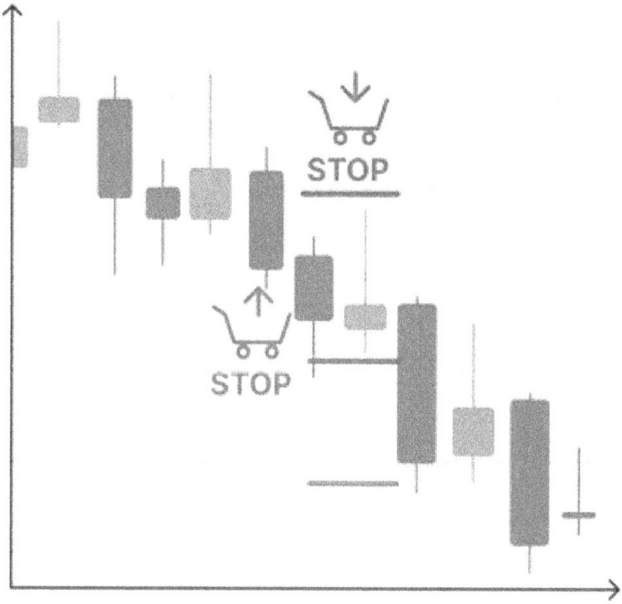

Place your buy stop entry 2 pips above the signal candle's high - again, only after the candle's close at 5 PM EST/10 PM GMT.

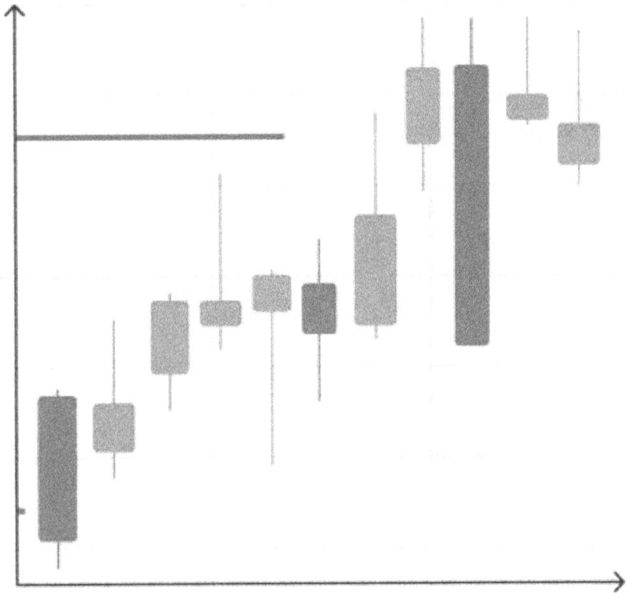

Your protective sell stop goes 2 pips below the signal candle's low. Your sell limit target maintains that same 1:1 risk-to-reward ratio.

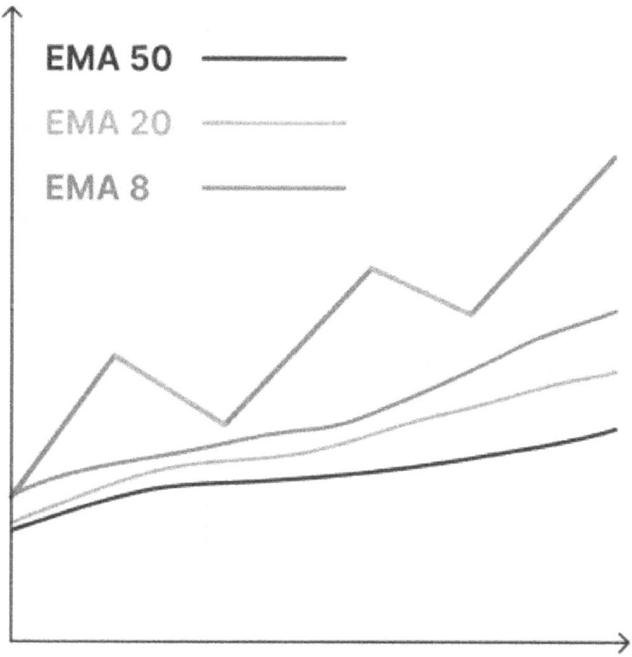

These trades can take several days to complete on the daily timeframe. That's perfectly normal - good trading is about patience and precision.

Quiz time!

Let's test your understanding of the complete strategy. What three conditions must be met for a valid bearish setup?

Answer: Remember, we need specific conditions for a high-probability setup. Random patterns or incorrect EMA alignments won't give us the edge we're looking for. We need a bearish market, properly fanned EMAs (8/20/50), and our signal candle must close in the lower 30% while touching or being above the 8 EMA.

Awesome work! See? It doesn't feel so complicated after going over it all again, right? With practice, you'll be nailing this strategy like it's second nature!

In our next lesson, we'll put this knowledge into practice with real chart examples. Get ready to spot these setups in real market conditions!

Lesson 2: Strategy in Action

Let's see it in action!

Now it's time to look at some real examples! I'll show you exactly how this strategy plays out in actual market conditions using recent chart data from the past 12 months.

Here's a daily chart of the GBP/USD. Notice how the moving averages are fanning out nicely - the 8 EMA below the 20 EMA, and the 20 EMA below the 50 EMA, all in perfect order.

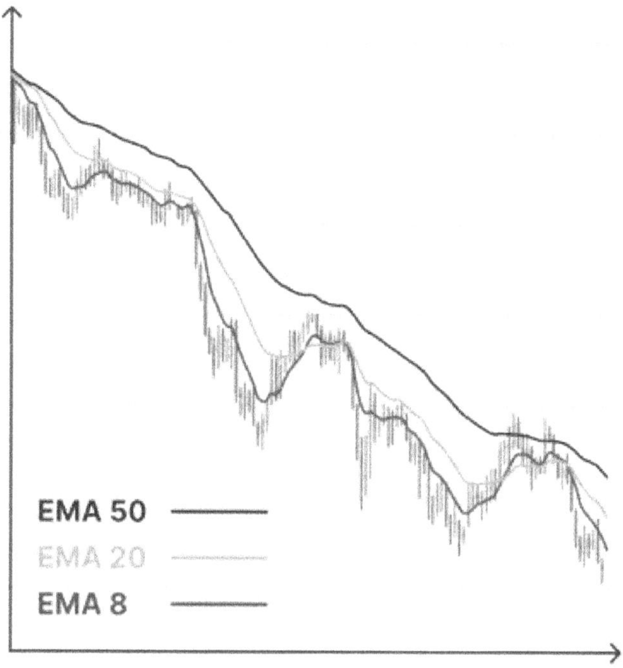

See these areas where the EMAs crossed over? These are zones where we wouldn't look for setups. Remember, we need clean fanning of our EMAs to confirm trend strength.

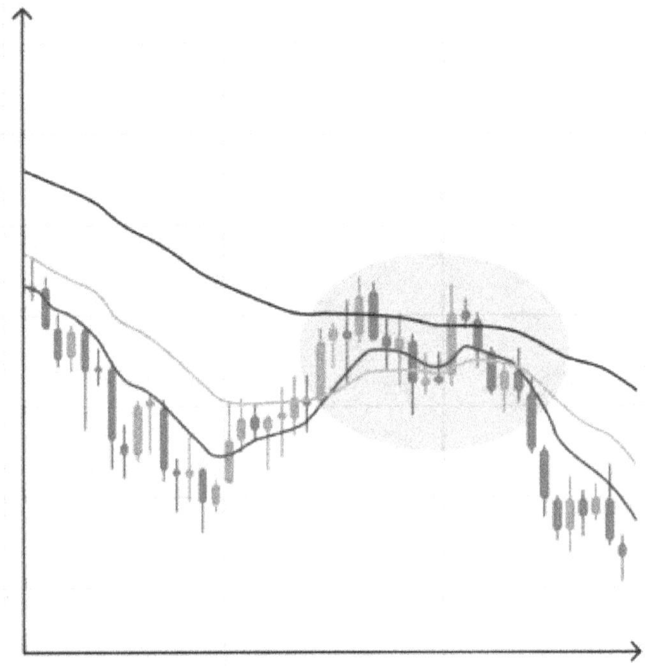

Let's analyze our first potential setup. This candle might look like a valid signal at first glance, but let's zoom in and check our criteria carefully.

Using our Fibonacci tool to measure, we can see this candle actually closes in the 50% range, not the lower 30% we require. This is why precise measurement is crucial - no eyeballing!

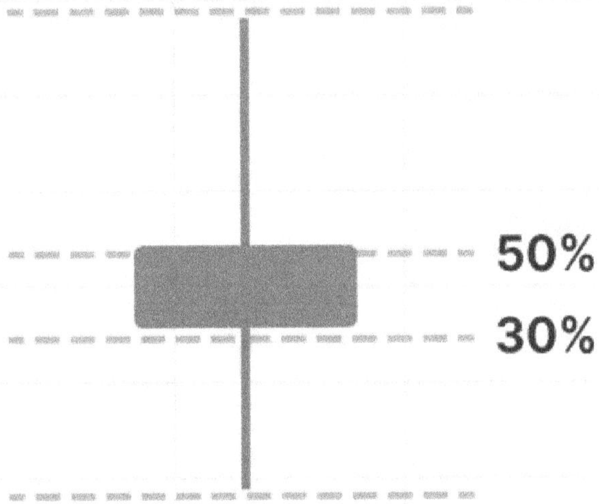

Here's another example that looks close but isn't quite right. The open and close are at about 35% - remember, we want below 30% for optimal probability.

Now, here's a perfect setup! The EMAs are fanned out correctly, we've pulled back to test the 8 EMA, and our signal candle has closed in the lower 30%.

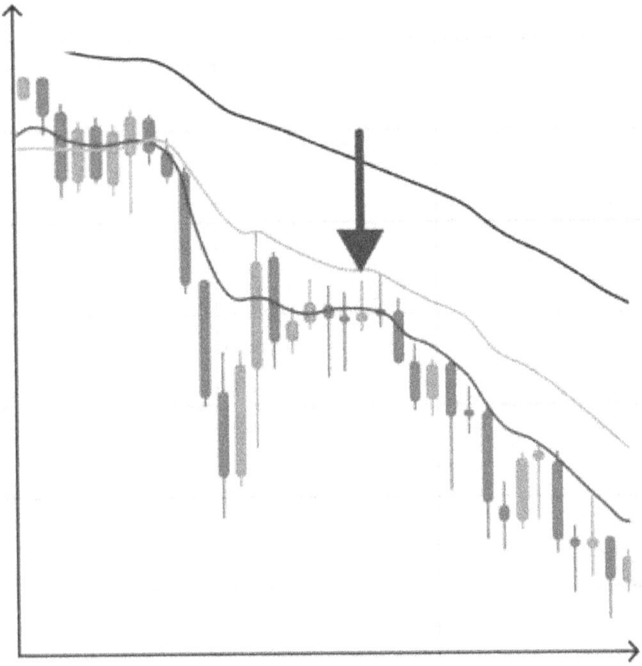

Watch what happens next - we place our sell stop order, but the next day doesn't trigger our entry. That's trading! But look what follows - another valid setup forms immediately after.

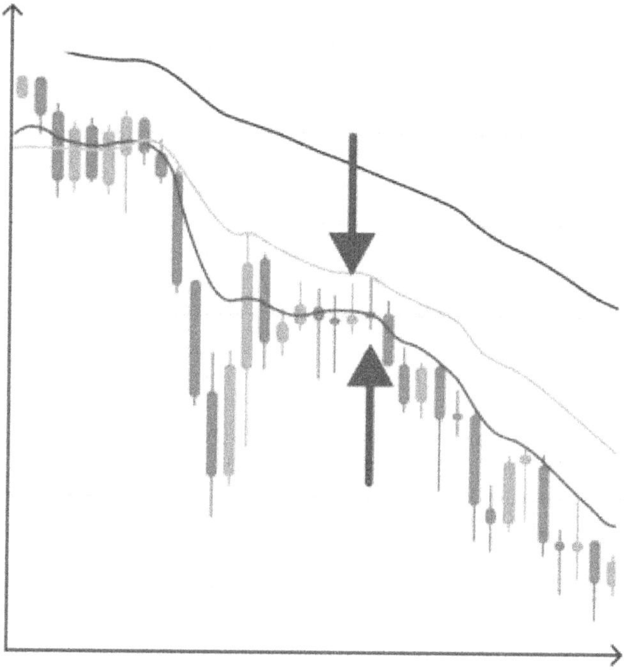

Our sell stop order (entry) goes 2 pips below the low at 22.43, our buy stop order (stop loss) 2 pips above the high at 22.35, and our buy limit order (profit target)at equal distance for our 1:1 ratio.

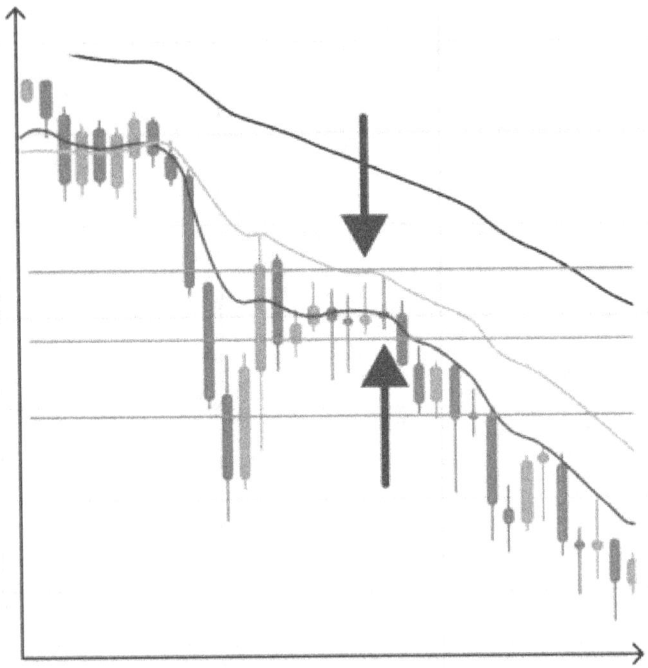

Here's another great example where multiple valid signals appeared in sequence. Each one met our criteria: proper EMA fanning, touch of 8 EMA, and correct candle formation.

Remember, once you're out of a trade, don't stop looking for new setups. As long as the EMAs maintain their proper fanning, new opportunities can emerge.

In this six-month period on GBP/ USD alone, we found about six valid opportunities - roughly one per month. Now imagine applying this across multiple pairs and markets!

One of the best parts of this strategy? It only takes about five minutes each day to scan for setups. You can check multiple markets efficiently once you know what you're looking for.

Final quiz!

Let's test your practical application skills. What should you do if you spot a candle that looks like a valid signal but hasn't closed yet?

Answer: Even if a setup looks perfect, we must follow our rules consistently. Jumping in early can lead to unnecessary losses. Always wait for the candle to close at the daily cutoff time (5 PM EST/10 PM GMT) and confirm ALL criteria before placing any orders.

Remember: this strategy works because it's based on strict rules and patience. It's not about catching every move - it's about catching high-probability setups that fit our criteria exactly.

Your homework:

- Start paper trading this strategy. Track every setup you spot, whether it triggers or not. Build your confidence before risking real money.

- Continue to research and study trading from other books and Youtube videos.

Congratulations! You now have a complete, professional trading strategy that you can implement right away.

Thank you for joining me on this journey! Remember, success in trading comes from consistency and discipline. Now go out there and start spotting those setups!

Good luck, have fun, and make money from trading!

Don't miss out!

Visit the website below and you can sign up to receive emails whenever Andy Hai Dinh publishes a new book. There's no charge and no obligation.

https://books2read.com/r/B-A-YYJBB-KTCYF

BOOKS 2 READ

Connecting independent readers to independent writers.

Did you love *A Beginner's Guide to Trading - Stock and Forex Technical Analysis*? Then you should read *WIN MORE, TRADE BETTER - A Practical Guide to Trading and Investing*[1] by Andy Hai Dinh!

[2]

Win More, Trade Better - A Practical Guide to Trading and Investing is your essential roadmap to mastering the markets with confidence. Whether you're a beginner looking to build a strong foundation or an experienced trader seeking to refine your strategies, this book delivers actionable insights, proven techniques, and real-world examples to help you trade smarter and invest more effectively.

Inside, you'll discover:

- How to develop a winning mindset and disciplined approach

---

1. https://books2read.com/u/brEDJA
2. https://books2read.com/u/brEDJA

- Practical strategies for stocks, forex, options, and crypto trading
- Risk management techniques to protect your capital
- Technical and fundamental analysis made simple
- Common pitfalls and how to avoid them

With a clear, no-nonsense approach, ***Win More, Trade Better*** cuts through the noise to provide you with the tools and knowledge needed to achieve consistent success in the financial markets. Whether you're trading part-time or aiming for a full-time career, this book will help you navigate the complexities of investing with clarity and confidence.

Andy Hai Dinh

Read more at https://pensight.com/x/lona.

Also by Andy Hai Dinh

ACRYLIC AND DIPPING POWDER - Product Knowledge and Applications
The Nail technician's Career Guide
A Beginner's Guide to Trading - Stock and Forex Technical Analysis
WIN MORE, TRADE BETTER - A Practical Guide to Trading and Investing

Watch for more at https://pensight.com/x/lona.

About the Author

Andy Hai Dinh is a market researcher and business consultant in the beauty industry. He is also a part-time trader profiting from swing trading stocks and Forex currencies.

www.ingramcontent.com/pod-product-compliance
Lightning Source LLC
LaVergne TN
LVHW052217200926
848481LV00001B/136
9798227515308